APPLETONS' SCHOOL READERS.

THE

FOURTH READER.

BY

WILLIAM T. HARRIS, A.M., LL.D.,
SUPERINTENDENT OF SCHOOLS, ST. LOUIS, MO.

ANDREW J. RICKOFF, A.M.,
SUPERINTENDENT OF INSTRUCTION, CLEVELAND, OHIO.

MARK BAILEY, A.M.,
INSTRUCTOR IN ELOCUTION, YALE COLLEGE.

NEW YORK, BOSTON, AND CHICAGO:
D. APPLETON AND COMPANY.
1880.

CONTENTS.

THE PREPARATORY NOTES.

The work to be done by the pupil is included under:

I. Biographical, historical, geographical, scientific, and literary allusions or references. The notes under this head are intended to suggest topics for discussion in the recitation, and the pupil is not required to study these, although he may read them with some profit.

II. Spelling and pronunciation. In the Appendix to this volume will be found suggested a method of teaching spelling by analysis. If preferred, the old method of oral or written spelling will suffice.

III. Language-lesson on the principles of written or printed language as found in the lesson. If carefully learned, the pupil will acquire a practical knowledge of grammatical forms, without the usual technicalities. He will learn to write and speak correctly. But the logic of language as given in technical grammar is not attempted here.

IV. Definitions, synonyms, and paraphrases, to be given by the pupil in his own language, i. e., in such words as he uses in every-day life, and not in words borrowed from the dictionary. He must find the words in the piece and study their connection with the rest, and give the special sense of the words as there used, not the general definition. This method will secure the most rapid mastery of a good vocabulary on the part of the pupil.

(Numbers II., III., and IV. are to be studied by the pupil, and he may be held responsible for the work required.)

V. Style and thought of the piece. The notes under this head should be read and discussed in the recitation, and they will answer a useful purpose in sharpening the pupil's faculty of criticism, even if the thoughts advanced are condemned and refuted.

It is evident that each selection from classic literature furnishes work enough for three, four, or five recitations. *First*, the pupil should learn the spelling, pronunciation, peculiarities of form, and meaning of the words in the lesson (II., III., IV.); *second*, the references and allusions made in the piece (I.); *third*, the thought and the style of expression (V.); *fourth*, the proper rendering of it as taught in the lessons on elocution.

The work here suggested is intended only as an auxiliary, and may be omitted for other topics presented by the teacher. Only a few hints are risked on the more important phases of each piece, and no attempt is made to exhaust the proper field of inquiry. It is safe to say that a thorough study of each literary piece in the higher Readers will be of more benefit to the pupil, in giving him an insight into human life, and directive power and influence among his fellow men, than all that he will or can learn from the other branches taught in the schools.

FOURTH READER.

I.—THE WHISTLE.

1. When I was a child, seven years old, my friends, on a holiday, filled my pockets with coppers. I went directly to a shop where they sold toys for children; and, being charmed with the sound of a whistle that I met by the way in the hands of another boy, I voluntarily offered him all my money for one.

2. I then came home, and went whistling all over the house, much pleased with my whistle, but disturbing all the family. My brothers, and sisters, and cousins, understanding the bargain I had made, told me I had given four times as much for it as it was worth.

3. This put me in mind what good things I might have bought with the rest of the money; and they laughed at me so much for my folly that I cried with vexation.

4. This, however, was afterward of use to me, the impression continuing on my mind; so that often, when I was tempted to buy some unnecessary thing, I said to myself, "Don't give too much for the whistle"; and so I saved my money.

5. As I grew up, came into the world, and observed the actions of men, I thought I met with many, very many, who gave too much for the whistle.

6. When I saw any one too ambitious of the favor of the great, wasting his time in attendance on public dinners, sacrificing his repose, his liberty, his virtue, and perhaps his friends, to attain it, I have said to myself, "This man gives too much for his whistle."

7. When I saw another fond of popularity, constantly employing himself in politics, neglecting his own affairs, and ruining them by that neglect, "He pays, indeed," said I, "too much for this whistle."

8. If I knew a miser, who gave up every kind of comfortable living, all the pleasure of doing good to others, all the esteem of his fellow-citizens, and the joys of benevolent friendship, for the sake of accumulating wealth, "Poor man," said I, "you do indeed pay too much for your whistle."

9. When I met a man of pleasure, sacrificing the improvement of his mind, or of his fortune, to mere bodily comfort, "Mistaken man," said I, "you are providing pain for yourself, instead of pleasure: you give too much for your whistle."

10. If I saw one fond of fine clothes, fine furniture, fine horses, all above his fortune, for which he contracted debts, and ended his career in prison, "Alas!" said I, "he has paid dear, very dear, for his whistle."

11. In short, I believed that a great part of the miseries of mankind were brought upon them by the false estimates they had made of the value of things, and by their giving too much for their whistles.

Adapted from Benjamin Franklin.

FOR PREPARATION.—I. Allusions, historical, geographical, and literary. II. Spelling and pronunciation; words to be copied, and marked with diacritical marks, hyphens, and accents. III. Language-lesson. IV. Words and phrases to be explained in the pupil's own words, giving the meaning as used in the lesson (*not* the general definition). V. Style and thought. Numbers I. and V. to suggest topics of conversation on the reading-lesson; Numbers II., III., and IV. to be prepared by the pupil. There may be some points in Numbers I. and V. that are too difficult for many of the pupils for whom this Reader is intended. The teacher will use his discretion in selecting topics from these numbers for explanation to his class.

I. Benjamin Franklin, an eminent American philosopher and statesman, born at Boston, Mass., January 17, 1706. His father was a soap and candle maker. Benjamin learned the printer's trade, and removed to Philadelphia. He discovered the identity of lightning and electricity. His efforts secured the alliance of the French with America in the Revolution. He also assisted in making important treaties, and in forming the Constitution of the United States. (See Lesson LXV.)

II. Write out and mark the pronunciation of friĕnds, fĭlled, whĭs′-tle, lăughed, un-nĕç′-es-sa-ry, neg-lĕct′-ing. (See Webster's diacritical marks on page 98, and in the introduction to the spelling lessons of the Appendix.)

III. "Children"—what change is necessary to make this word refer to only one? What meaning does *ing* give to the word *whistling?* Find other words in which it makes the word refer to continued action. Dr. Franklin wrote "says I" (7, 8, 9, 10) for "said I"—why incorrect?

IV. "Coppers"—what coin does this mean? What does "charmed" mean (1)? "Voluntarily"? (willingly, of his own accord.) "Disturbing" means what? Who is a *cousin?* What is a *bargain?* What is *folly?* —*vexation?* "Impression continuing on my mind"? (i. e., I remembered it.) "Ambitious of the favor of the great"? "Fond of popularity"? (in this case, desiring the people's votes.) Who is a *miser?* What is the meaning of *esteem?—benevolent?*—"accumulating wealth"?—comfortable? —"contracted debts"? (ran in debt.) "Ended his career" means what? "False estimates they had made of the value of things"? (i. e., made mistakes about the worth of things.)

V. Do you think of any other examples to add to these of Dr. Franklin, in which people have "given too much for the whistle"? Write out such a case in your own words. What is meant by "the great"? How can they bestow "favor"?

II.—THE KITTEN AND THE FALLING LEAVES.

1. See the kitten on the wall,
Sporting with the leaves that fall,
Withered leaves—one, two, and three—
From the lofty elder-tree!

2. Through the calm and frosty air
Of this morning bright and fair,
Eddying round and round, they sink
Softly, softly:

3. One might think,
From the motions that are made,
Every little leaf conveyed
Sylph or fairy hither tending,
To this lower world descending,
Each invisible and mute,
In his wavering parachute.

4. But the kitten, how she starts,
Crouches, stretches, paws, and darts!
First at one, and then its fellow,
Just as light and just as yellow:
There are many now—now one;
Now they stop, and there are none.

5. What intenseness of desire
In her upward eye of fire!
With a tiger-leap half-way
Now she meets the coming prey,
Lets it go as fast, and then
Has it in her power again:

"See the kitten on the wall,
Sporting with the leaves that fall."

(" *The Kitten and the Falling Leaves,*" p. 10.)

6. Now she works with three or four,
Like an Indian conjurer;
Quick as he in feats of art,
Far beyond in joy of heart.

7. Were her antics played in the eye
Of a thousand standers-by,
Clapping hands with shout and stare,
What would little Tabby care
For the plaudits of the crowd?
Over-happy to be proud,
Over-wealthy in the treasure
Of her own exceeding pleasure!

William Wordsworth.

For Preparation.—I. Like an "Indian conjurer" (i. e., possessing great skill in tossing up balls and catching them, keeping several in the air at a time).

II. Păr′-a-chute (păr′a-shoot), a-gain′ (-gĕn′), prey (distinguish from *pray*), trĕas′-ūre (trĕzh′ụr), cŏn′-ju-rer (kŭn′-), crouch′-es, plāyed, ex-çeed′-ing.

III. Tell some differences that you have noticed between a poem and a piece in prose. (Lines of regular length? Capitals, where placed? Accented syllables occur how often? Difference in the order of words in the sentence? etc.) Change the second paragraph to prose, beginning, "They sink softly and slowly through the calm," etc.

IV. Give the meaning as used in the poem, in your own words, of "withered leaves," "eddying round and round," "conveyed (carried) sylph or fairy hither tending" (i. e., riding down from the sky on the falling leaf), invisible (not to be seen), mute (making no sound), "wavering parachute" (like a large umbrella, used to descend with, in safety, from a balloon), crouches, its fellow (leaf), "intenseness of desire" (*very* desirous), prey, "feats of art" (quickness of hand, and ability to do difficult things), antics (funny actions), plaudits (clapping of hands, etc.).

V. "Upward eye of fire"—real fire, or only a shining in her eyes that looks like fire? What is referred to by "clapping hands," etc.?—by "little Tabby"? Give some other names used in naming kittens. Where is the kitten represented as standing, in this poem?

III.—THE DISCONTENTED PENDULUM.

1. An old Clock, that had stood for fifty years in a farmer's kitchen without giving its owner any cause of complaint, early one summer's morning, before the family was stirring, suddenly stopped. Upon this the Dial-plate (if we may credit the fable) changed countenance with alarm; the Hands made an ineffectual effort to continue their course; the Wheels remained motionless with surprise; the Weights hung speechless. Each member felt disposed to lay the blame on the others.

2. At length the Dial instituted a formal inquiry into the cause of the stop, when Hands, Wheels, Weights, with one voice, protested their innocence. But now a faint tick was heard from the Pendulum, who thus spoke:

3. "I confess myself to be the sole cause of the present stoppage, and am willing, for the general satisfaction, to assign my reasons. The truth is, that I am tired of ticking." Upon hearing this, the old Clock became so enraged that it was on the point of striking.

4. "Lazy Wire!" exclaimed the Dial-plate.—"As to that," replied the Pendulum, "it is vastly easy for you, Mistress Dial, who have always, as everybody knows, set yourself up above me—it is vastly easy for you, I say, to accuse other people of laziness—you who have nothing to do all your life but to stare people in the face, and to amuse yourself with watching all that goes on in the kitchen.

5. "Think, I beseech you, how you would like to be shut up for life in this dark closet, and wag backward and forward year after year, as I do."—"As to that," said the Dial, "is there not a window in your house on purpose for you to look through?"

6. "But what of that?" resumed the Pendulum. "Although there is a window, I dare not stop, even for an instant, to look out. Besides, I am really weary of my way of life; and, if you please, I'll tell you how I took this disgust at my employment.

7. "This morning I happened to be calculating how many times I should have to tick in the course only of the next twenty-four hours. Perhaps some of you above there can tell me the exact sum?"—The Minute-hand, being quick at figures, instantly replied, "Eighty-six thousand four hundred times."—"Exactly so," replied the Pendulum.

8. "Well, I appeal to you all if the thought of this was not enough to fatigue one? And when I began to multiply the strokes of one day by those of months and years, really it is no wonder if I felt discouraged at the prospect. So, after a great deal of reasoning and hesitation, thought I to myself, 'I'll stop!'"

9. The Dial could scarcely keep its countenance during this harangue; but, resuming its gravity, thus replied: "Dear Mr. Pendulum, I am really astonished that such a useful, industrious person as yourself should have been overcome by this suggestion.

10. "It is true, you have done a great deal of work in your time; so have we all, and are likely to do; and though this may fatigue us to *think* of, the question is, Will it fatigue us to *do?* Would you now do me the favor to give about half a dozen strokes, to illustrate my argument?"—The Pendulum complied, and ticked six times at its usual pace.

11. "Now," resumed the Dial, "was that exertion fatiguing to you?"—"Not in the least," replied the Pen-

what we are to read, until we understand it as well as what we say in conversation.

Suppose a school-visitor came in here, and, after hearing a few lessons, said, "That little boy reads well," we should know just what he meant by the word he spoke *loudest.*

If he said, "That little boy reads *well*"—emphasizing the last word only—he would mean to tell us *how* he reads. He would make that idea stand out *distinctly,* above all the rest. He reads, not badly or indifferently, but "*well.*"

Suppose he said, "That little boy *reads* well," then our attention would be specially called to the *reading.* That emphasis makes the *reading itself* stand out distinct from any other lesson. Whatever else he may do poorly, he "*reads*" well.

If he said, "That little *boy* reads well," he would mean that the *boy*, instead of the *girl*, or others, reads well.

[illegible] That *little* boy reads well," means that the *little* boy, i[illegible] of the *larger* boy, reads well.

[illegible]*at* little boy reads well," means that *that one* little [illegible] as distinct from some *other* little boy or boys, reads w[illegible]

[illegible]ow, give the *emphasis* so as to make us *think*—

1. Of the "*boy*" instead of the girl.
2. Of the "*little*" instead of the larger boy.
3. Of *some* "*one*" particular little boy.
4. Of the "*reading*" exercise.
5. Of "*how*" he reads.

Thus, by changing the emphasis, *five different meanings* and *readings* have been given to that line of five words; and we learn that the *emphasis* depends on the *sense*, and the *sense* on the *emphasis.*

Observe, also, that, in each reading, the *important* word is that which expresses the *distinctive idea;* and when the idea in any given word is *not distinctive*, the word is *not emphatic;* and, when trying to think out the meaning of your reading-lessons, keep in mind, to aid you, this first principle of "*Logical Analysis*":

THE DISTINCTIVE IDEAS ARE EMPHATIC.

PART II.

First, there must be some *distinct* "*thing*" we are to read about, and attention should be called to it by emphasis, as "winter," or "summer"; then, there must be something "*said*" about it, *distinct* from all other sayings, which needs emphasis: as, "*Winter* has *gone*, and *summer* has *come*"*;* or, "*Winter* is often too *cold*, and *summer* too *warm;* and so *spring* and *autumn* are *pleasanter* seasons of the year."

The last words, "seasons of the year," should not be emphasized; for winter and summer are "seasons of the year" too. That idea, then, is not distinctive of "spring" and "autumn," and is not emphatic. The writer did not intend to tell us that they are "seasons of the year" (he supposed we knew that), but merely that they are "pleasanter."

Hence the second principle of "*Logical Analysis*":

WHAT IS WELL KNOWN, OR UNDERSTOOD, NEEDS NO EMPHASIS.

Emphasis is too valuable to be wasted. Its great use is to INTRODUCE to hearers the NEW *important* ideas. And so, when an idea has been introduced *once*, it does not need to be emphasized right over again, any more than a man needs to be introduced to the same person over and over again. Nor do persons well acquainted with each other need *any* introduction. No more do ideas, familiar and well understood, need emphasis.

If we add to the thought above, that spring is pleasanter than winter, too, "because the *birds* and *flowers* come then," the ideas of "spring" and "winter," and that the one is "pleasanter" than the other, having all been given with emphasis once, only the *new* reason—that the "birds and flowers come then"—requires the "extra force."

"The light shines."

Both "light" and "shines" are new, and need emphasis.

"The moon shines." "The stars shine."

"Shines" was emphasized before, and only "moon" and "stars" are new.

"The stars shine dimly to-night."

Now both "stars" and "shine" are understood, and only *how* they shine, viz., "dimly," needs emphasis.

"The stars shine dimly to-night, because the moon is so bright."

All is understood now, and unemphatic, except the reason why they shine so dimly, "because the *moon* is so *bright*."

PART III.

Read this verse from the story of the "Prodigal Son," in the New Testament:

"But the father said to his servants, Bring forth the best robe, and put it on him; and put a ring on his hand, and shoes on his feet."

What did the father order his servants to bring forth?

The "*best robe*," and a "*ring*," and "*shoes*."

These, then, are emphatic, because they are all *dis-*

tinctive points; for the poor prodigal was *ragged*, and his hands and feet were *bare*. But if we try to make "hands" and "feet" distinctive (reading, "and put a ring on his *hand*, and shoes on his *feet*," as we too often hear it), we put, in the place of the gracious command, a most absurd and foolish one: as if the servants needed to be told *just where* to put the ring, lest they put it in one ear, or in his nose; or *just where* to put the shoes, lest they put them on his hands! Often we can not tell how to read a line until we look at what is before and after it.

"You have done *that* you should be *sorry* for,"

would be the right reading of Brutus's words to Cassius in the quarrel-scene from "Julius Cæsar," if these words stood thus alone. But when we read, just before these, the words of Cassius,

"Do not presume too much upon my love;
I may do that I shall be sorry for,"

we learn that the words "that" and "sorry" are not distinctive at all, but common to both sayings, while "have" and "should" stand out in sharp contrast to "may" and "shall"; and that the true reading of this reply must therefore be,

"You *have* done that you *should* be sorry for."

Read these few lines from the "Pickwick Papers":

"'What's your name, sir?' inquired the judge. 'Sam Weller, my lord,' replied that gentleman. 'Do you spell it with a "V" or a "W"?' inquired the judge. 'That depends upon the taste and fancy of the speller, my lord,' replied Sam; 'I never had occasion to spell it more than once or twice in my life, but *I* spells it with a

"*V.*"' Here a voice in the gallery exclaimed aloud, 'Quite right, too, Samivel—quite right! Put it down a "we," my lord; put it down a "we."' "

Thus we see that *anything*, from a single letter to a thought in Shakespeare or in the Bible, may be the distinctive idea requiring *emphasis*.

A general rule has been given that a word once read with "extra force" needs it no more. But sometimes a word or phrase is repeated for the very purpose of *more* emphasis; then, of course, the word is spoken more and more earnestly as it is repeated. "You *must* not, you MUST not go so near the edge of the steep bank!" "Oh, how *beautiful*, how BEAUTIFUL the rainbow is!" "Come *over*, come OVER the river to me!" "Oh, *dear mamma!* oh, DEAR MAMMA!" So, too, words like "himself," "itself," "yourself," etc., are used for the sole purpose of emphasizing another word, as, "*He* did it *himself*"; "*You yourselves* are to blame"; "It is an attribute to *God himself*."

V.—THE SPIDER AND THE FLY.

1. "Will you walk into my parlor?" said the Spider to the Fly;
"'Tis the prettiest little parlor that ever you did spy.
The way into my parlor is up a winding stair,
And I have many curious things to show when you are there."
"Oh no, no," said the little Fly; "to ask me is in vain,
For who goes up your winding stair can ne'er come down again."

2. "I'm sure you must be weary, dear, with soaring up so high;
Will you rest upon my little bed?" said the Spider to the Fly.
"There are pretty curtains drawn around; the sheets are fine and thin,
And if you like to rest awhile, I'll snugly tuck you in!"
"Oh no, no," said the little Fly, "for I've often heard it said,
They never, never wake again who sleep upon your bed!"

3. Said the cunning Spider to the Fly: "Dear friend, what can I do
To prove the warm affection I've always felt for you?
I have within my pantry good store of all that's nice;
I'm sure you're very welcome—will you please to take a slice?"
"Oh no, no," said the little Fly; "kind sir, that can not be:
I've heard what's in your pantry, and I do not wish to see!"

4. "Sweet creature!" said the Spider, "you're witty and you're wise;
How handsome are your gauzy wings! how brilliant are your eyes!
I have a little looking-glass upon my parlor shelf;
If you'll step in one moment, dear, you shall behold yourself."
"I thank you, gentle sir," she said, "for what you're pleased to say,
And, bidding you good morning now, I'll call another day."

5. The Spider turned him round about, and went into his den,
For well he knew the silly Fly would soon come back again:
So he wove a subtle web in a little corner sly,
And set his table ready to dine upon the Fly;
Then came out to his door again, and merrily did sing:
"Come hither, hither, pretty Fly, with the pearl and silver wing;
Your robes are green and purple; there's a crest upon your head;
Your eyes are like the diamond bright, but mine are dull as lead!"

6. Alas, alas! how very soon this silly little Fly,
Hearing his wily, flattering words, came slowly flitting by;
With buzzing wings she hung aloft, then near and nearer drew,
Thinking only of her brilliant eyes and green and purple hue,
Thinking only of her crested head. Poor, foolish thing! At last
Up jumped the cunning Spider, and fiercely held her fast;

7. He dragged her up his winding stair, into his dismal den,
Within his little parlor—but she ne'er came out again!

And now, dear little children, who may this story read,
To idle, silly, flattering words, I pray you, ne'er give heed;

Unto an evil counselor close heart and ear and eye,
And take a lesson from this tale of the Spider and the
Fly.
Mary Howitt.

FOR PREPARATION.—I. Is the spider a "cunning" animal? Is the fly a vain animal, pleased with the attentions of others, or only a greedy animal, that likes sweet things to eat?

II. Wạlk, pär′-lor, pret′-ti-est (prĭt′-), stâir, eū′-ri-oŭs, wīnd′-ing, wēa′-ry, sōar′-ing, eûr′-tainṣ, a-whīle′, hēard, friĕnd, prọve, ereat′-ūre (-yụr), gạuz′-y, brĭll′-iant, new (nū), plēaṣed, sŭb′-tle (sŭt′l), pēarl, pûr′-ple, dī′-a-mond, bŭzz′-ing, fiērçe′-ly, eoun′-sel-or.

III. What letters are omitted in *ne'er, I'm, I'll, I've, that's, you're, what's, you'll, there's?*

IV. Winding stair, curious, soaring, snugly, cunning, prove, pantry, welcome, "gauzy wings," behold, "wove a subtle web," crest, wily, flitting, dismal, counselor, flattering.

V. Note what the Spider said to persuade the Fly, in the first stanza (a beautiful parlor; then, curious things to see up the winding stair). Second stanza (a bed, with pretty curtains and fine sheets; kind attentions promised by the Spider, who tries to show how anxious he is for the Fly's comfort). Third stanza (fine things to eat in his pantry—sugar and molasses, so tempting to flies, doubtless; but the Fly knows better). Fourth stanza (praises the wit and wisdom of the Fly; then her personal beauty, gauzy wings, brilliant eyes; has a looking-glass for her use. The Fly, who knew so well what was in the pantry, now concludes to believe that he has a looking-glass, and promises to call; thinks that it will be too sudden a change of mind to go in at once). Fifth stanza (the Spider has found the weak side of the vain Fly, and now sings about her beauty and his own plainness). Sixth stanza (flattery of her wings and eyes secures the Spider's victim).

VI.—STEPPING-STONES.

1. When Nat went into school on Monday morning, he quaked inwardly, for now he thought he should have to display his ignorance before them all. But Mr. Bhaer

gave him a seat in the deep window, where he could turn his back on the others, and Franz heard him say his lessons there, so that no one could hear his blunders, or see how he blotted his copy-book. He was truly grateful for this, and toiled away so diligently that Mr. Bhaer said, smiling, when he saw his hot face and inky fingers:

2. "Don't work so hard, my boy; you will tire yourself out, and there is time enough."

"But I *must* work hard, or I can't catch up with the others. They know heaps, and I don't know anything," said Nat, who had been reduced to a state of despair by hearing the boys recite their grammar, history, and geography with what he thought amazing ease and accuracy.

3. "You know a good many things which they don't," said Mr. Bhaer, sitting down beside him, while Franz led a class of small students through the intricacies of the multiplication-table.

"Do I?" and Nat looked utterly incredulous.

"Yes. For one thing, you can keep your temper, and Jack, who is quick at numbers, can not; that is an excellent lesson, and I think you have learned it well. Then, you can play the violin, and not one of the lads can, though they want to do it very much. But, best of all, Nat, you really care to learn something, and that is half the battle. It seems hard at first, and you will feel discouraged; but plod away, and things will get easier and easier as you go on."

4. Nat's face had brightened more and more as he listened, for, small as the list of his learning was, it cheered him immensely to feel that he had anything to fall back upon. "Yes, I can keep my temper—father's beating taught me that; and I can fiddle, though I don't know where the bay of Biscay is," he thought, with a

sense of comfort impossible to express. Then he said aloud, and so earnestly that Demi heard him:

5. "I *do* want to learn, and I *will* try. I never went to school, but I couldn't help it; and, if the fellows don't laugh at me, I guess I'll get on first-rate—you and the lady are so good to me."

"They sha'n't laugh at you. If they do, I'll—I'll—tell them not to," cried Demi, quite forgetting where he was.

The class stopped in the middle of 7 times 9, and every one looked up to see what was going on.

6. Thinking that a lesson in learning to help one another was better than arithmetic just then, Mr. Bhaer told them about Nat, making such an interesting and touching little story out of it, that the good-hearted lads all promised to lend him a hand, and felt quite honored to be called upon to impart their stores of wisdom to the chap who fiddled so capitally. This appeal established the right feeling among them, and Nat had few hindrances to struggle against, for every one was glad to give him a "boost" up the ladder of learning.

Louisa M. Alcott.

FOR PREPARATION.—I. Have you read Miss Alcott's "Little Men"? This extract from "Little Men" describes the kind manner in which a poor homeless boy was received into the private school at Plumfield. Nat Blake had been found in a damp cellar, sick and friendless, mourning for his dead father and his lost violin, with which he had earned his scanty living as a street musician.

II. Eaş'-i-er, bright'-ened (brī'tnd), lĭst'-ened (lĭs'nd), toŭch'-ing, hŏn'-ored (ŏn'urd), Bhaer (pronounced like "bâre"), Franz (frănts).

III. Nat is a nickname (for Nathaniel). *Easy, easier, easiest:* what change in the meaning does the addition of *er* and *est* make? "Father's beating"—what does *'s* express? What is omitted in *can't?—sha'n't* (*ll* and *o*)?

IV. Ignorance, diligently, reduced, despair, accuracy, students, intricacies, incredulous, discouraged, plod, immensely, established, appeal, hindrances.

V. "Quaked inwardly" (i. e., his heart beat hard with fear)? Notice the acts of kindness: having him say his lessons where the others could not hear his blunders (such an act shows what is called a "delicate consideration" for Nat's feelings; it is not sufficient to be kindly disposed toward others, but we should delicately consider their feelings); then, the gentle manner of encouraging the boy to self-respect, by giving him credit for what he already knew, such as playing the violin. Notice the expressions: "They know heaps," "get on first-rate," "fiddle," "sha'n't," "boost." (These expressions do not shock us when we hear them spoken by boys and uneducated people; but when we see them in print we mark them as slang, or "vulgarisms," because they are only "colloquial," and are avoided by refined people. The writer of a story is obliged to use these expressions in order to paint the characters of the persons of the story; but we should learn to avoid them in writing, and even in conversation.)

VII.—THE VOICE OF SPRING.

1. I come, I come! ye have called me long;
I come o'er the mountains, with light and song.
Ye may trace my step o'er the waking earth
By the winds which tell of the violet's birth,
By the primrose stars in the shadowy grass,
By the green leaves opening as I pass.

2. I have breathed on the South, and the chestnut-flowers
By thousands have burst from the forest bowers,
And the ancient graves and the fallen fanes
Are veiled with wreaths on Italian plains;
But it is not for me, in my hour of bloom,
To speak of the ruin or the tomb!

3. I have looked o'er the hills of the stormy North,
And the larch has hung all his tassels forth;

The fisher is out on the sunny sea,
And the reindeer bounds o'er the pastures free,
And the pine has a fringe of softer green,
And the moss looks bright, where my step has been.

4. I have sent through the wood-paths a glowing sigh,
And called out each voice of the deep blue sky,
From the night-bird's lay through the starry time,
In the groves of the soft Hesperian clime,
To the swan's wild note by the Iceland lakes,
When the dark fir-branch into verdure breaks.

5. From the streams and founts I have loosed the chain;
They are sweeping on to the silvery main,
They are flashing down from the mountain brows,
They are flinging spray o'er the forest boughs,
They are bursting fresh from their sparry caves,
And the earth resounds with the joy of waves.

Felicia Hemans.

For Preparation.—I. Eight of the thirteen verses of this piece are omitted. Can you describe the plants mentioned—violet, primrose, chestnut, larch, pine, moss? "Hesperian clime" (refers to the western countries of Europe, which have a mild climate through the influence of the ocean-winds that blow from the west in the temperate zones).

II. An'-cient (ān'shent), veiled (vāld), wrēatheṣ (reethz), rein'-deer, sīgh (sī), bough (bou), voiçe, brīght (brīt), mount'-ainṣ (-inz).

III. Make a list of the *name-words* in the first and second stanzas (words used as names of objects; e. g., mountains, light, song, step, earth, winds, violet's, birth, stars, grass, leaves, etc.).

IV. Trace, bowers, glowing, clime, verdure, "silvery main," "loosed the chain," resounds, "fallen fanes" (ruined temples).

V. How is the approach of spring to be known? ("Trace my steps by soft winds, primroses, green leaves.") Is the reindeer referred to (3) the one used in Lapland instead of the horse or the cow, or one kept in a park as a curiosity? (Mrs. Hemans lived in the north of Wales. Reference to the "Iceland lakes" shows that she thought of the effect of spring on the northern, winter-bound countries.)

VIII.—DAN, THE FIREBRAND.

1. "Please, ma'am, could I speak to you? It is something very important," said Nat, popping his head in at the door of Mrs. Bhaer's room.

It was the fifth head which had popped in during the last half-hour; but Mrs. Jo was used to it, so she looked up, and said briskly:

"What is it, my lad?"

2. Nat came in, shut the door carefully behind him, and said, in an eager, anxious tone:

"Dan has come!"

"Who is Dan?"

"He's a boy I used to know when I fiddled 'round the streets. He sold papers, and was kind to me. I saw him the other day in town, and told him how nice it was here, and he's come."

3. "But, my dear boy, that is rather a sudden way to pay a visit."

"Oh, it isn't a visit; he wants to stay, if you will let him!" said Nat, innocently.

"Well, but I don't know about that," began Mrs. Bhaer, rather startled by the coolness of the proposition.

4. "Why, I thought you liked to have poor boys come and live with you, and be kind to them, as you were to me," said Nat, looking surprised and alarmed.

"So I do; but I like to know something about them first. I have to choose them, because there are so many. I have not room for all. I wish I had."

"I told him to come because I thought you'd like it; but if there isn't room, he can go away again," said Nat, sorrowfully.

5. The boy's confidence in her hospitality touched Mrs. Bhaer, and she could not find the heart to disappoint his hope and spoil his kind little plan; so she said:

"Tell me about this Dan."

"I don't know anything, only he hasn't got any folks, and he's poor, and he was good to me; so I'd like to be good to him, if I could."

6. "Excellent reasons, every one. But really, Nat, the house is full, and I don't know where I could put him," said Mrs. Bhaer, more and more inclined to prove herself the haven of refuge he seemed to think her.

"He could have my bed, and I could sleep in the barn. It isn't cold now, and I don't mind. I used to sleep anywhere with father," said Nat, eagerly.

7. Something in his speech and face made Mrs. Jo put her hand on his shoulder, and say, in her kindest tone:

"Bring in your friend, Nat; I think we must find room for him without giving him your place."

Nat joyfully ran off, and soon returned, followed by a most unprepossessing boy, who slouched in and stood looking about him, with a half-bold, half-sullen look, which made Mrs. Bhaer say to herself, after one glance:

"A bad specimen, I am afraid."

8. "This is Dan," said Nat, presenting him as if sure of his welcome.

"Nat tells me you would like to come and stay with us," began Mrs. Jo, in a friendly tone.

"Yes," was the gruff reply.

"Have you no friends to take care of you?"

"No."

"Say 'No, ma'am,'" whispered Nat.

"Sha'n't, neither!" muttered Dan.

9. "How old are you?"

"About fourteen."

"You look older. What can you do?"

"'Most anything."

"If you stay here, we shall want you to do as the others do—work and study, as well as play. Are you willing to agree to that?"

"Don't mind trying."

10. "Well, you can stay a few days, and we will see how we get on together.—Take him out, Nat, and amuse him till Mr. Bhaer comes home, when we will settle about the matter," said Mrs. Jo, finding it rather difficult to get on with this cool young person, who fixed his big black eyes on her with a hard, suspicious expression, sorrowfully unboyish.

Louisa M. Alcott.

FOR PREPARATION.—I. A short time after Nat had been received into the school at Plumfield, the events described in this and the next piece took place.

II. Plēaṣe, dūr′-ing, ăn̤x′-io̤ŭs (ănk′shus), ĭn′-no-çent-ly, to̤ŭched (tŭcht), rēa′-ṣonṣ (rē′zns), ēa′-ḡer (ē′-), shōul′-der, friĕnd′-ly, whĭs′-pered.

III. Make a list of ten of the name-words of this piece, and change them so as to make each of them express more than one (need, needs; door, doors; room, rooms; lad, lads, etc.).

IV. Lad, choose, folks, bold, presenting, reply, muttered, agree, amuse, difficult, important, briskly, alarmed, surprised, confidence, hospitality, disappoint, excellent, inclined, "haven of refuge," returned, unprepossessing, slouched, sullen, specimen, welcome, gruff, suspicious.

V. Notice the language that the boys use: "Hasn't got any folks," "Sha'n't, neither," "'Most anything," "Don't mind trying." Point out the expressions which you consider improper, and suggest the proper ones.

IX.—DAN'S BULL-FIGHT.

1. One Saturday afternoon, as a party of the boys went out to play, Tommy said:

"Let's go down to the river and cut a lot of new fish-poles."

"Take Toby to drag them back, and one of us can ride him down," proposed Stuffy, who hated to walk.

"That means you, I suppose. Well, hurry up, lazy-bones!" said Dan.

2. Away they went, and, having got the poles, were about to go home, when Demi unluckily said to Tommy, who was on Toby, with a long rod in his hand:

"You look like the picture of the man in the bull-fight, only you haven't got a red cloth, or pretty clothes on."

"I'd like to see one; wouldn't you?" said Tommy, shaking his lance.

3. "Let's have one. There's old Buttercup, in the big meadow: ride at her, Tom, and see her run," proposed Dan, bent on mischief.

"No, you mustn't," began Demi, who was learning to distrust Dan's propositions.

"Why not, little fuss-button?" demanded Dan.

"I don't think Uncle Fritz would like it."

"Did he ever say we must not have a bull-fight?"

"No, I don't think he ever did," admitted Demi.

4. "Then hold your tongue.—Drive on, Tom, and here's a red flag to flap at the old thing. I'll help you to stir her up." And over the wall went Dan, full of the new game, and the rest followed like a flock of sheep—even Demi, who sat upon the bars, and watched the fun with interest.

5. Poor Buttercup was not in a very good mood, for she had lately been bereft of her calf, and mourned for the little thing most dismally. Just now she regarded all mankind as her enemies (and I do not blame her); so, when the matadore came prancing toward her with the red handkerchief flying at the end of his lance, she threw up her head and gave a most appropriate "Moo!"

6. Tommy rode gallantly at her, and Toby, recognizing an old friend, was quite willing to approach; but, when the lance came down on her back with a loud whack, both cow and donkey were surprised and disgusted. Toby backed with a bray of remonstrance, and Buttercup lowered her horns angrily.

"At her again, Tom! She's jolly cross, and will do it capitally!" called Dan, coming up behind with another rod, while Jack and Ned followed his example.

7. Seeing herself thus beset, and treated with such disrespect, Buttercup trotted around the field, getting more and more bewildered and excited every moment; for, whichever way she turned, there was a dreadful boy yelling, and brandishing a new and very disagreeable sort of whip. It was great fun for them, but real misery for her; but she soon lost patience, and turned the tables in a most unexpected manner.

8. All at once she wheeled short around and charged full at her old friend Toby, whose conduct cut her to the heart. Poor, slow Toby backed so precipitately that he tripped over a stone, and down went horse, matadore, and all, in one ignominious heap; while distracted Buttercup took a surprising leap over the wall, and galloped wildly out of sight down the road.

9. "Catch her!—stop her!—head her off! Run, boys, run!" shouted Dan, tearing after her at his best pace; for she was Mr. Bhaer's pet Alderney, and, if anything happened to her, Dan feared it would be all over with him. Such a running, and racing, and bawling, and puffing, as there was before she was caught! The fish-poles were left behind. Toby was trotted nearly off his legs in the chase; and every boy was red, breathless, and scared.

10. They found poor Buttercup, at last, in a flower-garden, where she had taken refuge, worn out with the long run. Borrowing a rope for a halter, Dan led her home, followed by a party of very sober young gentlemen; for the cow was in a sad state, having strained her shoulder in jumping, so that she limped, her eyes looked wild, and her glossy coat was wet and muddy.

Louisa M. Alcott.

FOR PREPARATION.—I. Continuation of the story of Dan. "Alderney" (fine breed of cows). "Măt′-a-dōre" (the man who kills the bull in the bull-fight).

II. Mĕad′-ōw, mĭs′-chief (-chif), tongue (tŭng), caught (kawt), scared, fŏl′-lōwed, dŏn′-key.

III. Make a list of ten name-words in this piece that express more than one object each, and change them so as to express only one (poles, pole, etc.).

IV. Lance, proposed, distrust, admitted, flap, interest, mood, bereft, mourned, dismally, regarded, enemies, blame, prancing, appropriate, gallantly, recognizing, willing, approach, whack, bray, remonstrance, capitally, beset, bewildered, disagreeable, misery, patience, unexpected, charged, conduct, precipitately, ignominious, distracted, galloped, pace, refuge, halter, limped.

V. "Lot of fish-poles"—use a better expression for "lot," and also for "lazy-bones," "haven't got," "fuss-button," "old thing," "jolly cross."

X.—THE FOX AND THE CAT.

1. The Fox and the Cat, as they traveled one day,
With moral discourses cut shorter the way.
"'Tis great," says the Fox, "to make justice our guide."
"How godlike is mercy!" Grimalkin replied.

2. While thus they proceeded, a Wolf from the wood,
Impatient of hunger and thirsting for blood,
Rushed forth—as he saw the dull shepherd asleep—
And seized for his supper an innocent sheep.
"In vain, wretched victim, for mercy you bleat;
When mutton's at hand," says the Wolf, "I must eat."

3. The Cat was astonished; the Fox stood aghast,
To see the fell beast at his bloody repast.
"What a wretch!" says the Cat. "'Tis the vilest of brutes!
Does he feed upon flesh, when there's herbage and roots?"
Cries the Fox: "While our oaks give us acorns so good,
What a tyrant is this, to spill innocent blood!"

4. Well, onward they marched, and they moralized still,
Till they came where some poultry picked chaff by a mill;
Sly Reynard surveyed them with gluttonous eyes,
And made, spite of morals, a pullet his prize.
A mouse, too, that chanced from her covert to stray,
The greedy Grimalkin secured as her prey.

5. A Spider, that sat in her web on the wall,
Perceived the poor victims, and pitied their fall:
She cried, "Of such murders how guiltless am I!"
Then ran to regale on a new-taken fly.

J. Cunningham.

" Eagerly he looked upward after the unwearied bird."

(" *The Lark*," p. 35.)

For Preparation.—I. You have read the story of "The Discontented Pendulum," "The Spider and the Fly," and now you come to "The Fox and the Cat." These stories are called *fables*, not because they tell merely what did not happen, but because they tell what never could happen. Franklin's story of "The Whistle," Wordsworth's "Kitten and the Falling Leaves," Miss Alcott's story of "Nat," etc., all may have happened—and similar things will happen. But a fable relates what could not possibly have happened. Its object is to bring out a moral.

II. Trăv′-eled, guīde (gīd), thĩrst′-ing, shĕp′-herd (-erd), seīzed, wrĕtch′-ed, a-ghăst′, hẽrb′-age (ẽrb′ej), pōul′-try, sur-veyed′, per-çeived′, brutes. (How is *u* pronounced after *r?*)

III. Make a list of five name-words which express more than one object by the addition of *s* or *es*, or by some other change (discourses, brutes, etc.). Change ten name-words that express one object each, so as to make them express more than one (foxes, cats, days, ways, etc.).

IV. Proceeded, impatient, hunger, victim, bleat, mutton, astonished, repast, "fell beast," brutes, tyrant, moralized, "spite of morals," pullet, covert, secured, prey, regale.

V. Do we laugh at the idea of a cat and a fox making "moral discourses" (like a preacher)? Why? What names are given to the cat besides Grimalkin? (See Lesson II.) Who is called Reynard? Difference between *sheep* and *mutton?*—between *hens* and *poultry?* Do the cat and the fox really like "herbage and roots and acorns" themselves? Were the poultry eating the chaff, or picking it over for the grain left in it? Difference between *greedy* and *gluttonous?* What is absurd in the words and actions of the spider? Are we not all more apt to see the evil deeds of others than we are to correct our own?

XI.—THE LARK.

1. A little child went into the meadow just sprinkled with dew, and a thousand little suns glanced up at him, and a Lark arose, warbling her morning lay.

2. This Lark announced the joys of the coming season, and awakened endless hopes; while she herself soared

circling higher and higher, till her song was at last like the voice of an angel far up in the clear, blue sky.

3. The child had seen the earth-colored bird soar on high, and it seemed to him as if the earth had sent her forth to announce her joy and her gratitude to the sun above, because he had in friendliness and love turned his beaming face again toward her.

4. The Lark warbled her joyous and exultant lay above the hopeful fields; she sang of the loveliness of the morning, and of the earliest sunbeams playing in youthful freshness; of the gladsome springing of the flowers, and of the joyful sprouting of the fruit-stalks; and the song pleased the child beyond measure.

5. But the Lark soared still higher in her circlings, and her song grew softer and fainter still; and she sang of pleasure-trips with a friend to free and sunny hill-tops, and of pleasing expectations that rise out of the blue and fragrant distance.

6. The child did not exactly understand what he heard, but would have been glad to understand it; for he was now in expectation of wonderfully glorious things. Eagerly he looked upward after the unwearied bird; but she was lost in the fragrance of spring.

7. Then the child bent his head, turning one ear to the sky, to learn whether the little messenger of spring was no longer singing. In her vanishing tones he heard how she sang of her longings after the pure and all-present light.

8. Much longer did he listen; for the notes of the song bore him away to regions which his thoughts had never before reached, and he felt himself happier than ever in that blissful, upward flight.

9. But now the Lark came quickly down again, because its little body was too heavy for the high air, and its wings were not strong nor large enough for the pure element.

10. Then the red Corn-Poppies laughed at the plain little bird, and cried out with a shrill voice to one another, and to the surrounding stalks of corn: "Now you see that nothing comes of flying so high, and striving for empty air, since one loses his time, and brings back nothing but weary limbs and an empty stomach.

11. "That ugly, ill-dressed little creature wished to exalt herself above us all, and kept up a mighty noise. It lies there now on the ground, and can scarcely breathe any longer. But we have kept our places at the feast, and have prudently stuck to the solid ground, and have grown a great deal fatter and stronger."

12. The other little Poppies loudly clapped applause, so that the child's ears tingled, and he was about to punish them for their malicious delight, when a sky-blue Flower, just in blossom, took the word, and with gentle voice thus addressed her younger companions: "Do not suffer yourselves, my dears, to be led astray by appearances, nor by talk based on outward show.

13. "True, the Lark is tired out, and it is but empty space into which she has soared; but it is not empty space that the Lark has sought, nor has she come empty home. She strove for freedom and light, and light and freedom has she praised in her song.

14. "Earth and its joys she left behind, but she drank instead the pure air of life, and learned that it is not the earth but the sun that is abiding. Her desire to sing and to soar to the sun will make men praise her name long

after these silly boasters shall have gone down into and been buried in the ground."

15. The Lark heard this kind-hearted speech, and, with strength renewed, she sprang again into the cheerful sky. The child clapped his little hands for joy that the bird had flown up again, and the Corn-Poppies were mute, and their red faces grew pale with shame.

Translated by J. C. Pickard from F. W. Carové.

FOR PREPARATION.—I. In what country is the lark found? What "little suns" glanced up at him? (shining dew-drops.)

II. Mĕad′-ōw, sēa′-ṣon (sē′zn), a-wāk′-ened (-nd), ẽar′-li-est, lĭst′-en (lis′n), rē′-gionṣ (-juns), vŏl′-a-tĭle, stŏm′-ach, creāt′-ūre (-yur), ex-tŏlled′.

III. Write out ten of the name-words in this piece, and change them so as to express possession (child's, meadow's, sun's, lark's, etc.).

IV. Warbling, lay, announced, soared, converse, gratitude, exultant, vanishing, presentiments, ether, exalt, prudently, applause, malicious, void, abiding, demanded, retain, mute.

V. Study out the meaning of the words in this piece, and then make short sentences, in your own words, describing what the Lark did: 1. The Lark warbled her morning song. 2. The Lark told of the joys of the coming summer. 3. The Lark made all who heard her hopeful. 4. The Lark soared higher and higher, in circles; etc.

XII.—THE COMPLAINT OF THE WILD FLOWERS.

1. In the corner of a large field, and close to a swift-running brook, grew a great many wild flowers. The farmer had not driven his plow near them; and, as it was not a meadow, the cows and sheep had not cropped them off. They had a very pleasant time of it. The sun shone on them all day long, the soft wind played with them. Many, by reaching over a little, could see themselves in the water, and they could all hear the sweet

songs of the birds, who had built their nests in a tree close by.

"How gay we look, in our snug little corner!" said the Daisy one day; "that last shower has made us all so fresh!"

2. "It is all very well," said a Dandelion who grew close by, "but this place is too dull for me. I want to go and see the world."

"That is very foolish!" said a piece of Ivy, who had been busy for the last three years covering up some large stones that were lying in a heap beside the brook; "wandering about is not the way to get on."

"Well," said the Daisy, "I should be quite content if only the little children would come and see us, and clap their hands, and say how pretty we are!"

3. A Lark, whose nest was close by, heard what the Daisy said, and loved her for it; so he flew up in the air, and sang as he went:

"The Daisy has a gold eye set round with silver. She looks always up into the sky like a little star; but she does not shine at night. When the dew begins to fall, the Daisy shuts her eye and sleeps. But the birds sing on, for they love the little flower, she is so meek and fair."

The Daisy heard what the Lark said, and blushed quite red. If you look well among the daisies, you will find some of them always blushing.

4. "It is quite true," said the Buttercup, when the Lark had flown so high they could no longer hear him. "Little children once loved us very much, but now they go by to school, and do not even look at us! I am as bright a yellow as any flower can be—so bright that they used to put me under their chins to see who loved butter. I made a little chin a bright yellow, and they laughed,

and said, 'See how he loves butter!' I was merry to hear how they laughed. They called me Buttercup because I was as yellow as butter."

5. "I hope I am yellow too," said the Dandelion, "and larger than Buttercup. The Lark called the Daisy a star; but I am like a small sun. I am not a single flower, like Buttercup, but a great many little flowers made into one large one. When I go to seed I shall have a round, white head; then my head will blow to pieces, and I shall set out on my travels. Wherever I stop I shall plant one of my seeds. There will be more dandelions than ever next year."

6. "Wait till you see if we leave you any room!" said a gruff voice, and they all knew that it was a Thistle who spoke. "My seeds fly about, Cousin Dandelion, like yours; and my prickly leaves take up so much room, I am not sure you will have space to grow."

That was true enough, for the thistle is larger than the dandelion, and, though its flower is pretty and red, no one can gather it without pricking himself.

7. "I am glad I have no prickles," said a sweet voice, that filled the air with scent. "I like to be plucked by the little children. I send out a sweet smell to meet them, and they cry, 'There is a Violet!' They lift up my green leaves gently one by one; they find me hidden there, and their eyes sparkle with pleasure as they carry me off."

"Every one loves you, dear Violet!" said the Daisy, "and your sweet scent attracts more even than your beautiful color and thick, green leaves."

8. "Yes, it must be the scent," said a Dog-Violet, who was growing where every one could see him; "for my

leaves are just like my sister's, and I have a larger blossom, yet no one cares to gather me. It surely can not be because I am a few shades lighter in color."

"No, no!" said a Cowslip, shaking his long, yellow bells; "it is scent you lack. But even we who have it are not loved by little children as we should be.

9. "When they named me Cowslip, because my breath is like that of the cow, so sweet and pure, they used always to gather me. The mothers made wine and tea of me, but the little children made me into cowslip-balls—round balls—bright-yellow balls. They threw me in the air, and I filled it with scent, and dropped down into their little hands again, giddy with my pleasant flight. But now," said the Cowslip, in a sad voice, "the little children do not know how to make cowslip-balls." All the flowers sighed, they were so sorry the little children did not love them.

For Preparation.—I. Dandelion (dent = tooth: tooth of the lion). Daisy (day's-eye). Cowslip (cow's-lip).

II. Fiēld (fēld), grew (grōō), plow, could (kŏŏd), rēach′-ing, mĕad′-ōw, bu̇ilt (bĭlt), dāi′-ş̧y, läughed, piēç′-es, coŭş′-in (kŭz′n), sīghed (sīd), show′-er, dăn′-de-lī-on, thĭs′-tle (thĭs′sl), eȳes (īz), beaū′-ti-fụl (bū′-), sçĕnt (also cent and sent).

III. Certain words are used for the speaker, or the person spoken to or spoken of, to avoid repetition of name-words (these are: I, thou, you, he, she, it); they are called pronouns. Find eight pronouns in this piece.

IV. Gruff, scent, plucked, gently, sparkle, attracts, complaint, merry, blushed, giddy, flight, wandering, content, "the way to get on."

V. In what way does ivy cover up stones? Is the song of the Lark about the Daisy true? Do you know any other wild flowers besides those mentioned here? Was there anything envious in the speech of the Dog-Violet? What is envy? Was the Cowslip envious too?

XIII.—ALICE FELL.

1. The post-boy drove with fierce career,
   For threatening clouds the moon had drowned,
When suddenly I seemed to hear
   A moan, a lamentable sound.

2. As if the wind blew many ways,
   I heard the sound, and more and more;
It seemed to follow with the chaise,
   And still I heard it as before.

3. At length I to the boy called out;
   He stopped his horses at the word;
But neither cry, nor voice, nor shout,
   Nor aught else like it, could be heard.

4. The boy then smacked his whip, and fast
   The horses scampered through the rain;
And soon I heard upon the blast
   The voice, and bade them halt again.

5. Said I, alighting on the ground,
   "What can it be, this hideous moan?"
And there a little girl I found,
   Sitting behind the chaise alone.

6. "My cloak!"—no other word she spoke,
   But loud and bitterly she wept,
As if her little heart would burst;
   And down from off her seat she leapt.

7. "What ails you, child?"—She sobbed, "Look here!"
   I saw it in the wheel entangled,
A weather-beaten rag as e'er
   From any garden scarecrow dangled.

8. 'Twas twisted between nave and spoke;
   Her help she lent, and, with good heed,
Together we released the cloak—
   A miserable rag indeed!

9. "And whither are you going, child,
   To-night, along these lonesome ways?"
"To Durham," answered she, half wild.
   "Then come with me into the chaise."

10. She sat like one past all relief;
   Sob after sob she forth did send
In wretchedness, as if her grief
   Could never, never have an end.

11. "My child, in Durham do you dwell?"
   She checked herself in her distress,
And said: "My name is Alice Fell;
   I'm fatherless and motherless;

12. "And I to Durham, sir, belong!"
   Again, as if the thought would choke
Her very heart, her grief grew strong,
   And all was for her tattered cloak!

13. The chaise drove on; our journey's end
   Was nigh; and, sitting by my side,
As if she had lost her only friend
   She wept, nor would be pacified.

14. Up to the tavern-door we post;
   Of Alice and her grief I told,
And I gave money to the host,
   To buy a new cloak for the old.

15. "And let it be of duffel gray,
As warm a cloak as man can sell!"
Proud creature was she the next day,
The little orphan, Alice Fell.

William Wordsworth.

FOR PREPARATION.—I. The story of a poor little orphan girl who tries to ride behind the chaise to Durham on a rainy night. Her miserable cloak gets entangled in the wheels, and her moans attract the attention of a kind old gentleman inside the coach. Wordsworth loved to write poems describing kind acts done to the poor and suffering. Find, on the map, Durham in England.

II. Fiērçe, nēi′-ther, re-lief′, ereāt′-ūre, blew (blū) (and blue), çhāişe (shāz), nāve (and knave).

III. Make a list of ten *action-words* in this piece (words which tell what the objects expressed by the "name-words" do; as, drove, had drowned, seemed, hear, blew, heard, follow).

IV. "Fierce career," threatening, suddenly, halt, alighting, hideous, bitterly, entangled, scarecrow, dangled, ails, spoke, heed, released, lonesome, dwell, checked, nigh, pacified, tavern, host, "duffel gray" (coarse woolen cloth having a thick nap).

V. "A moan, a lamentable sound" (he says "moan," and then adds a description of it). "As if the wind blew many ways" (carrying the sound with different degrees of clearness).

XIV.—WHAT ALICE SAID TO THE KITTEN.

1. One thing was certain: that the white kitten had had nothing to do with it; it was the black kitten's fault entirely. For the white kitten had been having its face washed by the old cat for the last quarter of an hour (and bore it pretty well, considering): so you see that it couldn't have had any hand in the mischief.

2. The way Dinah washed her child's face was this: First she held the poor thing down by its ear with one

paw, and then with the other paw she rubbed its face all over, the wrong way, beginning at the nose; and just now, as I said, she was hard at work on the white kitten, which was lying quite still and trying to purr—no doubt feeling that it was all meant for its good.

3. But the black kitten had been finished with earlier in the afternoon; and so, while Alice was sitting curled up in a corner of the great arm-chair, half talking to herself and half asleep, the kitten had been having a grand game of romps with the ball of worsted that Alice had been trying to wind up, and had been rolling it up and down till it had all come undone again; and there it was, spread over the hearth-rug, all kinds of tangles, with the kitten running after its own tail in the middle.

4. "Oh, you wicked, wicked little thing!" cried Alice, catching up the kitten, and giving it a kiss to make it understand that it was in disgrace. "Really, Dinah ought to have taught you better manners!—You ought, Dinah; you know you ought!" she added, looking reproachfully at the old cat, and speaking in as cross a voice as she could manage; and then she scrambled back into the arm-chair, taking the kitten and the worsted with her, and began winding up the ball again.

5. But she didn't get on very fast, as she was talking all the time, sometimes to the kitten and sometimes to herself. Kitty sat very demurely on her knee, pretending to watch the progress of the winding, and now and then putting out one paw and gently touching the ball, as if it would be glad to help, if it might.

6. "Do you know what to-morrow is, kitty?" Alice began. "You'd have guessed if you'd been up in the window with me; only Dinah was making you tidy, so

you couldn't. I was watching the boys getting in sticks for the bonfire; and it takes plenty of sticks, kitty! But it got so cold, and it snowed so, they had to leave off.

7. "Never mind, kitty; we'll go and see the bonfire to-morrow." Here Alice wound two or three turns of the worsted round the kitten's neck, just to see how it would look: this led to a scramble, in which the ball rolled down upon the floor, and yards and yards of it got unwound again.

8. "Do you know, I was so angry, kitty," Alice went on, as soon as they were comfortably settled again, "when I saw all the mischief you had been doing, I was very nearly opening the window and putting you out into the snow? And you'd have deserved it, you little, mischievous darling! What have you got to say for yourself? Now, don't interrupt me!" she went on, holding up one finger. "I'm going to tell you all your faults. Number One: You squeaked twice while Dinah was washing your face this morning.

9. "Now, you can't deny it, kitty; I heard you! What's that you say?"—pretending that the kitten was speaking.—"Her paw went into your eye? Well, that's your fault, for keeping your eyes open. If you'd shut them tight up, it wouldn't have happened. Now, don't make any more excuses, but listen. Number Two: You pulled Snowdrop away by the tail, just as I had put down the saucer of milk before her.—What? you were thirsty, were you? How do you know she wasn't thirsty too? Now for Number Three: You unwound every bit of the worsted while I wasn't looking!

10. "That's three faults, kitty, and you've not been punished for any of them yet. You know, I'm saving up

all your punishments for Wednesday week.—Suppose they had saved up all *my* punishments," she went on, talking more to herself than to the kitten, "what would they do at the end of a year? I should be sent to prison, I suppose, when the day came. Or—let me see—suppose each punishment was to be going without a dinner? Then, when the miserable day came, I should have to go without fifty dinners at once. Well, I shouldn't mind that much. I'd far rather go without them than eat them."

Lewis Carroll.

For Preparation.—I. From "Through the Looking-Glass." "One thing was certain: that the white kitten had had nothing to do with it" (tangling up Alice's worsted). "Snowdrop" is the name of the white kitten. "Dinah" is the old cat.

II. Mĭs′-chief (-chif), ēar′-li-er, tạlk′-ing (tawk′-), wọrst′-ed (wo͝ost′-), a-gain′ (-gĕn′), heärth (härth), wĭck′-ed, cătch′-ing, knee (nee), toŭch′-ing (tŭch′-), fạults, thĭrst′-y̆.

III. When an action-word is used, it tells something that an object does. Make a list of ten of the action-words in this piece, and write before each the name of the object which it tells about (Dinah—washed, held, etc.).

IV. Certain, considering, tangle, disgrace, reproachfully, manage, demurely, pretending, progress, bonfire, deserved, interrupt, excuses, punished, miserable, "Wednesday week" (i. e., a week from next Wednesday).

V. "Wicked little thing." Is *wicked* a word that can be applied to animals? Why not? Is it laughable to apply it to animals? Is it laughable to speak of a kitten as the cat's "child"—of a kitten "feeling that it was all meant for its good"—as if the kitten were human, and could think? Find the other laughable expressions which speak of the animals as though they had human thoughts and feelings ("Dinah ought to have taught you better manners," etc.). We sometimes laugh at a person who says or thinks one thing and does another: was it laughable for Alice to call the kitten "wicked," and then kiss it? Find other absurd things like this ("mischievous darling," etc.).

XV.—THE SPIDER.

1. A child went with his father into the vineyard, and there saw a bee in the web of an ugly spider. The spider was just opening his fangs to attack the bee, when the child took his stick, broke the web, and set the little prisoner free.

2. When his father saw this, he asked the boy how he could be so regardless of the toilsome and beautiful web which the spider had prepared with so much ingenuity.

3. The child replied, "Has the spider not directed all his ingenuity to blood and malice, while the bee collects honey and wax, from which man derives much pleasure and benefit?"

4. "But," said the father, "perhaps you have done the spider injustice; for, see how his web protects the grapes from flies and wasps, that otherwise would do much mischief!"

5. "Ah!" said the boy, "it is not with the intent to shield the grapes, but to satisfy his thirst for blood, that the spider labors with so much dexterity."

"True," said the father; "probably the spider has little reason to be concerned about the grapes."

6. "Then," said the boy, "the good the spider does is of no avail to his spiteful character; for a good intention is certainly the only merit in a good deed."

7. "True," said the father; "but Nature, you see, knows how to apply even malicious things for the preservation of the good and useful."

8. "And why," asked the boy, "does the spider not work his web in social union, like the bees, that live together with so much comfort and happiness?"

9. "Dear child," said the father, "only for good ends can multitudes associate. The bond of malice and selfishness carries the seed of destruction within itself; but Nature has placed the hostile and the friendly, the malicious and the good, side by side, so that the contrast might be the greater, and thus convey a lesson to those who are willing to learn."

F. A. Krummacher.

FOR PREPARATION.—I. Is this story a fable, or could the event here described have actually happened? (See Lesson X.)

II. Vīne′-yard (vĭn′-), beaū′-ti-fụl (bū′-), ūn′-ion, ăs-sō′-ci-ate (-shĭ-āt), hŏn′-ȇy, mĭs′-chief (-chĭf).

III. Action-words express the time in which the action is performed. To express past time, some add *ed;* some make other changes. Make a list of ten action-words in this piece that express past time, and write opposite each the word expressing present time (went—go; saw—see; was—is; took—take; broke—break; set—set; asked—ask, etc.).

IV. Ugly, fangs, attack, regardless, toilsome, web, replied, directed, malice, derives, benefit, avail, spiteful, intention, merit, apply, malicious, social, multitudes, destruction, hostile. (The stiff, pompous language into which this fable is translated should all be paraphrased into such words as the pupil uses. It will make a good language-lesson.)

V. The spider's labors are spoken of as showing "ingenuity," "dexterity," and what else? Illustrate the meaning of these words by telling what the spider does that shows dexterity, etc. What do you think of the reason which the father gives for the fact that spiders do not work together in company? ("social union.") Do not wolves hunt in droves, and robbers and burglars work together? But, on the other hand are evil men likely to be faithful and kind toward each other?

XVI.—ALICE'S DREAM OF THE CHESS-QUEENS.

1. "I didn't know I was to have a party at all," said Alice; "but if there is to be one, I think I ought to invite the guests."

"We gave you the opportunity of doing it," the Red Queen remarked; "but I dare say you've not had many lessons in manners yet."

2. "Manners are not taught in lessons," said Alice. "Lessons teach you to do sums, and things of that sort."

"Can you do addition?" the White Queen asked. "What's one and one, and one and one, and one and one, and one and one, and one and one?"

3. "I don't know," said Alice. "I lost count."

"She can't do addition," the Red Queen interrupted. —"Can you do subtraction? Take nine from eight."

"Nine from eight! I can't, you know," Alice replied, very readily; "but—"

4. "She can't do subtraction," said the White Queen. —"Can you do division? Divide a loaf by a knife—what's the answer to that?"—"I suppose—" Alice was beginning; but the Red Queen answered for her: "Bread and butter, of course. Try another subtraction sum: Take a bone from a dog, what remains?"

5. Alice considered. "The bone wouldn't remain, of course, if I took it; and the dog wouldn't remain—it would come to bite me; and I'm sure I shouldn't remain!"

"Then you think nothing would remain?" said the Red Queen.

"I think that's the answer."

6. "Wrong, as usual," said the Red Queen; "the dog's temper would remain."

"But I don't see how—"

"Why, look here!" the Red Queen cried. "The dog would lose his temper, wouldn't he?"

"Perhaps he would," Alice replied, cautiously.

7. "Then, if the dog went away, his temper would remain!" the Red Queen exclaimed, triumphantly.

Alice said, as gravely as she could, "They might go different ways." But she couldn't help thinking to herself, "What dreadful nonsense we're talking!"

"She can't do sums a bit!" the queens said together, with great emphasis.

8. "Can *you* do sums?" Alice said, turning suddenly on the White Queen; for she didn't like being found fault with so much.

The queen gasped, and shut her eyes. "I can do addition," she said, "if you give me time; but I can't do subtraction under any circumstances."

9. "Of course you know your A B C?" said the Red Queen.

"To be sure I do!" said Alice.

"So do I," the White Queen whispered; "we'll often say it over together, dear. And I'll tell you a secret: I can read words of one letter! Isn't that grand? However, don't be discouraged; you'll come to it in time."

10. Here the Red Queen began again. "Can you answer useful questions?" she said. "How is bread made?"

"I know that!" Alice cried, quickly. "You take some flour—"

"Where do you pick the flower?" the White Queen asked—"in a garden, or in the hedges?"

"Well, it isn't picked at all," Alice explained; "it's ground—"

"How many acres of ground?" said the White Queen. "You mustn't leave out so many things."

11. "Fan her head!" the Red Queen anxiously interrupted. "She'll be feverish after so much thinking."

So they set to work, and fanned her with branches of leaves, till she had to beg them to leave off, it blew her hair about so.

"She's all right again now," said the Red Queen. "Do you know languages? What's the French for 'fiddle-de-dee'?"

"'Fiddle-de-dee' is not English," Alice replied, gravely.

"Who ever said it was?" asked the Red Queen.

12. Alice thought she saw a way out of the difficulty this time. "If you'll tell me what language 'fiddle-de-dee' is, I'll tell you the French for it!" she exclaimed, triumphantly.

But the Red Queen drew herself up rather stiffly, and said, "Queens never make bargains."

"I wish queens never asked questions," Alice thought to herself.

13. "Don't let us quarrel," the White Queen said, in an anxious tone. "What is the cause of lightning?"

"The cause of lightning," Alice said, very decidedly, for she felt quite certain about this, "is the thunder—no, no!" she hastily corrected herself; "I meant the other way."

"It's too late to correct it," said the Red Queen; "when you've once said a thing, that fixes it, and you must take the consequences." *Lewis Carroll.*

FOR PREPARATION.—I. From "Through the Looking-Glass," or Alice's dream of what she saw when she walked through the looking-glass into the room on the other side.

II. Guĕsts, quĭck′-ly, ex-plāined′, ā′-creş (ā′kerz), lăn′-gua-ġeş, cŏn′-se-quen-çes.

III. Make a list of five action-words in this piece that express past time with *ed;* of five expressing past time in other ways.

IV. Invite, opportunity, addition, interrupted, subtraction, replied, readily, division, remains, considered, usual, temper, cautiously, triumphantly, gravely, nonsense, fault, gasped, circumstances, secret, grand, discouraged, hedges, difficulty, bargains, quarrel, correct, fixes.

V. The opportunity for absurd and laughable situations is found in this story, in the fact that everything seen in a looking-glass is changed from right to left. There is a change of this sort even in the methods of thinking of the chess-queens that Alice meets.

XVII.—IN THE FOREST.

1. In the cottage it was dull and close and quiet, while out of doors everything seemed to smile and exult in the clear air and boundless world. So the child went out into the green wood, of which the dragon-fly had told him so many pleasant things.

2. There he found everything even more beautiful and lovely than he had been told. For, wherever he went, the tender mosses kissed his feet, the grasses clasped his knees, the flowers caressed his hands, the bushes stroked his cheeks kindly and coolingly, and the tall trees welcomed him to their fragrant shadow.

3. There was no end to his delight. The little birds of the forest piped and sang as well as they could, and skipped and flitted gayly about, and the little wood-flowers vied with each other in beauty and fragrance, and every sweet sound took a sweet odor by the hand, and so went down into the heart of the child and had a merry wedding-dance.

4. The nightingale and the lily of the valley led the dance. Each lived so entirely—single and alone—in the

heart of the other, that one could not tell whether the notes of the nightingale were winged lilies, or the lilies nightingale-notes visible like dew-drops.

5. The child was filled with joy. He sat down, and almost thought he must take root and dwell among the little plant-people, that he might take part more intimately in their tender joys.

6. For he had an inward satisfaction in the secret, quiet, obscure life of the moss and heather, which knew nothing of storm, nor of frost, nor of the burning heat of the sun; but were well content with their many neighbors and friends, refreshing themselves, in peace and good-fellowship, with the dew and the shadow bestowed upon them by the lofty trees.

7. For them indeed it was always a high festival when a sunbeam sought them out; while the tops of the tall trees above them found great delight only in the glowing red of morning and evening.

Translated by J. C. Pickard from F. W. Carové.

For Preparation.—I. In the "Story without an End," from which also the piece about "The Lark" (Lesson XI.) was taken, the child goes out into the forest to see for himself the wonderful things which the dragon-fly has described to him.

II. Cŏt′-tage, plĕaș′-ant, beaū′-ti-ful, whêr-ĕv′-er, de-līght′ (-līt′), could (kŏŏd), nīght′-in-gāle, lĭl′-y, văl′-ley, brēathed, naught (nawt), bowed (boud), lĭl′-ieș, thôught (thawt), pēo′-ple (pē′pl), hĕath′-er, neigh′-bors (nā′burz), grōwths, sôught (sawt).

III. Change the following so as to express present time: was, seemed, went, told, kissed, clasped. Find other action-words expressing past time, in the third, fourth, and fifth paragraphs.

IV. Exult, boundless, dragon-fly, clasped, "birds piped," vied, fragrance, visible, intimately, obscure.

V. In this story of the child's visit to the forest, and of his communion with the flowers and birds, the birds and flowers are represented as having human feelings and habits. The child is like a poet, and fancies animals and things to be alive, to possess souls, and to act like human beings.

XVIII.—EMPHASIS BY TIME.

We observed, in our first lesson, that we know the meaning of what is said to us by the *louder* tones given to the important words—that is, by the emphasis of "*force*." Listen to another way by which a word is made emphatic. "*Y-o-u* did that; I *k-n-o-w* you did."

Observe that "you" and "know" are spoken *more slowly* than the other words—that we give more *time* to them.

"*Time*," then, as well as "force," helps us to emphasize.

As louder force is represented to the eye by printing the emphatic words in *italics* and CAPITALS, so *longer time* may be represented to the eye by spacing the words to which it can be given, thus: "Y-o-u are the very s-o-u-l of *mischief*, and, if you don't behave *better*, I shall send you a-w-a-y."

We can not stretch out the long time on the syllable "*mis*" in mischief, or "*bet*" in better. And the reason is, that these syllables are short (by nature and good usage), and time long enough for good emphasis can be given only to the *longer* sounds. But, when the accented syllables are open and long, remember that the emphasis of time is much more thoughtful and graceful than that of force.

"'*Thanks!*' said the judge; 'a s-w-e-e-t-e-r draught
From a f-a-i-r-e-r hand was never quaffed.'"

"I had a brother once, a g-r-a-cious boy,

. . . . .

A summer b-l-o-o-m on his f-a-i-r cheeks, a s-m-i-l-e
Parting his innocent lips. In one short hour,
The pretty, h-a-r-m-less boy was s-l-a-i-n."

"Oh! you h-a-r-d hearts, you c-r-u-e-l men of Rome!"

"D-e-a-r, *gentle*, p-a-tient, n-o-b-l-e Nell was *dead*—n-o s-l-e-e-p so b-e-a-u-tiful and c-a-l-m."

"Gentle" and "dead" are short, and can not take long time; so they, like *all other short* syllables, must be emphasized by force and slide.

XIX.—THE SHIPWRECK OF ROBINSON CRUSOE.

1. Nothing can describe the confusion of thought which I felt when I sank into the water; for though I swam very well, yet I could not deliver myself from the waves so as to draw breath, till that wave, having driven me, or rather carried me, a vast way on toward the shore, and having spent itself, went back, and left me upon the land almost dry, but half dead with the water I took in.

2. I had so much presence of mind as well as breath left, that, seeing myself nearer the mainland than I expected, I got upon my feet, and endeavored to make on toward the land as fast as I could, before another wave should return and take me up again. But I soon found it was impossible to avoid it; for I saw the sea come after me as high as a great hill, and as furious as an enemy which I had no means or strength to contend with.

3. My business was to hold my breath, and raise myself upon the water, if I could; and so, by swimming, to

preserve my breathing and pilot myself toward the shore, if possible: my greatest concern now being, that the wave, as it would carry me a great way toward the shore when it came on, might not carry me back again with it when it gave back toward the sea.

4. The wave that came upon me again buried me at once twenty or thirty feet deep in its own body, and I could feel myself carried with a mighty force and swiftness toward the shore, a very great way; but I held my breath, and assisted myself to swim still forward with all my might. I was ready to burst with holding my breath, when, as I felt myself rising up, so, to my immediate relief, I found my head and hands shoot out above the surface of the water; and though it was not two seconds of time that I could keep myself so, yet it relieved me greatly, and gave me breath and new courage.

5. I was covered again with water a good while, but not so long but I held it out; and, finding the water had spent itself, and began to return, I struck forward against the return of the wave, and felt ground again with my feet. I stood still a few moments to recover breath, and till the water went from me, and then took to my heels and ran, with what strength I had, farther toward the shore. But neither would this deliver me from the fury of the sea, which came pouring in after me again; and twice more I was lifted up by the waves and carried forward as before, the shore being very flat.

6. The last time of these two had well-nigh been fatal to me; for the sea, having hurried me along, as before, landed me, or rather dashed me, against a piece of a rock, and that with such force that it left me senseless, and indeed helpless as to my own deliverance; for the blow, taking my side and breast, beat the breath, as it were, quite

out of my body; and, had it returned again immediately, I must have been strangled in the water: but I recovered a little before the return of the wave, and, seeing I should again be covered with the water, I resolved to hold fast by a piece of the rock, and so to hold my breath, if possible, till the wave went back.

7. Now, as the waves were not so high as the first, being nearer land, I held my hold till the wave abated, and then fetched another run, which brought me so near the shore that the next wave, though it went over me, yet did not so swallow me up as to carry me away; and, the next run I took, I got to the mainland, where, to my great comfort, I clambered up the cliffs of the shore, and sat me down upon the grass, free from danger, and quite out of the reach of the water. *Daniel De Foe.*

For Preparation.—I. Have you read the "Adventures of Robinson Crusoe"?

II. En-dĕav′-ored, bus′-i-ness (bĭz′-ness), re-liēved′, coŭr′-age (kŭr′ej), con-fū′-sion (-zhun), rāise (rāz), brĕath, tō′-ward (tō′ard), bur′-ied (bĕr′id), mīght′-y (mīt′-ĭ), a-gain′ (-gĕn′).

III. Change, so as to express present time, these words: *sunk, swam, carried, driven, went, left, took, had, got, found, was, saw, came, gave.* Past forms of *stand, walk, run?*

IV. Confusion, deliver, presence of mind, furious, concern, surface, fatal, abated, fetched, contend, pilot, recover, resolved, clambered.

V. How many waves did Crusoe encounter before he reached the land? What was the nature of the shore of the island upon which Crusoe was wrecked? (steep and precipitous, or flat? See § 7.) Can you explain what causes waves? Notice old-fashioned expressions and uses of words in this piece, and change them to such expressions as we use in ordinary life; e. g., "water I took in"; "make on toward the land"; "held it out"; "the blow taking my side and breast"; "gave back"; "fetched another run"; "sat me down."

"The antlered monarch of the waste
Sprang from his heathery couch in haste."

("*The Chase*," p. 59.)

With anxious eye he wandered o'er
Mountain and meadow, moss and moor,
And pondered refuge from his toil
By far Lochard or Aberfoyle.

7. But nearer was the copse-wood gray
That waved and wept on Loch Achray,
And mingled with the pine-trees blue
On the bold cliffs of Ben Venue.
Fresh vigor with the hope returned;
With flying foot the heath he spurned,
Held westward with unwearied race,
And left behind the panting chase.

Sir Walter Scott.

For Preparation.—I. From the beginning of the "Lady of the Lake." "Monan's rill" (branch of the Tēith, which empties into the Firth of Forth), Glenart'ney, Uam-Vär', Ben Voirlich (vōr'lik), Mentēith', Lŏchärd', Aberfoyle (ă-ber-foil'), Loch Achray, Ben Venūe' (places among the Scottish Highlands, sixty miles northwest of Edinburgh).

II. Fōe'-men, fal'-con (faw'kn), câirn, piērç'-ing, ănx'-ioŭs (ănk'-shus), bēa'-con (bē'kn), kĭn'-dled (-dld), hēaths (a word used much in Scotland, a flowering shrub), e'er.

III. Number of poetic feet in each line? "The *stag* | at *eve* | had *drunk* | his *fill*." Accent on the first or second syllable of each foot? Distinction between roe and doe?

IV. Lair, "hoof and horn," warder, "antlered monarch," waste, crested, dale, glen, cavern, response, covert, rout (clamorous throng of huntsmen), ken (view), din, linn (mountain brook), sylvan, gallant, perforce, shrewdly, mettled, realms, varied, copse. Meaning of *Ben* (a mountain) and *Loch* (a lake).

V. What time is meant by the "sun kindling his beacon red," etc.? (1.) "Opening pack"? (of hounds.) "Less loud the sounds," etc.? (5.) What explanation given of this in the last eight lines of the stanza?

XXI.—DRIVING BEES.

1. In former times all the bees in a hive had to be destroyed before the honey could be got. This cruel method has now been abandoned, and the honey is secured without killing a single bee. The new mode was publicly exhibited at a bee-show in the Crystal Palace, near London, in September, 1874, and is thus described:

2. A few puffs from a pipe caused the bees to retreat among the combs, and the hive was gently turned upside down. A new and empty hive was then placed above the other so as to cover it completely; then the chief bee-master drummed with his fist upon the lower hive, and waited for the rush of the bees to the upper hive.

3. At the first disturbance of their hive, the bees had all run to fill their bags with honey. Thus they were heavy and good-tempered, and even those who escaped through the gap between the two hives did not sting the bee-master, although his face and hands were unprotected.

4. After the lapse of a few minutes a rushing sound was heard. This proved that the bees had begun to move upward. Whenever the queen-bee passed up, the others immediately followed. It was now safe to lift up the edge of the top hive, so that what was going on inside could be distinctly seen.

5. Like soldiers swarming up the walls of a city which they were about to take by storm, the bees were seen hurrying upward in thousands, climbing over each other's bodies several deep, without ever regarding the open space between the two hives, by which they might easily have escaped into the open air.

6. The combs were then taken out of the old and deserted hive, and put into frames and placed in a machine for extracting the honey. This machine is turned rapidly round by a handle, and the speed with which it makes the combs revolve drives all the honey out of the cells. As the honey flies out of the combs it is dashed against the inside of the vessel, and falls down to the bottom, whence it drops into the jar placed below to collect it.

7. The next thing is to tie up with tape the old combs, some emptied of their honey, and some still full, in new frames, and to place them in the new hive. In twenty-four hours, or at most forty-eight, the tape will be no longer needed, for the bees, with cement and wax, will have built the combs into the new frames, and will quickly proceed to fill them anew with honey.

8. By thus making use a second time of the old combs the time of the bees is saved, and they give to honey-making the precious days of summer, which would otherwise require to be devoted to the building up of fresh waxen cells. The whole process of driving the bees from the old to the new hive occupied less than an hour's time.

London Correspondent.

For Preparation.—I. "Crystal Palace, near London"—what was this building erected for? Why called "Crystal"?

II. Hŏn'ey, pŭb'-lic-ly, ex-hĭb'-it-ed, combs (kōmz), ĕmp'-ty, chiēf, wāit'-ed, hĕav'-y, găp, ĕdge (ĕj), climb'-ing (klīm'-), ma-chīne' (-sheen'), a-gainst' (-gĕnst'), çĕm'-ent, quĭck'-ly.

III. For the following action-words write corresponding name-words of which the actions are told: Could be got (honey), has been abandoned (method), was exhibited (mode), caused (puffs), turned, placed, drummed, waited, passed, were seen.

IV. Method, abandoned, retreat, hive, completely, disturbance, escaped, unprotected, lapse, proved, immediately, distinctly, swarming, deserted, extracting, revolve, precious, require, devoted, process, occupied.

V. "A few puffs"—of what? (tobacco-smoke.) "Fill their bags with honey" (what bags do bees have?) What is a "queen-bee"? What is gained by the process of saving the honey-comb and using it over again?

XXII.—THE HUNTSMAN.

1. Alone, but with unbated zeal,
The horseman plied the scourge and steel;
For, jaded now and spent with toil,
Embossed with foam and dark with soil,
While every gasp with sobs he drew,
The laboring stag strained full in view.
2. Two dogs of black Saint Hubert's breed,
Unmatched for courage, breath, and speed,
Fast on his flying traces came,
And all but won that desperate game:
For, scarce a spear's length from his haunch,
Vindictive toiled the bloodhounds stanch;
3. Nor nearer might the dogs attain,
Nor farther might the quarry strain.
Thus up the margin of the lake,
Between the precipice and brake,
O'er stock and rock their race they take.

4. The hunter marked that mountain high,
The lone lake's western boundary,
And deemed the stag must turn to bay,
Where that huge rampart barred the way;
Already glorying in the prize,
Measured his antlers with his eyes;
5. For the death-wound, and death-halloo,
Mustered his breath, his whinyard drew.

But, thundering as he came prepared,
With ready arm and weapon bared,
The wily quarry shunned the shock,
And turned him from th' opposing rock;
6. Then, dashing down a darksome glen,
Soon lost to hound and hunter's ken,
In the deep Trossach's wildest nook
His solitary refuge took.
7. There, while, close couched, the thicket shed
Cold dews and wild flowers on his head,
He heard the baffled dogs in vain
Rave through the hollow pass amain,
Chiding the rocks that yelled again.

8. Close on the hounds the hunter came,
To cheer them on the vanished game;
But, stumbling in the rugged dell,
The gallant horse exhausted fell.
9. The impatient rider strove in vain
To rouse him with the spur and rein;
For the good steed, his labors o'er,
Stretched his stiff limbs to rise no more.
Then, touched with pity and remorse,
He sorrowed o'er the expiring horse:
10. "I little thought, when first thy rein
I slacked upon the banks of Seine,
That Highland eagle e'er should feed
On thy fleet limbs, my matchless steed!
Woe worth the chase, woe worth the day,
That costs thy life, my gallant gray!"

Sir Walter Scott.

FOR PREPARATION.—I. This is another extract from "The Lady of the Lake," continuing "The Chase" (Lesson XX.). The King of Scotland is hunting among the Highlands of Scotland, and gets lost in the wilds; his steed dies of over-exertion. Where is the Seine River?

II. Coŭr′-aġe (kŭr′ej), hău̇nch, rei̱n (rān), fleet, ex-ha̤ust′-ed (egz-hawst′ed).

III. Explain what time is denoted in the following action-words, and tell how you know it by the spelling: *plied, spent, drew, strained, came, won, toiled, might, take, fell, strove, costs, thought.*

IV. Unbated zeal, jaded, embossed, desperate, brake, stanch, bay, quarry, wily, shunned, ken, solitary refuge, couched, thicket, baffled, amain, chiding, rugged dell, spur, remorse, slacked, steed, gallant.

V. "Plied the scourge and steel" (scourge = the whip, and steel = the spurs). "All but won"—express this in other words. "The hunter marked" —what meaning has *marked* here? "Huge rampart" (the mountain is called a "rampart," as though it "barred the way," like the wall of a fort). "Measured his antlers" (the hunters saved the antlers, or branching horns, of their game, as trophies of their success). "Whinyard" (he drew his sword and rode up to strike the deer, but the deer turned in a different direction from the "rampart," and escaped down a dark, narrow valley). "Woe worth the chase!" (worth means *betide*, or *be to:* Woe be to the chase!)

XXIII.—SOLON.

1. Solon was one of the wise men of Greece. He it was who gave that clever answer to Crœsus, King of Lydia. Crœsus was so rich, that even now it is common to say, "as rich as Crœsus." This king showed his wealth to Solon, and then asked "if he did not think the possessor of so much gold the happiest of men." "No," replied the philosopher; "I know a happier man: an honest laborer who has just enough to live on."

2. "And who the next happiest?" said the king, expecting himself to be named. "The next happiest," answered Solon, "are two virtuous sons who were remarkable for their duty and kindness to their mother."—"And think you not that I am happy?" exclaimed the

disappointed monarch.—"No man can be deemed happy till his death," said the sage; meaning, I suppose, that according as his life was spent could his state be judged.

3. When Crœsus afterward was taken prisoner by Cyrus, and was about to be burnt, he recollected this conversation, and cried out, "O Solon, Solon!" Cyrus inquired the meaning of this exclamation; and when the cause of it was explained, he set Crœsus at liberty, and owned himself instructed by the hint of Solon. So the philosopher saved the life of one king and improved another.

4. Thespis was the first poet who performed comedies at Athens. They had no play-houses, but used to act upon an open cart, somewhat as our Merry-Andrews do now. Solon did not disapprove of these shows, but went himself to see them. When the play was over, he called Thespis, who had been acting various characters, and asked him if he was not ashamed to speak so many lies. Thespis replied, "It was all in jest."

5. Admire, I beseech you, the answer of Solon. Striking his staff on the ground violently, he cried: "If we encourage ourselves to speak falsely in jest, we shall run the chance of acquiring a habit of speaking falsely in serious matters." Had he never spoken any other words than these, he would have deserved the character of a wise man.

6. Æsop, who wrote so many ingenious fables, was much caressed by King Crœsus; while Solon, for his bluntness, was little noticed. Æsop therefore said: "A man should not converse with kings, if he does not choose to say what is agreeable to them."

You rascal! for an hour have I been grubbing,
Giving my crying whiskers here a scrubbing
With razors just like oyster-knives.
Sirrah! I tell you, you're a knave,
To cry up razors that can't shave!"

6. "Friend," quoth the razor-man, "I'm not a knave.
As for the razors you have bought,
Upon my word, I never thought
That they would shave."
"Not think they'd shave!" quoth Hodge, with wondering eyes,
And voice not much unlike an Indian yell:
"What were they made for, then?—you scamp!" he cries.
"Made!" quoth the fellow, with a smile—"To SELL!"

John Wolcott.

FOR PREPARATION.—I. John Wolcott (called "Peter Pindar"). "Eighteen pence" English money (about thirty-six cents of our money. Razors at three cents apiece—"wondrous cheap," indeed!).

II. Mū'-ṣi-cal, rā'-zorṣ, broad (brawd), be-nēath', pāid, sīghed (sīd), friĕnd, bôught (bawt), would (wŏŏd).

III. What do quotation-marks (" ") inclose? Tell whose words are included between them in the first place where they are used;—in the second place, etc.

IV. Fellow, offered, "eighteen pence," certainly, cheap, bumpkin (blockhead), rascal, knave, provided, enormous, prize, lathered, grinning, grub, "hedger cutting furze," impostors, rogue, scamp, quoth.

V. Was it quite honest in Hodge to buy the razors if he thought they were stolen? Is there any need of "most" before "enormous"? Why is the bumpkin called a "clown"? "Flay themselves" (i. e., the razor scratched the skin off, but would not cut the beard).

XXV.—ROBINSON CRUSOE'S MANUFACTURE OF POTTERY.

1. I had long studied, by some means or other, to make myself some earthen vessels—which, indeed, I wanted much, but knew not where to come at them. However, considering the heat of the climate, I did not doubt but, if I could find out any clay, I might botch up some such pot as might, being dried in the sun, be hard and strong enough to bear handling, and to hold anything that was dry, and required to be kept so; and as this was necessary in the preparing corn-meal, etc., which was the thing I was upon, I resolved to make some as large as I could, and fit only to stand like jars, to hold what should be put into them.

2. It would make the reader pity me, or rather laugh at me, to tell how many awkward ways I took to shape this jar; what odd, misshapen, ugly things I made; how many of them fell in, and how many fell out—the clay not being stiff enough to bear its own weight; how many cracked by the over-violent heat of the sun, being set out too hastily; and how many fell in pieces with only removing, as well before as after they were dried; and, in a word, how, after having labored hard to find the clay, to dig it, to temper it, to bring it home, and work it, I could not make above two large earthen, ugly things (I can not call them jars) in about two months' labor.

3. However, as the sun baked these two very dry and hard, I lifted them very gently, and set them down again in two great wicker baskets, which I had made on purpose for them, that they might not break; and, as between the pot and the basket there was a little room to

spare, I stuffed it full of the rice and barley straw; and these two pots, being to stand always dry, I thought would hold my dry corn, and perhaps the meal, when the corn was bruised.

4. Though I succeeded so poorly in my design for large pots, yet I made several smaller things with better success, such as little round pots, flat dishes, pitchers, and pipkins, and anything my hand turned to; and the heat of the sun baked them very hard.

5. But all this would not answer my end, which was to get an earthen pot to hold liquids and bear the fire, which none of these could do. It happened some time after, making a pretty large fire for cooking my meat, when I went to put it out after I had done with it, I found a broken piece of one of my earthenware vessels in the fire, burnt as hard as a stone, and red as a tile. I was agreeably surprised to see it, and said to myself that certainly they might be made to burn when whole, if they would burn when broken.

6. This set me to study how to order my fire so as to make it burn some pots. I had no notion of a kiln, such as the potters burn in, or of glazing them with lead, though I had some lead to do it with; but I placed three large pipkins and two or three pots in a pile, one upon another, and placed my fire-wood all around it, with a great heap of embers under them.

7. I plied the fire with fresh fuel round the outside and upon the top, till I saw the pots in the inside red-hot quite through, and observed that they did not crack at all. When I saw them clear red, I let them stand in that heat about five or six hours, till I found one of them, though it did not crack, did melt or run; for the sand

which was mixed with the clay melted by the violence of the heat, and would have run into glass if I had gone on.

8. So I slacked my fire gradually, till the pots began to abate of the red color; and watching them all night, that I might not let the fire abate too fast, in the morning I had three very good—I will not say handsome—pipkins, and two other earthen pots, as hard burnt as could be desired; and one of them perfectly glazed with the running of the sand.

9. After this experiment, I need not say that I wanted no sort of earthenware for my use; but as to the shapes of them, they were very indifferent (as any one may suppose), as I had no way of making them but as the children make dirt-pies, or as a woman would make pies who had never learned to raise paste.

10. No joy at a thing of so mean a nature was ever equal to mine, when I found I had made an earthen pot that would bear the fire; and I had hardly patience to stay till they were cold, before I set one on the fire again with some water in it, to boil me some meat, which it did admirably well; and with a piece of a kid I made some very good broth, though I wanted oatmeal and several other ingredients requisite to make it as good as I would have had it.

Daniel De Foe.

FOR PREPARATION.—I. After Crusoe had escaped from the sea (Lesson XIX.), he tried to make himself comfortable. He made a house out of a cave; planted some seeds that he recovered from the wreck; tamed some goats, etc. This extract tells us how he learned to make crockery from clay.

II. Nĕç′-es-sa-ry, pre-pâr′-ing, awk′-ward, weight (wāt), lā-bored, lĭq′-uid, piēçe, kĭln (kĭl).

III. In the following, which word is the name of the object, and which one the description of it?—*some means, earthen vessels, any clay, awkward ways, ugly things, little room.* Notice the old-fashioned expressions and uses of words: "come at them" and "I was upon" (1); "answer my end" (purpose) (5); "wanted" for *needed* (10). (All sentences containing unusual modes of expression should be paraphrased by the pupil in his own words.)

IV. Considering, climate, botch, required, temper, bruised, design, tile, notion, glazing, pipkins, embers, fuel, violence, slacked, gradually, abate, experiment, indifferent, patience, admirably, ingredients, requisite.

V. Write in your own words the sixth, seventh, and eighth paragraphs, and try to tell the particulars in fewer words.

XXVI.—A PSALM OF LIFE.

1. Tell me not, in mournful numbers,
   Life is but an empty dream!
   For the soul is dead that slumbers,
   And things are not what they seem.

2. Life is real! life is earnest!
   And the grave is not its goal;
   Dust thou art, to dust returnest,
   Was not spoken of the soul.

3. Not enjoyment, and not sorrow,
   Is our destined end or way;
   But to act, that each to-morrow
   Find us farther than to-day.

4. Art is long, and Time is fleeting,
   And our hearts, though stout and brave,
   Still, like muffled drums, are beating
   Funeral marches to the grave.

5. In the world's broad field of battle,
   In the bivouac of life,
   Be not like dumb, driven cattle—
   Be a hero in the strife!

6. Trust no future, howe'er pleasant;
   Let the dead past bury its dead!
Act, act in the living present,
   Heart within, and God o'erhead!

7. Lives of great men all remind us
   We can make our lives sublime,
And, departing, leave behind us
   Footprints on the sands of time:

8. Footprints that perhaps another,
   Sailing o'er life's solemn main,
A forlorn and shipwrecked brother,
   Seeing, shall take heart again.

9. Let us, then, be up and doing,
   With a heart for any fate;
Still achieving, still pursuing,
   Learn to labor and to wait.

Henry W. Longfellow.

FOR PREPARATION.—I. "Dust thou art" (Eccl. iii. 20: "All go to one place; all are of dust, and all turn to dust again").

II. Bĭv′-ouăc (bĭv′wăk), dŭmb (dŭm), eăt′-tle, a-chiēv′-ing.

III. What words are used to describe "numbers," "dream," "life," "marches," "field," "cattle," "brother"?

V. Slumbers, goal, returnest, destined, fleeting, muffled, stout, funeral, hero, strife, present, remind, sublime, departing, "sands of time," "solemn main," forlorn, pursuing.

V. "Mournful numbers" (poetry is divided into feet, of which there are a certain *number* in each line; hence poetry is sometimes called "numbers"). The thought of the first stanza is: Do not say, Life is a *dream*, for a dream occurs in sleep, and the sleep of the soul is death, in which there are *no* dreams. Then, again, in a dream things only *seem*—they do not *exist*. But such things *are* not; hence life, which is a real thing, is not a dream. "The grave is not its goal" (i. e., the soul does not find its end in the grave—does not return to dust). "Like muffled drums are beating," etc. ("Brave hearts" would seem to refer to the soul, but "beating" must refer to the heart in the body; otherwise the soul would be here described as marching to the grave. It is the idea of the muffled drum that suggests "brave and stout" as a soldierly contrast.) In the battle and in the bivouac (in action and in rest). "Sands of time" (as, on the sands of the sea-shore, whatever marks are made are soon effaced by the waves, so time soon effaces the memory of events, especially if they are of little account. But the lives of great men show us that we may, by heroic action, leave footprints which will remain to be seen by others, and so encourage them).

XXVII.—AN ELEPHANT-HUNT.

1. On the 2d of September, 1832, intelligence was brought to the collector of Tinnevelly that some wild elephants had appeared in the neighborhood. A hunting party was immediately formed, and a large number of native hunters were engaged. We left the tents, on horseback, at half-past seven o'clock in the morning, and rode three miles to an open spot, flanked on one side by rice-fields, and on the other by a jungle.

2. After waiting some time, Captain B—— and myself walked across the rice-fields to the shade of a tree. There we heard the trumpet of an elephant; we rushed across the rice-fields up to our knees in mud, but all in vain, though we came upon the track of one of the animals, and then ran five or six hundred yards into the jungle.

3. After various false alarms, and vain endeavors to discover the objects of our chase, the collector went into the jungle, and Captain B—— and myself into the bed of the stream, where we had seen the tracks; and here it was evident the elephants had passed to and fro. Disappointed and impatient, we almost determined to give

up the chase and go home; but shots fired just before us reanimated us, and we proceeded, and found that the collector had just fired twice.

4. Off we went through forest, over ravine, and through streams, till at last, at the top of the ravine, the elephants were seen. This was a moment of excitement! We were all scattered. The collector had taken the middle path; Captain B——, some huntsmen, and myself took the left; and other hunters scrambled down that to the right. At this moment I did not see anything but what I took to be a native hut roofed with leaves; but, after advancing a few yards, the huge head of an elephant shaking above the jungle, within ten yards of us, burst suddenly upon my view.

5. Captain B—— and a hunter were just before me; we all fired at the same moment, and in so direct a line that the percussion-cap of my gun hit the hunter, whom I thought at first I had shot. This accident, though it proved slight, troubled me a little. The great excitement occasioned by seeing, for the first time, a wild beast at liberty and in a state of nature, produced a sensation of hope and fear that was intense.

6. The startling appearance of such a huge creature, and our being scattered and separated, created for an instant a slight dismay, which may be better understood than described. The beast gave one of his horrid trumps, and charged somebody whom I could not see; but I followed him, and the next instant beheld the collector running, without hat or gun, and the elephant after him. I fired instantly, intending to hit a vital part, which is under the ear; the shot struck, but, unfortunately, without taking proper effect.

7. My servant-boy, with a reserve gun, was ten or twelve yards off—a long way at such a moment; but no more time was lost than could be avoided in exchanging guns with him. I turned back as quickly as possible, and at this instant the elephant seized the collector and lifted him off the ground. I instantly leveled my gun, in the hope that a chance of saving him might offer.

8. The beast turned partly around the tree, still holding the collector in the grasp of his trunk, and I saw that I had a clear shot at his head. I fired, and struck him, the ball entering his left eye. He staggered, stumbled, let the collector fall, and made off without trampling on him. I then rushed forward, intending to discharge my second barrel; but, some objects coming between the elephant and me, he escaped, and I lost sight of him entirely.

9. The collector now lay apparently lifeless on the ground. A painful sensation of dizziness nearly overpowered me. I went toward him: he moved, and assisted himself by taking hold of a tree. I then hastened, and found him like one risen from the grave, pale as death. I saw blood—but it was that of the elephant—dropping from his brow.

10. Never shall I forget my feelings when I saw the monster rushing on him, still less those when I saw the brute's huge trunk twine round and take him up. All this occurred in less than a minute. The collector was, of course, very faint. We gave up the pursuit, and got some brandy-and-water, which revived him. He told us that he had advanced till within six yards of the elephant, and then fired, thinking that, as usual, it would retreat, instead of which it charged him.

11. He then fired a second time, within three yards of the beast, and fled; but the animal gained upon him: he threw his gun at it, and tried to run round a tree; but it was too cunning, and ran round the tree also, seized him by the neck, and threw him down. It then attempted to gore him. Luckily, the tusks stuck into the ground on each side of him, and thus he was preserved.

12. The collector then felt the brute take him up in his trunk; he heard my shot, and immediately found himself on the ground. He quietly lay there a second or two, then inclined himself slightly, and perceived that the elephant's back was toward him. The animal must have carried away at least twenty balls. Perhaps he was led to select the collector on account of his being dressed in bright white jean.

13. Four days after our exploit, a report reached us that some hunters had killed the elephant, which had continued to wander about the place where he had been wounded. It was fourteen feet long from the root of the tail to the joining of the trunk to the head, and eleven feet high. My balls had struck in the neck and left eye, and the head was terribly marked with shots.

Library of Entertaining Knowledge.

For Preparation.—I. Find, on your map, Tinnevelly, in the southern part of Hindostan. What European nation governs this part of India? (English.)

II. Neigh′-bor-hood (nā′-), pro-çeed′-ed, sĕp′-a-rāt-ed, hās′-tened (hās′nd), pur-suit′ (-sūt′).

III. Arrange a list of the action-words in the first three paragraphs, writing out their several forms in parallel columns: in the first column, write the form denoting present time and a single person spoken of; in the second column, present time and more than one person spoken of; in the third column, past time. E. g.:

is	are	was
brings	bring	brought
has	have	had

IV. Intelligence, flanked, jungle, reanimated, collector, ravine, excitement, slight, accident, occasioned, sensation, intense, percussion-cap, dismay, trumps, vital, reserve, avoided, leveled, revived, gore, tusks, inclined, jean, report, mangled.

V. Write an analysis of this piece (merely naming the several items, thus: September 2, 1832, wild elephants appear near Tinnevelly; hunting party formed; ride to the place—rice-fields and jungle; delay; elephants heard, tracks seen, but no elephant; false alarms; impatience; shots fired by the collector; elephants seen up the ravine, etc.).

XXVIII.—THE BAREFOOT BOY.

1. Blessings on thee, little man—
Barefoot boy, with cheek of tan!
With thy turned-up pantaloons,
And thy merry whistled tunes;
With thy red lip, redder still,
Kissed by strawberries on the hill;
With the sunshine on thy face,
Through thy torn brim's jaunty grace;
From my heart I give thee joy!
I was once a barefoot boy!

2. Oh, for boyhood's painless play,
Sleep that wakes in laughing day,
Health that mocks the doctor's rules;
Knowledge, never learned of schools;
Of the wild-bee's morning chase,
Of the wild flower's time and place,

Flight of fowl, and habitude
Of the tenants of the wood;
How the tortoise bears his shell,
How the woodchuck digs his cell,
And the ground-mole sinks his well;

3. How the robin feeds her young,
How the oriole's nest is hung;
Where the whitest lilies blow,
Where the freshest berries grow,
Where the ground-nut trails its vine;
Where the wood-grape's clusters shine;
Of the black wasp's cunning way,
Mason of his walls of clay.

4. Oh, for boyhood's time of June,
Crowding years in one brief moon,
When all things I heard or saw
Me, their master, waited for!
I was rich in flowers and trees,
Humming-birds and honey-bees;
For my sport the squirrel played,
Plied the snouted mole his spade;

5. Laughed the brook for my delight,
Through the day and through the night,
Whispering at the garden-wall,
Talked with me from fall to fall;
Mine the sand-rimmed pickerel-pond,
Mine the walnut-slopes beyond.

6. Oh, for festal dainties spread,
Like my bowl of milk and bread—

Pewter spoon and bowl of wood,
On the door-stone, gray and rude!
O'er me, like a regal tent,
Cloudy-ribbed, the sunset bent,
Purple-curtained, fringed with gold,
Looped in many a wind-swung fold;
While for music came the play
Of the pied frogs' orchestra;
And, to light the noisy choir,
Lit the fly his lamp of fire.
I was monarch: pomp and joy
Waited on the barefoot boy!

7. Cheerily, then, my little man,
Live and laugh, as boyhood can!
Though the flinty slopes be hard,
Stubble-speared the new-mown sward,
Every morn shall lead thee through
Fresh baptisms of the dew;
Every evening from thy feet
Shall the cool wind kiss the heat.

8. All too soon these feet must hide
In the prison-cells of pride,
Lose the freedom of the sod,
Like a colt's for work be shod,
Made to tread the mills of toil,
Up and down in ceaseless moil:
Happy, if their track be found
Never on forbidden ground;
Happy, if they sink not in
Quick and treacherous sands of sin.
Ah! that thou couldst know thy joy,
Ere it passes, barefoot boy!

John G. Whittier.

For Preparation.—I. A part only of this poem is given in this place. Why is the black wasp called a "mason"? What spade does the mole use? Why called "pickerel-pond"? What fly "lights his lamp"?

II. Tôr′-toise (-tĭs), wo͝od′-chŭck, ō′-ri-ōle's nĕst, choir (kwīr) (and quire).

III. What meaning is given by *'s* in brim's, boyhood's, bee's? Explain *est* in whitest; *ies* in berries. Explain the abbreviations *i. e.*, *e. g.*

IV. "From fall to fall," "frogs' orchestra," "ceaseless moil."

V. "Cheek of tan" (made out of tan, or only cheek of tan-color?). "Redder still" (because he had stained his lips with strawberry-juice). "Mocks the doctor's rules" (neglects his rules, or has no need of them—which?). What does he mean by all things waiting for him, their master? "Oh, for festal dainties" (that he could enjoy with such relish as he did his bowl of bread and milk). The sky at sunset (6) was like a royal tent with beautiful curtains. "Flinty slopes" and "stubble-speared" (the trials of the boy with bare feet are to walk over a field of stubble or over flinty stones). Explain how shoes may be called "prison-cells of pride."

XXIX.—THE STORY OF A WAVELET.

1. The child had sunk into a dream of delight, and was thinking how gladly he would be a sunbeam or a moonbeam. He would have liked to hear more from the dragon-fly. When all grew still, and remained so, he opened his eyes and looked around for his dear guest; but she had flown away into the wide world.

2. As the child did not care to sit alone any longer, he arose and went down to the purling brook. This was flowing along right joyously, and bustling on in a comical way to plunge into the river, just as if the huge mountain were following close upon its heels—the mountain from which it had run away but a little while before, escaping only by a perilous leap.

3. Then the child talked to the little waves, and asked them whence they came. For a long time they would

give him no answer, but rolled away, one over another, until at last one tiny wave, clear as crystal, dropped down, and stopped behind a stone so as not to grieve the friendly child. From her he heard very strange stories, some of which he did not understand; for she told him of her earlier adventures, and of the inside of the mountain.

4. "A long time ago," she said, "I dwelt with countless sisters in a great sea, in peace and unity. We enjoyed many a pastime: now we mounted as high as a house, and peeped at the stars. We saw how the coral-builders worked themselves tired, in order to come at length to the sweet light of day.

5. "But I was proud, and thought myself much better than my sisters. So once, when the sun had sunk down into the sea, I clung to one of his warm rays, and thought I should now mount even to the stars, and be like one of them. But I had not risen far when the sunbeam shook me off, and, not caring what might become of me, let me fall into a dark cloud.

6. "Soon there was a flash of fire through the cloud, and I was in great peril; but the whole cloud settled down upon a mountain, and I escaped, after much anxiety. Now I hoped to be out of danger, when all of a sudden I slipped upon a pebble, and fell from one stone to another, deeper and deeper down into the mountain, till at last it grew dark as night about me, and I could hear and see nothing more.

7. "Then I found, indeed, that 'pride goeth before a fall.' I resigned myself to my fate; and as I had already, while in the cloud, laid aside all pride, so here, now, humility came to be my portion. At length, after many

purifications by means of the mysterious virtues of metals and minerals, I was allowed to come again into the open and pleasant air. I wish now to return to my sisters in the ocean, and there patiently wait till I am called to something better."

8. She had scarcely done speaking when the roots of a forget-me-not caught her, and drew her in, that she might become a flower, and sweetly shine, a little blue star in the green firmament of earth.

Translated by J. C. Pickard from F. W. Carové.

For Preparation.—I. From the "Story without an End." Lesson XI., the story of "The Lark," is the thirteenth chapter of the same book; Lesson XVII., "In the Forest," is the fifth; and this one, "The Story of a Wavelet," is the second. The dragon-fly has finished his account of the world, and now the child hears the wavelet's story.

II. De-līght′ (-līt′), tī′-ny, crȳs′-tal, cŏr′-al, re-ṣīgned′ (-zīnd′).

III. Arrange the three forms of the action-words that you find in the fourth and fifth paragraphs, in columns. Arrange "said" and "dwelt," for example, thus:

now	*now*	*then*
(he)	(they)	(he or they)
says	say	said
dwells	dwell	dwelt

IV. Purling, bustling, comical, huge, perilous, adventures, unity, anxiety, austere, humility, purifications, mysterious.

V. "Coral-builders" (little animals, incorrectly called "insects," that secrete a stony substance in such quantities as to build the coral formations from the bottom of the sea up toward the surface). The wavelet "clung fast to a ray." Have you seen water "dry up"—i. e., be taken up or absorbed by the air when exposed to the warm sun? What was the "flash of fire through the cloud"? (6.) "Purifications by means," etc.—i. e., water is filtered through sand and other substances. Read Longfellow's poem, "Flowers," and note the allusion to this story: "When he called the flowers, so blue and golden, stars that in earth's firmament do shine."

XXX.—EMPHASIS BY SLIDES.

PART I.

Listen again, and notice still *another* way by which words are emphasized. "Are you *coming'?*" "*Yes*\`, in a moment." "Shall we *read'* together, or *talk*\`?" "Let us *read*\`." "Will *you'* read to *me'?* or shall *I*\` read to *you*\`?"

Observe how the voice slides *up* on some emphatic words, and *down* on others.

When I say, "Will *you'* read to *me'?*" my voice slides upward on "*you*" and on "*me*"; and when I say, "Or shall *I*\` read to *you*\`?" my voice slides downward on "*I*" and on "*you.*"

These emphatic tones, which we use in asking and answering direct questions, are called "THE SLIDES." On the simple question, the "*rising slide*" is heard (marked thus [']); as, "Do you *hear'?*" On the answer, the "*falling slide*" is heard (marked thus [\`]); as, "*Yes*\`, I *hear*\` you."

For the right use of these rising and falling slides in reading, we must divide emphatic ideas into two classes, which we will call *positive* and *negative* ideas. The most important ideas are positive statements; as,

> "Life is *real*\`, life is *earnest*\`."
> "Art is *long*\`, and Time is *fleeting*\`."

The less important ideas are negative statements, often in contrast with positive ideas; as,

> "Be not like dumb, driven *cattle'*—
> Be a *hero*\` in the strife."

The last line is a positive statement.

"Do *right*\`, and you will be *happy*\`," are both positive.

"If you do *right'*, you will be *happy`*." Here the first idea of doing right is not a command—is not certain, but doubtful—is not positive, but *negative*, and must be read with the rising slide. Hence the *general principle* for the *slides:*

POSITIVE IDEAS SHOULD BE READ WITH THE FALLING SLIDE.

NEGATIVE IDEAS SHOULD BE READ WITH THE RISING SLIDE.

"Will you take *tea'* or *coffee'?*" "No, I thank you; I will take *water`* or *milk`*, if you please."

The *rising* slide is given to tea and to coffee because both are *negative.* The person asking the question is in *doubt* on both points. But suppose it were *certain* that one of the two would be taken; then one idea is (in the mind of the person asking the question) *positive,* and one of the slides must *fall.* "Will you take *tea'*, or *coffee`?*" "I will take *coffee`*."

"Shall we go to the mountains', or to the seaside`?" This gives us, also, one positive idea. We are going to one place or the other. But, "Shall we go to the mountains' or seaside' this summer?" makes both "*mountains*" and "*seaside*" negative. The person asking is in doubt on each point, and so each has the rising slide. But the answer, "We are going to the mountains`, or, "We are going to the seaside`," or, "We shall stay at home`," is positive, and therefore requires the falling slide.

"Will you', or you', or you' do me this favor?"

These are all negative ideas. The person asking is not sure that any one will favor him, and so the rising slide must be given to each and all. But if it is positively believed that one of the three will do the favor, then the last one appealed to will take the falling slide: "Will you′, or you′, or you‵ do me this favor?"

"Is your brother′ at home?" "No‵, sir; he has sailed for Europe‵." "Has he gone for pleasure′, or for study‵?" "He has gone for both‵"; or, "He has gone for his health‵, rather than for pleasure′ or study′."[1]

"The GOLDEN RULE‵ is the very *life* and *soul*‵ of *politeness*‵."

"Come, *read*‵ to me some *poem*‵—
Some *simple*‵ and *heart*‵-felt lay,

. . . . . .

Not from the *grand* old *masters*′,
Not from the bards *sublime*′.

. . . . . .

Read from some *humbler*‵ poet,
Whose songs gushed from his *heart*‵,
As *showers*‵ from the *clouds* of *summer*‵,
Or *tears*‵ from the *eyelids*‵ start."

A fine example of the positive and negative slides is seen in these beautiful words of Dickens, after the death of little Nell:

"She seemed a creature *fresh*‵ from the hand of God, and *waiting*‵ for the breath of life; not one who *had*′ lived, and suffered *death*′."

PART II.

SIMPLE AND COMPOUND QUESTIONS.

The simple question is, from its very nature, a negative idea. It asserts nothing; it only *asks* something,

[1] The rule, so commonly given, that "the voice must fall when the sense is completed," fails here, and often elsewhere, because the sense is completed with the negative idea, which must have the *rising* slide, even at the end of the sentence.

and is therefore to be read with the rising slide; as, "Do you *understand'* me?" "Is it *clear'?*" But if this usual interrogative sense changes to a positive appeal, the question must be read, like any other positive idea, with the falling slide: "That is not right, *is'* it?" "I would not do that, would *you'?*" The question is not asked in doubt, but with the certainty in the speaker's mind that the one appealed to will agree with him.

"I said an *elder'* soldier, *not* a *better'*;
Did' I say better?"

"Isn't that a *splendid'* story you are reading?"

Thus we see that the *sense*, and not the *form*, of the sentence must determine the right reading.

Compound questions, such as, "Where are you *going'?*" "What are you *doing'?*" take the *falling* slide. *Why?* Because every such question has one *positive* idea, which comes last, and is *emphasized.*

"You are *going'* somewhere," is positive. "Will you tell me *where'?*" "Where" only is interrogative, and this is not emphasized when the question is read with the falling slide. "Where are you *going'?* Where are you GOING'?" It is generally given as a rule that, when such questions as these are repeated, they take the rising slide. This is not true in *fact* or *principle;* for, when such a question is not heard the first time, it is repeated in the very same way, with more positive emphasis, until the person spoken to is forced to hear it. *Then* only, if his answer is not distinctly heard, the question may be given with the rising slide; but not until the emphasis is taken from the positive, and put on the *negative*—the *interrogative*—idea; as, "*Where'* are you going?"

Thus any such double-idea'd question — beginning with when, where, who, what, why, which, etc.—may be analyzed and read.

XXXI.—BETH'S SICKNESS.

1. Beth had the scarlet fever, and was much sicker than any one, except Hannah and the doctor, suspected. The girls knew nothing about illness, and Mr. Lawrence was not allowed to see her; so Hannah had everything her own way, and busy Dr. Bangs did his best, but left a good deal to the excellent nurse.

2. Meg staid at home, lest she should infect the Kings, and kept house, feeling very anxious, and a little guilty when she wrote letters in which no mention was made of Beth's illness. She could not think it right to deceive her mother; but she had been bidden to mind Hannah, and Hannah would not hear of "Mrs. March bein' told, and worried just for sech a trifle." Jo devoted herself to Beth day and night—not a hard task, for Beth was very patient, and bore her pain uncomplainingly as long as she could control herself.

3. But there came a time when, during the fever-fits, she began to talk in a hoarse, broken voice, to play on the coverlet as if on her beloved little piano, and try to sing with a throat so swollen that there was no music left; a time when she did not know the familiar faces around her, but addressed them by wrong names, and called imploringly for her mother. Then Jo grew frightened, Meg begged to be allowed to write the truth, and even Hannah said she "would think of it, though there was no danger yet." A letter from Washington added to

their trouble, for Mr. March had had a relapse, and could not think of coming home for a long while.

4. How dark the days seemed now! how sad and lonely the house! and how heavy were the hearts of the sisters as they worked and waited, while the shadow of death hovered over the once happy home! Then it was that Margaret, sitting alone, with tears dropping often on her work, felt how rich she had been in things more precious than any luxuries money could buy—in love, protection, peace, and health, the real blessings of life.

5. Then it was that Jo, living in the darkened room, with that suffering little sister always before her eyes, and that pathetic voice sounding in her ears, learned to see the beauty and sweetness of Beth's nature, to feel how deep and tender a place she filled in all hearts, and to acknowledge the worth of Beth's unselfish ambition to live for others, and make home happy by the exercise of those simple virtues which all may possess, and which all should love and value more than talent, wealth, or beauty.

6. And Amy, in her exile, longed eagerly to be at home, that she might work for Beth, feeling now that no service would be hard or irksome, and remembering, with regretful grief, how many neglected tasks those willing hands had done for her. Laurie haunted the house like a restless ghost, and Mr. Lawrence locked the grand piano, because he could not bear to be reminded of the young neighbor who used to make the twilight pleasant for him.

7. Every one missed Beth. The milkman, baker, grocer, and butcher inquired how she did; poor Mrs. Hummel came to beg pardon for her thoughtlessness,

and to get a shroud for Minna; the neighbors sent all sorts of comforts and good wishes; and even those who knew her best were surprised to find how many friends shy little Beth had made.

8. Meanwhile she lay on her bed, with old Joanna at her side; for even in her wanderings she did not forget her forlorn *protégée*. She longed for her cats, but would not have them brought, lest they should get sick; and, in her quiet hours, she was full of anxiety about Jo. She sent loving messages to Amy, bade them tell her mother that she would write soon, and often begged for pencil and paper to try to say a word, that her father might not think she had neglected him.

9. But soon even these intervals of consciousness ended, and she lay hour after hour tossing to and fro, with incoherent words on her lips, or sank into a heavy sleep which brought her no refreshment. Dr. Bangs came twice a day; Hannah sat up at night; Meg kept a telegram in her desk, all ready to send off at any minute; and Jo never stirred from Beth's side.

10. The 1st of December was a wintry day indeed to them, for a bitter wind blew, snow fell fast, and the year seemed getting ready for its death. When Dr. Bangs came that morning, he looked long at Beth, held the hot hand in both his own a minute, and laid it gently down, saying in a low tone to Hannah, "If Mrs. March can leave her husband, she'd better be sent for."

FOR PREPARATION.—I. This extract is from "Little Women" (Chapter XVIII.). While the mother, Mrs. March, is away nursing the father in a hospital in Washington, Beth is taken sick with the scarlet fever. At first they hesitate to inform the absent parents of the state of the case. Mrs. Hummel's baby, "Minna," had died of the scarlet fever, and Beth had been exposed to the disease while at Mrs. Hummel's.

II. Nŏth′-ing (nŭth′-), bus̤′-y (bĭz′y), guĭlt′-y, pā′-tient (-shent), dūr′-ing, thrōat, (thrōt), fa mĭl′-iar, frĭght′-ened (frīt′nd), hĕav′-y, wāit′-ed, vĭrt′-ūes̤, văl′-ūe, ēa′-ḡer-ly, häunt′-ed, ghōst (gōst), neigh′-bor (nā′-), should (shŏŏd), ċŏm′-forts (kŭm′furts), rĕad′-y.

III. Describing-words are frequently changed to express comparison (*sicker* compares with another one; *sickest* would compare with more than one).

IV. Suspected, allowed, excellent, infect, anxious, mention, deceive, trifle, devoted, uncomplainingly, control, hoarse, addressed, imploringly, relapse, pathetic, tender, acknowledge, ambition, possess, exile, service, irksome, regretful, neglected tasks, reminded, twilight, inquired, shy, *protégée* (prō-tā-zhā′—one under the care of another), forlorn, intervals, incoherent, consciousness.

V. Notice the stages in the progress of the disease, as described here: The gradual increase in the interest of all as the case grows critical; the pathetical mention of Beth's thoughtfulness of her parents, sisters, and even of her cats; the traits of character exhibited by the nurse and the doctor.

XXXII.—BETH'S SICKNESS (Continued).

1. It was past two o'clock when Jo, who stood at the window thinking how dreary the world looked in its winding-sheet of snow, heard a movement by the bed, and, turning quickly, saw Meg kneeling before their mother's easy-chair, with her face hidden. A dreadful fear passed coldly over Jo as she thought, "Beth is dead, and Meg is afraid to tell me!"

2. She was at her post in an instant, and to her excited eyes a great change seemed to have taken place. The fever-flush and the look of pain were gone, and the beloved little face looked so pale and peaceful in its utter repose, that Jo felt no desire to weep or to lament. Leaning low over this dearest of her sisters, she kissed the damp forehead with her heart on her lips, and softly whispered, "Good-by, my Beth—good-by!"

3. As if waked by the stir, Hannah started out of her sleep, hurried to the bed, looked at Beth, felt her hands, listened at her lips, and then, throwing her apron over her head, sat down to rock to and fro, exclaiming under her breath: "The fever's turned! She's sleepin' nat'ral! Her skin's damp, and she breathes easy! Praise be given! O my goodness me!"

4. Before the girls could believe the happy truth, the doctor came to confirm it. He was a homely man, but they thought his face quite heavenly when he smiled, and said, with a fatherly look at them: "Yes, my dears, I think the little girl will pull through this time. Keep the house quiet. Let her sleep; and, when she wakes, give her—"

5. What they were to give, neither heard; for both crept into the dark hall, and, sitting on the stairs, held each other close, rejoicing with hearts too full for words. When they went back to be kissed and cuddled by faithful Hannah, they found Beth lying, as she used to do, with her cheek pillowed on her hand, the dreadful pallor gone, and breathing quietly, as if just fallen asleep.

"If mother would only come now!" said Jo, as the winter night began to wane.

6. "See!" said Meg, coming up with a white, half-opened rose, "I thought this would hardly be ready to lay in Beth's hand to-morrow, if she—went away from us. But it has blossomed in the night, and now I mean to put it in my vase here; so, when the darling wakes, the first thing she sees will be the little rose and mother's face."

7. Never had the sun risen so beautifully, and never had the world seemed so lovely, as it did to the heavy eyes of Meg and Jo as they looked out in the early morning, when their long, sad vigil was done.

8. "It looks like a fairy world," said Meg, smiling to herself, as she stood behind the curtain, watching the dazzling sight.

"Hark!" cried Jo, starting to her feet.

Yes, there was a sound of bells at the door below, a cry from Hannah, and then Laurie's voice, saying, in a joyful whisper: "Girls—she's come—she's come!"

Louisa M. Alcott.

FOR PREPARATION.—I. Meanwhile Laurie has telegraphed for the mother, and brings word that Mr. March is better. Mrs. March is expected to arrive at two in the morning. The doctor says that a change for better or worse will take place at midnight. Midnight has passed, but the sisters are still in doubt.

II. Drēar′-y, kneel′-ing (neel′-), a-frāid′, lĭst′-ened (lĭs′nd), ā′-pron (ā′purn), vāse, hĕav′-y, watch′-ing, sīght (sīt).

III. Explain the *'s* in "the fever's turned"; in "skin's damp"; in "she's come"; in "mother's face."

IV. "Winding-sheet," instant, "utter repose," desire, lament, homely, pallor, dazzling, vigil.

V. Correct "She's sleepin' nat'ral." Use a better expression for "pull through." What does "O my goodness me!" express? (Anything more than joyful surprise and relief?)

XXXIII.—THE RAINY DAY.

The day is cold, and dark, and dreary;
It rains, and the wind is never weary;
The vine still clings to the moldering wall,
But at every gust the dead leaves fall,
    And the day is dark and dreary.

My life is cold, and dark, and dreary;
It rains, and the wind is never weary;
My thoughts still cling to the moldering past,
But the hopes of youth fall thick in the blast,
    And the days are dark and dreary.

Be still, sad heart, and cease repining;
Behind the clouds is the sun still shining;
Thy fate is the common fate of all;
Into each life some rain must fall:
Some days must be dark and dreary.

H. W. Longfellow.

For Preparation.—I. Have you read this author's poem, "Afternoon in February"? (See Lesson LXI.) Note the resemblances and differences. The day, cold, dark, dreary, rainy, with dead leaves falling, corresponds to the life within, the thoughts, hopes, etc. In the poem referred to (LXI.) there is a similar correspondence.

II. Drēar′-y, wēa′-ry.

III. Correct: *It rain; the vine cling.*

IV. "Moldering past," repining.

V. What is the consolation which the poem mentions? What, in the second stanza, corresponds to *the day, the vine, the dead leaves*, in the first stanza?

XXXIV.—AX-GRINDING.

1. When I was a little boy, I remember, one cold winter's morning, I was accosted by a smiling man with an ax on his shoulder. "My pretty boy," said he, "has your father a grindstone?"

"Yes, sir," said I.

"You are a fine little fellow!" said he. "Will you let me grind my ax on it?"

2. Pleased with the compliment of "fine little fellow," "Oh, yes, sir," I answered. "It is down in the shop."

"And will you, my man," said he, patting me on the head, "get me a little hot water?"

How could I refuse? I ran, and soon brought a kettleful.

3. "How old are you?—and what's your name?" continued he, without waiting for a reply. "I'm sure you are one of the finest lads that I have ever seen. Will you just turn a few minutes for me?"

4. Tickled with the flattery, like a little fool, I went to work, and bitterly did I rue the day. It was a new ax, and I toiled and tugged till I was almost tired to death. The school-bell rang, and I could not get away. My hands were blistered, and the ax was not half ground.

5. At length, however, it was sharpened, and the man turned to me with, "Now, you little rascal, you've played truant! Scud to the school, or you'll rue it!"

"Alas!" thought I, "it was hard enough to turn a grindstone this cold day, but now to be called a little rascal is too much."

6. It sank deep into my mind, and often have I thought of it since. When I see a merchant over-polite to his customers, begging them to take a little brandy, and throwing his goods on the counter, thinks I, "That man has an ax to grind."

7. When I see a man flattering the people, making great professions of attachment to liberty, who is in private life a tyrant, methinks, "Look out, good people! That fellow would set you turning grindstones!"

8. When I see a man hoisted into office by party spirit, without a single qualification to render him either respectable or useful, "Alas!" methinks, "deluded people, you are doomed for a season to turn the grindstone for a booby."

Benjamin Franklin.

For Preparation.—I. Who wrote this piece? (See the signature at the end.) Supposing that the event described actually occurred in the life of the author of this piece, about what year was it? (See Lessons I. and LXV. for the date of his birth.)

II. Write, with diacritical marks (as here indicated), dividing into syllables, marking the accent and the pronunciation of the important vowels, the following words: Shōul′-der, pret′-ty (prĭt′-), said (sĕd), ăn′-swered (serd), brôught (brawt), pēo′-ple (pē′pl), mĭn′-utes (-ĭts), ăx. Write these words in a column, and explain in each case the difficulties of spelling and pronunciation, as in the following model. (See spelling-lessons in the Appendix for fuller directions.)

WORDS.	EXPLANATION OF DIFFICULTIES OF SPELLING, ETC.
Shōul′-der........	uses the combination ou to represent the sound ō. It is more common to use o, oa, or ow; less common to use oe, oo, eau, ew, eo, or au.
Pret′-ty (prĭt′ty)....	uses e for ĭ; more common to use i, y, ui, or u; less common, ee, ie, or o.
said..............	uses ai for ĕ; more common, e or ea; less common, æ, a, ei, eo, ie, u, or ue.
ăn′-s*w*er*e*d........	w is silent; also an e in the final syllable.
brôu*gh*t..........	uses ou for a̤; more common, aw, au, or o; less common, oa. The gh also is silent.
mĭn′-utes (mĭn′ĭts)..	uses u for ĭ (see above, "pretty"); also e silent.
pēo′-pl*e*...........	uses eo for ē; more common, e, ea, ee, ie, ei, i, ey, and æ; less common, uay.
ăx...............	spelled by English authorities, and by Worcester, *axe*.

Webster's Diacritical Marks: ā, ē, ī, ō, ū, ȳ, long; ă, ĕ, ĭ, ŏ, ŭ, y̆, short; câre, fär, låst, fa̤ll, wha̤t; thêre, ve̱il, tẽrm; pïque, fïrm; dône, fôr, do̤, wo̤lf, fōōd, fo͝ot; fûrl, ru̱de, pu̱sh; silent letters in italics; ç as s; ç͟h as sh; c, ch, as k; ġ as j; g̅ as in g̅et; s̶ as z; x̶ as gz; n̲ as in lin̲ger, lin̲k; th as in thine.

III. Explain the use of the apostrophe in winter's, what's, you've;—the use of the hyphen in over-polite, and its omission in grindstone. What is the use of *s* in minutes? "Look out, good people!"—why is capital L used, and why the ! at the end?

IV. Define compliment, accosted, scud, rue, flattery, blistered, booby; use synonyms for these in the sentences where they occur, if possible.

V. Why "a *smiling* man"? (i. e., why did he smile?) Explain the motive for the use of the words, "fine little fellow," "my man," "how old are you?" etc. Why did he pat the boy on the head? (Dr. Franklin's style is regarded as a model of purity and simplicity. It contains many colloquial expressions, however, that should not be approved in writing; e. g., he frequently uses such phrases as "says I," "thinks I.") Point out some sentence in this piece which you think particularly clear and strong in style. What is the thought of the piece, stated in your own words? Compare the style and thought of this piece with that of Lesson I., on "The Whistle." Each conveys a moral.

XXXV.—MARCH.

1. The cock is crowing,
   The stream is flowing,
   The small birds twitter,
   The lake doth glitter,
The green field sleeps in the sun;
   The oldest and youngest
   Are at work with the strongest;
   The cattle are grazing,
   Their heads never raising;
There are forty feeding like one!

2. Like an army defeated,
   The snow hath retreated,
   And now doth fare ill
   On the top of the bare hill;
The plowboy is whooping anon, anon.
   There's joy in the mountains;
   There's life in the fountains;
   Small clouds are sailing,
   Blue sky prevailing;
The rain is over and gone!

William Wordsworth.

For Preparation.—I. Have you read any other selection from Wordsworth? (Lesson II., "The Kitten and the Falling Leaves"; Lesson XIII., "Alice Fell.") He is famed for deep thought, but sometimes wrote childish and whimsical pieces.

II. Plow′-boy, whōōp′-ing (hōōp′-), pre-vāil′-ing, smạll.

III. Explain the *th* in *doth* (expresses present time and person addressed); *s* in *sleeps* (present time and person spoken of); *est* in *oldest* (what form of the describing-word would you use, if only two things were compared?); *ing* in *grazing; ed* in *defeated; ne* in *gone* (past time). Difference in meaning between *is* and *are?* When do you use *is*, and when *are?*

IV. "Twitter"—does this word indicate its meaning by its sound? What does "anon" mean? ("anon, anon"—again and again.)

V. Notice the rhymes, *fare ill* and *bare hill*. Do the English pronounce the *h* as strongly as we do? *Anon* rhymes with *gone:* this is the way the English pronounce *gone*. We ought to say *gŏn*, and not *gôn*. "Forty feeding like one"—what effect does this sentence have in painting the picture? Can you see, in imagination, how the scene looked? Why were the cattle so intent on eating? Was it the taste of the new grass growing after the shower, and the fact that the cattle had had no fresh grass all winter?

XXXVI.—THE CAREFUL OBSERVER.

1. A dervise was journeying alone in a desert, when two merchants suddenly met him. "You have lost a camel," said he to the merchants. "Indeed we have," they replied.

2. "Was he not blind in his right eye, and lame in his left leg?" said the dervise. "He was," replied the merchants. "Had he not lost a front tooth?" "He had," said the merchants. "And was he not loaded with honey on one side, and with wheat on the other?" "Most certainly he was," they replied; "and, as you have seen him so lately, and marked him so particularly, you can, in all probability, conduct us to him."

3. "My friends," said the dervise, "I have never seen your camel, nor ever heard of him, but from you!" "A pretty story, truly," said the merchants; "but where are the jewels which formed a part of his burden?" "I

have seen neither your camel nor your jewels," repeated the dervise.

4. On this, they seized his person, and forthwith hurried him before the cadi; but, on the strictest search, nothing could be found upon him, nor could any evidence whatever be adduced to convict him either of falsehood or of theft.

5. They were about to proceed against him as a sorcerer, when the dervise, with great calmness, thus addressed the court: "I have been much amused with your surprise, and own that there has been some ground for your suspicions; but I have lived long and alone, and I can find ample scope for observation even in a desert.

6. "I knew that I had crossed the track of a camel that had strayed from its owner, because I saw no mark of any human footstep on the same route. I knew that the animal was blind of one eye, because it had cropped the herbage only on one side of its path; and that it was lame in one leg, from the faint impression which that particular foot had produced upon the sand.

7. "I concluded that the animal had lost one tooth, because, wherever it had grazed, a small tuft of herbage had been left uninjured in the center of its bite. As to that which formed the burden of the beast, the busy ants informed me that it was corn on the one side; and the clustering flies, that it was honey on the other."

Colton.

For Preparation.—I. Who is a dervise? (spelled also dervis and dervish—a Turkish or Persian monk.) What country does he inhabit? (Western Asia.) What deserts are found there? For what purposes are camels used on deserts, and why used instead of horses or oxen? Who is a cadi? (A Turkish "justice of the peace.")

II. Copy spelling and pronunciation, and give explanations (according to form in Lesson XXXIV.) of joŭr′-ney-ing (jûr′-ny-), (*ey* before *i*), hŏn′-ey (hŭn′y) (*o* as *ŭ* and *ey* as *ĭ*), friĕnds (frĕndz), sus-pĭ′-cioŭs (-pĭsh′us), crŏpped (*pped* pronounced *pt*), strāyed, sēized, route (*ou* as *oo*), bus′-y, (bĭz′y) eā′-dĭ, dēr′-vīse.

III. Explain the modification in meaning produced by the addition of *ed* in loaded, *ly* in lately, *s* in jewels, *n* in seen, *r* in your, *est* in strictest, *ness* in calmness, *er* in owner.

IV. Define sorcerer, ample, scope.

V. What persons, from their mode of life and the business that they are engaged in, are likely to become careful observers of the traces left by wild animals?—of the signs of change in the weather?—of the obstructions on railway-tracks?—of the signs of disease in men?—of errors in printing?—of signs of dishonesty among people on the street?—of the indications of strength and speed in horses?

XXXVII.—THE MARINER'S DREAM.

1. In slumbers of midnight the sailor-boy lay;
   His hammock swung loose at the sport of the wind,
But, watchworn and weary, his cares flew away,
   And visions of happiness danced o'er his mind.

2. He dreamed of his home, of his dear native bowers,
   And pleasures that waited on life's merry morn;
While Memory stood sidewise, half covered with flowers,
   And restored every rose, but secreted its thorn.

3. Then Fancy her magical pinions spread wide,
   And bade the young dreamer in ecstasy rise:
Now far, far behind him the green waters glide,
   And the cot of his forefathers blesses his eyes.

4\. The jessamine clambers in flowers o'er the thatch,
And the swallow chirps sweet from her nest in the wall;
All trembling with transport, he raises the latch,
And the voices of loved ones reply to his call.

5\. A father bends o'er him with looks of delight;
His cheek is impearled with a mother's warm tear;
And the lips of the boy in a love-kiss unite
With the lips of the maid whom his bosom holds dear.

6\. The heart of the sleeper beats high in his breast;
Joy quickens his pulses—all hardships seem o'er,
And a murmur of happiness steals through his rest:
"O God! thou hast blessed me; I ask for no more."

7\. Ah, what is that flame which now bursts on his eye?
Ah, what is that sound which now 'larms on his ear?
'Tis the lightning's red gleam, painting hell on the sky!
'Tis the crashing of thunders, the groan of the sphere!

8\. He springs from his hammock—he flies to the deck!
Amazement confronts him with images dire;
Wild winds and mad waves drive the vessel a wreck—
The masts fly in splinters—the shrouds are on fire!

9\. Like mountains the billows tremendously swell;
In vain the lost wretch calls on Mercy to save;
Unseen hands of spirits are ringing his knell,
And the Death-angel flaps his broad wings o'er the wave!

10. O sailor-boy, woe to thy dream of delight!
 In darkness dissolves the gay frost-work of bliss.
Where, now, is the picture that Fancy touched bright—
 Thy parents' fond pressure, and Love's honeyed kiss?

11. O sailor-boy, sailor-boy, never again
 Shall home, love, or kindred thy wishes repay!
Unblessed and unhonored, down deep in the main
 Full many a fathom, thy frame shall decay.

12. No tomb shall e'er plead to remembrance for thee,
 Or redeem form or frame from the merciless surge;
But the white foam of waves shall thy winding-sheet be,
 And winds, in the midnight of winter, thy dirge!

13. On a bed of green sea-flowers thy limbs shall be laid;
 Around thy white bones the red coral shall grow;
Of thy fair yellow locks, threads of amber be made;
 And every part suit to thy mansion below.

14. Days, months, years, and ages shall circle away,
 And still the vast waters above thee shall roll;
Earth loses thy pattern for ever and aye.
 O sailor-boy, sailor-boy, peace to thy soul!

William Dimond.

For Preparation.—I. For what people would this poem possess the most interest? (For a people living on an island—Great Britain—and furnishing multitudes of sailors? How many friends and relatives on that island have occasion every year to mourn those lost by shipwreck!) Do you think that the author of this poem was an American, or an Englishman?

II. Ec′-sta-sy, hòn′-eyed (hŭn′id), mĕr′-çi-less, mĕm′-o-ry.

III. Of what two words is *midnight* composed, and what does each mean? "O God! thou hast blessed me," etc.—whose words do the quotation-marks here indicate? "'Larms"—what is omitted? ("'Larums his ear" is another reading of this passage.) "Parents' fond pressure"—what does the *s'* indicate? What effect on the meaning, if it were changed to *'s*? "Many a fathom"—what does *a* mean after *many?* (It makes us think of each one of the number, and therefore makes it seem larger.) "Shall e'er plead"—what is omitted in *e'er?*

IV. Hammock, watchworn, jessamine, clambers (how can a plant be said to *clamber?*), transport, fathom, amber-threads, thy pattern, "for ever and aye," red coral.

V. Do you pronounce *wind* so as to rhyme with *mind?* (see first stanza.) "Memory stood sidewise." (Memory is *personified* here, or described as a person.) How could she stand so as to conceal the thorns, and show only the roses? Do all roses grow on thorny bushes? How is Fancy personified (as an angel) in the third stanza? What is meant by "groan of the sphere"? "Unblessed" (i. e., by parents, or by the clergyman) "and unhonored" (i. e., without the usual ceremonies in honor of the dead—without tombstone, etc.). Is this not a dreary poem—without any consolation?

XXXVIII.—HOW MUCH EMPHASIS.

The degree of emphasis of all kinds varies with the relative *worth* and *spirit* of the ideas. Mere *facts* call only for force, time, and slide enough to distinguish the more important words from the others.

"How many were *with*\` you on your excursion?" "Twenty\`."

"Where did you *go*\`?" "Where′? To the mountains\`."

Here the distinctive force, time, and slide are all *moderate.* But when earnest *feeling* is added to the facts, the degree of emphasis *increases* accordingly. "Did you enjoy′ the mountain-scenery?" "Oh, EVER\ so much! It was so W-I-L-D\ and G-R-A-N-D\! I never *saw*\ anything SO MAGNIFICENT\."

Here the "force" grows louder with the earnestness, the "slides" are longer, and the "time" (when applicable) is longer. But *gentle* ideas, *tenderness*, and *sadness* require *subdued* force—softer than that given to matter-of-fact ideas. The slides, also, are a half-tone shorter. But the *time* is longer, and fills more s-p-a-c-e, in *emphasizing* sacred or sad parts.

EXAMPLE.

Paul had never risen\ from his little bed\. . . .

"Floy! what *is*\ that?"

"Where\, dearest?" "There\, at the *bottom* of the *bed*\." "There's *nothing* there, except *papa′*." The figure lifted up its head, and rose¯, and, coming to the bedside, said¯: "*My—own—boy¯!* Don't you *know′ me?*".

"*Don't* be so sorry\ for *me*\, dear papa¯. Indeed, I am *quite* happy¯. Now, lay me down. And, Floy\, come *close*\ to me, and let me *see you*\." . . . .

"How *fast*\ the *river*\ runs, between its green banks and the rushes¯, Floy¯! But it's very *near—the—sea*\ now. I *hear* the *waves¯!* They *always*\ said so¯!"

Presently, he told her that the motion of the boat upon the stream was lulling him to *rest*\. Now, the boat was out at *sea*\; and now, there was a *shore*\ before him. *Who*\ stood on the bank? He put his hands together, as he had been used to do at his *prayers*\. He did not *remove* his *arms′* to do it, but they saw him fold them so behind his *sister's neck*\`. "*Mamma* is like *y-o-u*\`, Floy¯; I know¯ her by the *face*\` *!* The *light*¯ about the head¯ is *shining-on-me* as I *go*\` *!*"

From "Dombey and Son," by Dickens.

XXXIX.—THE DEATH OF THE FLOWERS.

1. The melancholy days are come, the saddest of the year,
   Of wailing winds, and naked woods, and meadows brown and sear.
   Heaped in the hollows of the grove, the autumn leaves lie dead;
   They rustle to the eddying gust, and to the rabbit's tread.
   The robin and the wren are flown, and from the shrubs the jay,
   And from the wood-top calls the crow through all the gloomy day.

2. Where are the flowers, the fair young flowers, that lately sprang and stood
   In brighter light and softer airs, a beauteous sisterhood?
   Alas! they all are in their graves—the gentle race of flowers
   Are lying in their lowly beds, with the fair and good of ours.
   The rain is falling where they lie; but the cold November rain
   Calls not from out the gloomy earth the lovely ones again.

3. The windflower and the violet, they perished long
ago,
And the brier-rose and the orchis died amid the summer glow;
But on the hill the goldenrod, and the aster in the
wood,
And the yellow sunflower by the brook in autumn
beauty stood,
Till fell the frost from the clear cold heaven, as falls
the plague on men,
And the brightness of their smile was gone from upland, glade, and glen.

4. And now, when comes the calm, mild day, as still
such days will come,
To call the squirrel and the bee from out their winter
home;
When the sound of dropping nuts is heard, though
all the trees are still,
And twinkle in the smoky light the waters of the
rill;
The South-wind searches for the flowers whose fragrance late he bore,
And sighs to find them in the wood and by the
stream no more.

5. And then I think of one who in her youthful beauty
died,
The fair, meek blossom that grew up and faded by
my side:
In the cold, moist earth we laid her, when the forests
cast the leaf,
And we wept that one so lovely should have a life so
brief;

Yet not unmeet it was that one, like that young friend
of ours,
So gentle and so beautiful, should perish with the
flowers.

William Cullen Bryant.

For Preparation.—I. What month is here described? Collect the assertions relating to plants and to animals which indicate the season.

II. Mĕl′-an-chŏl-y, săd′-dest, sēar (sere), beaū′te-oŭs (bū′-), plāgue (plāg), squir′-rel (pronounced in England squĭr′rel, or squĕr′rel; in this country we generally hear it pronounced skwŭr′rel).

III. Turn into prose the fourth stanza, using words of your own if required to make the expression clear and complete.

IV. Eddying, brier-rose, orchis, windflower, goldenrod, aster, brief, "glade and glen."

V. "The *mel*-an-*chol*-y *days* are *come*, the *sad*-dest *of* the *year*" (◡— | ◡— | ◡— | ◡— || ◡— | ◡— | ◡—). Contrast the regularity of the rhythm in this piece with that in XLIII. and LVI. Note the personification of South-wind in the fourth stanza, the description of melancholy external conditions affecting nature, and of the corresponding inward melancholy at the decease of a person—a young friend. (See XXXIII. and LXI. for a similar transition.)

XL.—THE TEMPEST.

1. There was a certain island in the sea, the only inhabitants of which were an old man, whose name was Prospero, and his daughter Miranda, a very beautiful young lady. She came to this island so young, that she had no memory of having seen any other human face than her father's.

2. They lived in a cave, or cell, made out of a rock. It was divided into several apartments, one of which Prospero called his study. There he kept his books, which chiefly treated of magic—a study at that time much affected by all learned men; and the knowledge of this art he found very useful to him, for, being thrown by a strange

chance upon this island, which had been enchanted by a witch called Sycorax, who died there a short time before his arrival, Prospero, by virtue of his art, released many good spirits that Sycorax had imprisoned in the bodies of large trees, because they had refused to execute her wicked commands. These gentle spirits were ever after obedient to the will of Prospero. Of these, Ariel was the chief.

3. The lively little sprite Ariel had nothing mischievous in his nature, except that he rather took too much pleasure in tormenting an ugly monster called Caliban; for he owed him a grudge because he was the son of his old enemy Sycorax. This Caliban Prospero found in the woods, a strange, misshapen thing, far less human in form than an ape. He took him home to his cell, and taught him to speak; and Prospero would have been very kind to him, but the bad nature which Caliban inherited from his mother Sycorax would not let him learn anything good or useful; therefore he was employed like a slave, to fetch wood, and do the most laborious offices; and Ariel had the charge of compelling him to do these services.

4. When Caliban was lazy and neglected his work, Ariel, who was invisible to all eyes but Prospero's, would come slyly and pinch him, and sometimes tumble him down in the mire; and then Ariel, in the likeness of an ape, would make mouths at him; then, swiftly changing his shape, in the likeness of a hedgehog, he would lie tumbling in Caliban's way, who feared the hedgehog's sharp quills would prick his bare feet. With a variety of such like vexatious tricks Ariel would often torment him, whenever Caliban neglected the work which Prospero commanded him to do.

5. Having these powerful spirits obedient to his will, Prospero could, by their means, command the winds and the waves of the sea. By his orders they raised a violent storm, in the midst of which, and struggling with the wild sea-waves, that every moment threatened to swallow it up, he showed his daughter a fine large ship, which, he told her, was full of living beings like themselves. "Oh, my dear father," said she, "if by your art you have raised this dreadful storm, have pity on their sad distress. See! the vessel will be dashed to pieces! Poor souls! they will all perish. If I had power, I would sink the sea beneath the earth, rather than that the good ship should be destroyed, with all the precious souls within her!"

6. "Be not so amazed, daughter Miranda," said Prospero; "there is no harm done. I have so ordered it that no person in the ship shall receive any hurt. What I have done has been in care of you, my dear child. You are ignorant who you are, or where you came from; and you know no more of me, but that I am your father, and live in this poor cave. Can you remember a time before you came to this cell? I think you can not, for you were then not three years of age."

7. "Certainly I can, sir," replied Miranda.

"By what?" asked Prospero; "by any other house, or person? Tell me what you can remember, my child."

Miranda said: "It seems to me like the recollection of a dream; but had I not once four or five women who attended upon me?"

Prospero answered: "You had, and more. How is it that this still lives in your mind? Do you remember how you came here?"

"No, sir," said Miranda; "I remember nothing more."

8. "Twelve years ago, Miranda," continued Prospero, "I was Duke of Milan, and you were a princess and my only heir. I had a younger brother, whose name was Antonio, to whom I trusted everything; and, as I was fond of retirement and deep study, I commonly left the management of my state affairs to your uncle, my false brother (for so, indeed, he proved). I, neglecting all worldly ends, buried among my books, did dedicate my whole time to the bettering of my mind.

9. "My brother Antonio, being thus in possession of my power, began to think himself the duke indeed. The opportunity I gave him of making himself popular among my subjects awakened in his bad nature a proud ambition to deprive me of my dukedom. This he soon effected with the aid of the King of Naples, a powerful prince, who was my enemy."

"Wherefore," said Miranda, "did they not that hour destroy us?"

10. "My child," answered her father, "they durst not, so dear was the love that my people bore me. Antonio carried us on board a ship, and, when we were some leagues out at sea, forced us into a small boat, without either tackle, sail, or mast. There he left us, as he thought, to perish; but a kind lord of my court, one Gonzalo, who loved me, had privately placed in the boat water, provisions, apparel, and some books, which I prize above my dukedom."

"Oh, my father," said Miranda, "what a trouble I must have been to you then!"

11. "No, my love," said Prospero; "you were a little cherub that did preserve me. Your innocent smiles made me bear up against my misfortunes. Our food lasted

till we landed on this desert island, since which time my chief delight has been in teaching you, Miranda; and well have you profited by my instructions."

"Heaven thank you, my dear father!" said Miranda. "Now, pray tell me, sir, your reason for raising this sea-storm."

"Know, then," said her father, "that by means of this storm my enemies, the King of Naples and my cruel brother, are cast ashore upon this island."

12. Having so said, Prospero gently touched his daughter with his magic wand, and she fell fast asleep; for the spirit Ariel just then presented himself before his master to give an account of the tempest, and how he had disposed of the ship's company; and, though the spirits were always invisible to Miranda, Prospero did not choose she should hear him holding converse, as would seem to her, with the empty air.

FOR PREPARATION.—I. This, and the following selections from the "Tales from Shakespeare," written by Charles Lamb and his sister Mary, give the greater part of the story forming the plot of Shakespeare's "Tempest." There are difficult passages in the piece, but the study necessary to master them will be rewarded. Some pupils, perhaps, will be induced to read at a future time the great drama of Shakespeare itself.

II. Isl′-and (īl′-), chiēf′-ly, mĭs′-chiev-oŭs (-che-vus), com-pĕl′-ling, drĕad′-fụl, hẹir (âr), bur′-ied (bĕr′-), lēagues̱ (lēgz), troŭb′-le, a-gainst′ (-gĕnst′), wạnd, Prŏs′-pe-ro, Sȳc′-o-răx, A′-rĭ-el, Mĭl′-an, Gon-zä′-lo.

III. Make a list of the action-words in the first two paragraphs, and write out four forms of each (e. g., is, are, was, being; comes, come, came, coming; has, have, had, having; lives, live, lived, living; makes, make, made, making).

IV. Apartments, chance, enchanted, witch, obedient, sprite, tormenting, "owed grudge," misshapen, ape, inherited, invisible, threatened, perish, precious, amazed, harm, recollection, "state affairs," dedicate, possession, popular, subjects, ambition, apparel, prize, cherub, preserve, converse.

V. "Treated of magic" (treated of an art which pretended to control the forces of nature). "A study much affected" (then much in fashion). "Four or five women who attended upon me" (7). Note the statement above (1), "had no memory of having seen," etc.

XLI.—THE TEMPEST (Continued).

1. "Well, my brave spirit," said Prospero to Ariel, "how have you performed your task?"

Ariel gave a lively description of the storm, and of the terrors of the mariners; and how the king's son, Ferdinand, was the first who leaped into the sea, and his father thought he saw this dear son swallowed up by the waves and lost. "But he is safe," said Ariel, "in a corner of the isle, sitting with his arms folded sadly, lamenting the loss of the king his father, whom he concludes drowned. Not a hair of his head is injured; and his princely garments, though drenched in the sea-waves, look fresher than before."

3. "That's my delicate Ariel!" said Prospero. "Bring him hither: my daughter must see this young prince. Where are the king and my brother?"

"I left them," answered Ariel, "searching for Ferdinand, whom they have little hopes of finding, thinking they saw him perish. Of the ship's crew, not one is missing, though each one thinks himself the only one saved; and the ship, though invisible to them, is safe in the harbor."

3. "Ariel," said Prospero, "thy charge is faithfully performed; but there is yet more work."

"Is there more work?" said Ariel. "Let me remind you, master, you have promised me my liberty. I pray,

The Prince followed with amazement the sound of Ariel's voice, till it led him to Prospero and Miranda.

("*The Tempest*," p. 114.)

remember I have done you worthy service, told you no lies, made no mistakes, served you without grudge or grumbling."

4. "How now?" said Prospero. "You do not recollect what a torment I freed you from."

"Pardon me, dear master," said Ariel, ashamed to seem ungrateful; "I will obey your commands."

"Do so," said Prospero, "and I will set you free." He then gave orders what further he would have him do; and away went Ariel, first to where he had left Ferdinand, and found him still sitting on the grass in the same melancholy posture.

5. "Oh, my young gentleman," said Ariel, when he saw him, "I will soon move you. You must be brought, I find, for the lady Miranda to have a sight of your pretty person. Come, sir, follow me." He then began singing:

"Full fathom five thy father lies:
  Of his bones are coral made;
Those are pearls that were his eyes:
  Nothing of him that doth fade,
But doth suffer a sea-change
Into something rich and strange.
Sea-nymphs hourly ring his knell:
Hark! now I hear them—ding-dong bell."

6. This strange news of his lost father soon roused the prince from the stupor into which he had fallen. He followed with amazement the sound of Ariel's voice, till it led him to Prospero and Miranda, who were sitting under the shade of a large tree. Now, Miranda had never seen a man before, except her own father.

"Miranda," said Prospero, "tell me what you are looking at yonder?"

7. "O father," said Miranda, in a strange surprise, "surely that is a spirit! How it looks about! Believe me, sir, it is a beautiful creature! Is it not a spirit?"

"No, girl," answered her father; "it eats, and sleeps, and has senses such as we have. This young man, you see, was in the ship. He is somewhat altered by grief, or you might call him a handsome person; he has lost his companions, and is wandering about to find them."

8. Miranda, who thought all men had grave faces and gray beards like her father, was delighted with the appearance of this beautiful young prince; and Ferdinand, seeing such a lovely lady in this desert place, and, from the strange sounds he had heard, expecting nothing but wonders, thought he was upon an enchanted island, and that Miranda was the goddess of the place, and, as such, began to address her. But she answered, timidly, that she was no goddess, but a simple maid.

9. Prospero left them, and called his spirit Ariel, who quickly appeared before him, eager to relate what he had done with Prospero's brother and the King of Naples. Ariel said he had left them almost out of their senses with fear at the strange things he had caused them to see and hear.

10. When fatigued with wandering about, and famished for want of food, he had suddenly set before them a delicious banquet, and then, just as they were going to eat, he appeared visible before them in the shape of a harpy, a voracious monster with wings, and the feast vanished away.

11. Then, to their utter amazement, this seeming harpy spoke to them, reminding them of their cruelty in driving Prospero from his dukedom, and leaving him

and his infant daughter to perish in the sea; saying that for this cause these terrors were suffered to afflict them.

12. The King of Naples, and Antonio, the false brother, repented the injustice they had done to Prospero; and Ariel told his master he was certain their penitence was sincere, and that he, though a spirit, could not but pity them.

"Then bring them hither, Ariel," said Prospero. "If you, who are but a spirit, feel for their distress, shall not I, who am a human being like themselves, have compassion on them? Bring them quickly, my dainty Ariel."

For Preparation.—I. Where are Milan and Naples?

II. Mĕl′-an-chŏl-y, cŏr′-al, pĕarls, knĕll (nĕl), wan′-der-ing, de-light′-ed (-lit′-), wŏn′-ders.

III. Make a list of the name-words in the first paragraph, and write the four forms of each (e. g., spirit, spirit's, spirits, spirits'; task, task's, tasks, tasks').

IV. Description, lamenting, remind, grudge, grumbling, recollect, ungrateful, posture, sea-nymphs, handsome, grave, desert, relate, delicious, famished, banquet, voracious, afflict, repented, sincere, compassion, dainty.

V. Are mariners more apt to be superstitious than other people? What reason for this? (Because they deal with an element—the ocean—which is easily stirred up by the winds and made frightfully dangerous. The wind can not be calculated upon; its causes and effects are not readily foreseen. Such uncertainty has a tendency to undermine the faith of sailors in natural causes.) "Full fathom five thy father lies" (the song in Shakespeare's "Tempest," Act. II., Scene 2).

XLII.—THE TEMPEST (Concluded.)

1. Ariel soon returned with the king, Antonio, old Gonzalo, and their train, who had followed him, wondering at the wild music he played in the air to draw them on to his master's presence. This Gonzalo was the same who formerly had so kindly provided Prospero with books and provisions, when his wicked brother left him, as he thought, to perish in an open boat in the sea.

2. Grief and terror had so stupefied their senses that they did not know Prospero. He first discovered himself to the good old Gonzalo, calling him the preserver of his life; and then his brother and the king knew that he was the injured Prospero.

3. Antonio, with tears and sad words of sorrow and true repentance, implored his brother's forgiveness; and the king expressed his sincere remorse for having assisted Antonio to depose him. Prospero forgave them; and, upon their engaging to restore his dukedom, he said to the King of Naples, "I have a gift in store for you too," and, opening a door, showed him his son Ferdinand, playing at chess with Miranda.

4. Nothing could exceed the joy of the father and the son at this unexpected meeting, for each thought the other drowned in the storm. "O wonder!" said Miranda; "what noble creatures these are! It must surely be a brave world that has such people in it."

5. The King of Naples was almost as much astonished at the beauty and excellent graces of the young Miranda as his son had been. "Who is this maid?" said he. "She seems the goddess that has parted us, and brought us thus together."

"She is the daughter to this Prospero, who is the famous Duke of Milan, of whose renown and evil fortune I have heard so much, but whom I never saw till now."

6. Prospero spoke kind words, meaning to comfort his brother, which so filled Antonio with shame and remorse that he wept, and was unable to speak. The kind old Gonzalo wept to see this joyful reconciliation, and prayed for blessings on the young couple.

7. Prospero now told them that their ship was safe in the harbor, and the sailors all on board her, and that he and his daughter would accompany them home the next morning.

8. Before Prospero left the island, he dismissed Ariel from his service, to the great joy of that lively little spirit; who, though he had been a faithful servant to his master, was always longing to enjoy his liberty, to wander uncontrolled in the air like a wild bird, under green trees, among pleasant fruits and sweet-smelling flowers. "My quaint Ariel," said Prospero to the little sprite when he made him free, "I shall miss you; yet you shall have your freedom."

9. "Thank you, my dear master," said Ariel; "but give me leave to attend your ship home with prosperous gales, before you bid farewell to the assistance of your faithful spirit; and then, master, when I am free, how merrily I shall live!" Here Ariel sung this pretty song:

"Where the bee sucks, there suck I;
In a cowslip's bell I lie;
There I couch when owls do cry;
On the bat's back I do fly
After summer merrily:
Merrily, merrily shall I live now
Under the blossom that hangs on the bough."

10. Prospero then buried deep in the earth his magical books and wand, for he was resolved never more to make use of the magic art. Having thus overcome his enemies, and being reconciled to his brother and the King of Naples, nothing now remained to complete his happiness but to revisit his native land, to take possession of his dukedom, and to witness the happy marriage of his daughter Miranda and Prince Ferdinand, which the king said should be instantly celebrated with great splendor on their return to Naples; at which place, under the safe convoy of the spirit Ariel, they, after a pleasant voyage, soon arrived. *Charles and Mary Lamb.*

FOR PREPARATION.—I. The scene of "The Tempest" is laid on an island somewhere in the Mediterranean Sea, but some of the incidents are taken from descriptions of voyages in the West Indies.

II. Fāith′-fu̧l, lĭb′-er-ty, wa̧n′-der, frui̤ts (fru̧ts), bur′-ied (bĕr′ĭd), com-plēte′.

III. Make a list of the describing-words in the first two paragraphs, and write the three forms of each one that admits of comparison (e. g., old, older, oldest; wild, wilder, wildest).

IV. Train, provided, formerly, stupefied, discovered, implored, remorse, depose, engaging, restore, unexpected, renown, reconciliation, uncontrolled, quaint, gale, revisit, witness, convoy.

V. "Where the bee sucks," etc. (from "The Tempest," Act V., Scene 1).

XLIII.—THE ADOPTED CHILD.

1. "Why wouldst thou leave me, O gentle child?
Thy home on the mountain is bleak and wild—
A straw-roofed cabin, with lowly wall;
Mine is a fair and a pillared hall,
Where many an image of marble gleams,
And the sunshine of pictures for ever streams."

2. "Oh! green is the turf where my brothers play,
Through the long, bright hours of the summer day;
They find the red cup-moss where they climb,
And they chase the bee o'er the scented thyme,
And the rocks where the heath-flower blooms they know—
Lady, kind lady, oh, let me go!"

3. "Content thee, boy, in my bower to dwell:
Here are sweet sounds which thou lovest well;
Flutes on the air in the stilly noon,
Harps which the wandering breezes tune,
And the silvery wood-note of many a bird,
Whose voice was ne'er in thy mountains heard."

4. "Oh! my mother sings, at the twilight's fall,
A song of the hills far more sweet than all;
She sings it under our own green tree,
To the babe half slumbering on her knee;
I dreamed last night of that music low—
Lady, kind lady, oh, let me go!"

5. "Thy mother is gone from her cares to rest,
She hath taken the babe on her quiet breast;
Thou wouldst meet her footsteps, my boy, no more,
Nor hear her song at the cabin-door.
Come thou with me to the vineyards nigh,
And we'll pluck the grapes of the richest dye."

6. "Is my mother gone from her home away?—
But I know that my brothers are there at play—
I know they are gathering the foxglove's bell,
Or the long fern-leaves by the sparkling well;
Or they launch their boats where the bright streams flow—
Lady, kind lady, oh, let me go!"

7. "Fair child, thy brothers are wanderers now:
They sport no more on the mountain's brow;
They have left the fern by the spring's green side,
And the stream where the fairy barks were tried.
Be thou at peace in thy brighter lot,
For thy cabin-home is a lonely spot."

8. "Are they gone, all gone from the sunny hill?
But the bird and the blue-fly rove o'er it still;
And the red-deer bound in their gladness free,
And the heath is bent by the singing bee,
And the waters leap, and the fresh winds blow—
Lady, kind lady, oh, let me go!"

Felicia Hemans.

For Preparation.—I. Mrs. Hemans lived for some time in the north of Wales. Do you think that the orphan child here described came from the mountainous districts of Wales, and that the poem is founded on some incident that took place there? Do you think that this poem is more pathetic (affecting, causing pity) than "The Mariner's Dream"? (Lesson XXXVII.)

II. Thȳme (tīm), sçĕnt′-ed, vĭne′-yard (vĭn′-), läunch.

III. Tell which lines in this poem included in quotation marks (" ") are spoken by the lady who has adopted the child, and which are spoken by the child. Why is the dash used after *know*, *low*, *away*, *play*, *flow*, *blow?* (Denotes abrupt change. The child breaks off his description of the scenes he loves so well, in order to beseech the lady to let him return to them.)

IV. Red cup-moss, scented thyme, heath-flower, foxglove's bell.

V. This poem is a most vivid picture of homesickness. Note how the child calls up the images of home, and describes them until he can restrain himself no longer, and bursts out with his prayer to the lady. The repetition of "Lady, kind lady, oh, let me go!" (in the second, fourth, sixth, and eighth stanzas), is called a *refrain*. Note the contrast in the pictures drawn by the child and by the lady: straw-roofed cabin contrasted with a fair and pillared hall; the bleak and wild home described by the lady, with the green turf, bright summer hours, the red-deer so free, and, more than all, the companionship of his brothers, and the voice of his mother, described by the child.

XLIV.—THE HEDGEHOG AND THE HARE.

1. This story, in telling it, sounds very like a fable, but nevertheless it is all perfectly true; for my grandfather, from whom I had it, used always to say, as he told it to me, chuckling with glee, "It must be true, my son; otherwise how could one tell it?" The story ran thus:

2. It was a holiday morning in harvest-time, just as the buckwheat was coming into blossom. The sun had risen into the sky, clear and bright; the morning wind swept over the stubble; the larks sang merrily as they rose into the air; the bees hummed busily in the buckwheat, and the country-folks were going to church, all dressed in their Sunday clothes. All creatures were merry-minded, and the Hedgehog too.

3. The Hedgehog stood before his door with his arms folded, looked up into the morning breeze, and hummed a little tune to himself, neither better nor worse than a Hedgehog is used to sing on a fine sunny morning; and, as he was thus singing to himself, it all at once came into his head that, while his wife was washing and dressing the children, he might as well take a ramble in the fields, and look after his crop of turnips. Now, the turnips were close by his house, and he used to eat them with his family; therefore he looked upon them as his own.

4. No sooner said than done. The Hedgehog fastened the door after him, and went his way into the field. He had not gone far from home, and was just waddling round a little copse-wood which lay before the turnip-field, when his neighbor, the Hare, crossed his path, who had come out on a like errand, to look after his cabbages. When the Hedgehog spied the Hare, he wished him a friendly

"Good morning." But the Hare, who was a great man in his way, and vastly proud, did not deign to return the Hedgehog's greeting, but, turning up his nose in a scornful manner, merely said to the Hedgehog: "How comes it that you are running about the fields so early in the morning?" "I am going to take a little walk," said the Hedgehog. "A walk, forsooth!" said the Hare, laughing; "methinks you might put your legs to some better use."

5. This answer disgusted the Hedgehog greatly. Anything else he could have borne, but of his legs he would not hear a word in disparagement, just because they were by nature short. "Do you flatter yourself," said he to the Hare, "that you can do more with your legs?" "I fancy so, indeed," said the Hare. "That remains to be seen," answered the Hedgehog; "I'll lay you a wager that I would beat you in a race." "Ha! ha! ha!" said the Hare, holding his sides with laughter; "you are a funny fellow, with your short legs! But, with all my heart, so let it be, if you are so anxious to be beaten. What shall the wager be?" "Three artichokes and three onions," said the Hedgehog. "Agreed!" said the Hare; "let us start at once." "Nay," said the Hedgehog, "not quite so fast, if you please. I have not tasted any food this morning, and will first go home and eat a bit of breakfast. In half an hour I will be here again."

6. So saying, the Hedgehog went his way home, as the Hare was content; and on his way he thought to himself: "The Hare trusts to his long legs, but I will be up with him nevertheless. He gives himself the airs of a fine gentleman, truly, yet he is but a sorry fellow after all. We shall see who will win the wager!"

7. Now, when the Hedgehog reached home he called to his wife, and said: "Wife, dress yourself quickly; you

must go with me into the field hard by." "What's in the wind now?" said his wife. The Hedgehog answered: "I have wagered with the Hare three artichokes and three onions that I will run a race with him, and you must stand by and see us run." "Mercy upon us, man!" cried his wife, "are you stark mad? How could you think for a minute of running a race with a Hare?" "Hold your tongue, wife!" said the Hedgehog; "that is my affair. Do not meddle and make in a man's business." What could the Hedgehog's wife do? She was obliged to follow, whether she would or no.

8. As they were jogging along together, the Hedgehog said to his wife: "Listen, now, to what I say. Look! we shall run our race up yonder long field. The Hare will run in one furrow, and I in another, and we shall start from the top of the field. Now, you have only to sit quietly in the furrow at the farther end, and, when the Hare comes up on the other side, call out to him, 'Here I am!'"

9. By this time they had reached the spot. The Hedgehog placed his wife in the furrow, and then went up to the end of the field. When he came there, the Hare was already on the ground. "Shall we start?" said the Hare. "With all my heart!" said the Hedgehog. "Make ready, then!" So each one took up his place in the furrow. The Hare counted, "One! two! three!" and away he went, like a flash of lightning, down the field. But the Hedgehog only ran about three steps, then squatted down in the furrow, and sat as still as a mouse.

10. Now, when the Hare, at full speed, reached the end of the field, the Hedgehog's wife called out, "Here I am, waiting for you!" The Hare started, and was not

a little amazed, fully believing that it was the Hedgehog himself who called to him; for, as every one knows, the Hedgehog's wife is for all the world like her husband.

11. But the Hare thought to himself, "There must be some mistake here." So he cried, "Turn about and run again!" and away he went, like an arrow from a bow, till his ears whistled in the wind. But the Hedgehog's wife staid quietly in her place.

12. Now, when the Hare came to the top of the field, the Hedgehog cried out, "Hallo! here I am. Where have you been all this while?" But the Hare was out of his wits, and cried out, "Once more—turn about, and away!" "By all means," answered the Hedgehog; "for my part, as often as you please."

13. So the Hare went on, running backward and forward three-and-seventy times. The seventy-fourth time, however, he did not reach the end of the field; in the middle of the furrow he dropped down dead. But the Hedgehog took the three artichokes and the three onions he had won, called his wife out of the furrow, and away they jogged merrily home together; and, if they are not dead, they are living still.

For Preparation.—I. (This is a good specimen of the popular stories, half fable, half fairy-tale, that are told to children from one generation to another. They resemble the fable in that they all have a moral—sometimes a very deep one—though it is not distinctly told at the end.) In what country is this scene laid? Where are found turnips, larks, buckwheat, hedgehogs, hares, etc.? Have you read Grimm's collection of fairy-tales? (These stories are sometimes fragments of old pagan religious myths.)

II. Chŭck′-ling, deign (dān), guĭn′-ea (gĭn′e), mĭn′-ute (-it), tongue (tŭng).

III. Buckwheat (beech-wheat, i. e., resembling the beech-nut); nevertheless (what three words compose it?—*never-the-less*).

IV. Waddling, copse-wood, disparagement, wagered, "gives himself the airs of a fine gentleman," "sorry fellow."

V. "For my grandfather used to say," etc.—is this a good reason, or a ridiculous one? Why? "Like a flash of lightning"—this is exaggeration, and is called *hyperbole.* Of course, no animal could run as fast as a flash of lightning. "Like an arrow from a bow . . . . ears whistled"—this, too, is hyperbole, but not so strong as before. Is it not absurd to compare this second race of the hare, which must have been swifter than the first, to an arrow, when the first was already compared to the lightning-flash? The moral of this story teaches how the cunning of mind is superior to brute force. Which is the more admirable, the swiftness of the hare, or the cunning of the hedgehog? Do you admire either very much?

XLV.—THE VILLAGE BLACKSMITH.

1. Under a spreading chestnut-tree
 The village smithy stands;
The smith, a mighty man is he,
 With large and sinewy hands;
And the muscles of his brawny arms
 Are strong as iron bands.

2. His hair is crisp, and black, and long;
 His face is like the tan;
His brow is wet with honest sweat;
 He earns whate'er he can,
And looks the whole world in the face,
 For he owes not any man.

3. Week in, week out, from morn to night,
 You can hear his bellows blow;
You can hear him swing his heavy sledge,
 With measured beat and slow,
Like a sexton ringing the village bell
 When the evening sun is low.

4. And children, coming home from school,
   Look in at the open door;
 They love to see the flaming forge,
   And hear the bellows roar,
 And catch the burning sparks that fly
   Like chaff from a threshing-floor.

5. He goes on Sunday to the church,
   And sits among his boys;
 He hears the parson pray and preach;
   He hears his daughter's voice
 Singing in the village choir,
   And it makes his heart rejoice.

6. It sounds to him like her mother's voice,
   Singing in Paradise!
 He needs must think of her once more—
   How in the grave she lies;
 And, with his hard, rough hand, he wipes
   A tear out of his eyes.

7. Toiling, rejoicing, sorrowing,
   Onward through life he goes;
 Each morning sees some task begin,
   Each evening sees it close;
 Something attempted, something done,
   Has earned a night's repose.

8. Thanks, thanks to thee, my worthy friend,
   For the lesson thou hast taught!
 Thus, at the flaming forge of life,
   Our fortunes must be wrought;
 Thus, on its sounding anvil, shaped
   Each burning deed and thought!

Henry W. Longfellow.

FOR PREPARATION.—I. "The Old Clock on the Stairs" (Lesson LVI.) may stand in the present residence of the poet Longfellow, at Cambridge, which is the house once used by Washington as his headquarters. Across the street, and farther in, on the road to Cambridge, stood the "village smithy" and "the spreading chestnut-tree."

II. Vĭl′-lage, sĭn′-ew-y (sĭn′yu-y), mŭs′-çles (mŭs′sls), ī′-ron (ī′urn), owes (ōz), fōrge, ēarned (ērnd), ăn′-vil.

III. What meaning does the syllable *ren* give to children?—*ing* to toiling? (present time and continued action.) Find other words in this lesson in which *ing* gives the same meaning.

IV. Smithy, brawny, "like the tan," sledge, chaff.

V. What connection has "For he owes not any man" with what goes before? What figures of speech—what metaphors—in the eighth stanza? ("Flaming forge of life," etc. A metaphor is a "figure of speech," in which one object is likened to another or compared with another directly, the words *as* or *like* being omitted. He does not use a "simile," and say, "Life is *like* a flaming forge, upon which we hammer out our fortunes, just as a blacksmith hammers out his iron," but he means it. He uses a metaphor instead of a comparison or simile.) Note the irregularity of meter in this piece, as compared with Bryant's poetry (XXXIX.) or Mrs. Hemans's (VII. and XLIII.).

XLVI.—ON STRESS.

Stress is the *quality*, rather than the quantity, of emphatic force. It is of two general kinds, viz., *smooth* and *abrupt.*

Smooth, swelling tones are pleasing to the ear. Abrupt, harsh tones are displeasing to the ear. What is agreeable to the ear, naturally expresses what is agreeable to the mind; and what is disagreeable to the ear, expresses what is disagreeable to the mind.

Hence, for the right use of stress in reading, we have this simple general principle:

PLEASING IDEAS REQUIRE THE SMOOTH STRESS.

DISPLEASING IDEAS REQUIRE THE ABRUPT STRESS.

EXAMPLES.

I.

(*Smooth Stress.*)

"Maud Muller, on a summer's day,
Raked the meadow sweet with hay.

"Beneath her torn hat glowed the wealth
Of simple beauty and rustic health.

"Singing, she wrought, and her merry glee
The mock-bird echoed from his tree.

. . . .

"The judge looked back as he climbed the hill,
And saw Maud Muller standing still.

"'A form more fair, a face more sweet,
Ne'er hath it been my lot to meet.

"'And her modest answer, and graceful air,
Show her wise and good as she is fair.

"'Would she were mine, and I to-day,
Like her, a harvester of hay!

(*Abrupt Stress.*)

"'No doubtful balance of rights and wrongs,
Nor weary lawyers with endless tongues,

(*Smooth Stress.*)

"'But low of cattle, and song of birds,
And health, and quiet, and loving words.'

(*Abrupt Stress.*)

"But he thought of his sisters, proud and cold,
And his mother, vain of her rank and gold.

"So, closing his heart, the judge rode on,
And Maud was left in the field alone."

From "Maud Muller," by Whittier.

II.

(*Very Abrupt Stress.*)

"'Curse on him!' quoth false Sextus;
'Will not the villain drown?
But for this stay, ere close of day,
We should have sacked the town!'

(*Smooth Stress.*)

"'Heaven help him!' quoth Lars Porsena,
'And bring him safe to shore;
For such a gallant feat of arms
Was never seen before.'"

From "Horatius at the Bridge," by Macaulay.

XLVII.—I REMEMBER, I REMEMBER.

1. I remember, I remember
The house where I was born—
The little window where the sun
Came peeping in at morn.
He never came a wink too soon,
Nor brought too long a day;
But now I often wish the night
Had borne my breath away!

2. I remember, I remember
   The roses red and white,
The violets and the lily-cups,
   Those flowers made of light!
The lilacs where the robin built,
   And where my brother set
The laburnum on his birthday—
   The tree is living yet!

3. I remember, I remember
   Where I was used to swing,
And thought the air must rush as fresh
   To swallows on the wing.
My spirit flew in feathers then,
   That is so heavy now;
And summer pools could hardly cool
   The fever on my brow!

4. I remember, I remember
   The fir-trees, dark and high;
I used to think their slender tops
   Were close against the sky.
It was a childish ignorance,
   But now 'tis little joy
To know I'm farther off from heaven
   Than when I was a boy.

Thomas Hood.

For Preparation.—I. This poem, like "The Adopted Child" of Mrs. Hemans (Lesson XLIII.), is an expression of the longing called homesickness. Note its expression in the closing lines of the first stanza (and where else?). This is a lyric poem, intended to be sung rather than read. The pupil should, however, learn to read properly even this species of poetry. He will find it necessary to use chiefly the "emphasis of time" in this poem. (See Lesson XVIII.)

The trapper setting fire to the prairie-grass.

("*The Prairie on Fire.*" p. 133.)

II. Bōrne, peep′-ing, brôught (brawt), nīght, brĕath, vī′-o-lĕts, lĭl′-y, flow′-ers, buĭlt (bilt), la-bûr′-num, thôught (thawt), fĕath′-ers.

III. Mark the feet of the first stanza, and the accented syllables, noting the difference between the first and other lines:

> "*I* re-*mem*-ber, *I* re-*mem*-ber
> The *house* where *I* was *born*," etc.

IV. Lily-cups; on the wing.

V. Why "made of light"? (lily-cups.) "Set the laburnum"—what is meant? Comparison hinted at between "spirit flew in feathers" ("feathers" of hope; "flew," like a bird) and "swallows on the wing," and contrast with its "heavy" present. What pun is implied in the fourth stanza, in using *heaven* as a synonym of *sky?* (When a child, I thought the sky so near that the tops of the fir-trees touched it. *Sky* is a synonym of *heaven;* but heaven means not only the sky, but also the future abode of the blessed. Such a confusion of two different applications of a word is a pun.)

XLVIII.—THE PRAIRIE ON FIRE.

1. "You have come to your recollections too late, miserable old man!" cried Middleton. "The flames are within a quarter of a mile of us, and the wind is bringing them down in this direction with dreadful rapidity."

2. "The flames! I care little for the flames. If I only knew how to circumvent the cunning of the Tetons, as I know how to cheat the fire of its prey, there would be nothing needed but thanks to the Lord for our deliverance. Do you call this a fire? If you had seen what I have witnessed in the eastern hills, when mighty mountains were like the furnace of a smith, you would have known what it was to fear the flames, and to be thankful that you were spared!

3. "Come, lads, come! it is time to be doing now, and to cease talking, for yonder curling flame is truly coming on like a trotting moose. Put hands upon this short and withered grass where we stand, and lay bare the earth."—"Would you think to deprive the fire of its victims in this childish manner?" exclaimed Middleton. A faint but solemn smile passed over the features of the old man as he answered: "Your grandfather would have said that, when the enemy was nigh, a soldier could do no better than to obey."

4. The captain felt the reproof, and instantly began to imitate the industry of Paul, who was tearing the decayed herbage from the ground in a sort of desperate compliance with the trapper's direction. Even Ellen lent her hands to the labor; nor was it long before Inez was seen similarly employed, though none among them knew why or wherefore.

5. When life is thought to be the reward of labor, men are wont to be industrious. A very few moments sufficed to lay bare a spot of some twenty feet in diameter. Into one edge of this little area the trapper brought the females, directing Middleton and Paul to cover their light and inflammable dresses with the blankets of the party.

6. So soon as this precaution was observed, the old man approached the opposite margin of the grass, which still environed them in a tall and dangerous circle, and, selecting a handful of the driest of the herbage, he placed it over the pan of his rifle. The light combustible kindled at the flash. Then he placed the little flame into a bed of the standing grass, and, withdrawing from the spot to the center of the ring, patiently awaited the result.

7. The subtle element seized with avidity upon its new fuel, and in a moment forked flames were gliding among the grass, as the tongues of ruminating animals are seen rolling among their food, apparently in quest of its sweetest portions. "Now," said the old man, holding up a finger, and laughing in his peculiarly silent manner, "you shall see fire fight fire! Ah me! many a time I have burned a smooth path from wanton laziness to pick my way across a tangled plain."

8. "But is this not fatal?" cried the amazed Middleton; "are you not bringing the enemy nigher to us, instead of avoiding it?"—"Do you scorch so easily? Your grandfather had a tougher skin. But we shall live to see; we shall all live to see." The experience of the trapper was in the right.

9. As the fire gained strength and heat, it began to spread on three sides, dying of itself on the fourth for want of aliment. As it increased, and the sullen roaring announced its power, it cleared everything before it, leaving the black and smoking soil far more naked than if the scythe had swept the place.

10. The situation of the fugitives would have still been hazardous had not the area enlarged as the flame encircled them. But by advancing to the spot where the trapper had kindled the grass, they avoided the heat, and in a very few moments the flames began to recede in every quarter, leaving them enveloped in a cloud of smoke, but perfectly safe from the torrent of fire that was still furiously rolling onward.

11. The spectators regarded the simple expedient of the trapper with that species of wonder with which the

courtiers of Ferdinand are said to have viewed the manner in which Columbus made his egg to stand on its end; though with feelings that were filled with gratitude instead of envy.

12. "Most wonderful!" said Middleton, when he saw the complete success of the means by which they had been rescued from a danger that he had conceived to be unavoidable. "The thought was a gift from Heaven, and the hand that executed it should be immortal."

13. "Old trapper," cried Paul, thrusting his fingers through his shaggy locks, "I have lined many a loaded bee into its hole, and know something of the nature of the woods; but this is robbing a hornet of his sting without touching the insect!"

14. "It will do—it will do!" returned the old man, who after the first moment of his success seemed to think no more of the exploit. "Let the flames do their work for a short half-hour, and then we will mount. That time is needed to cool the meadow, for these unshod beasts are as tender on the hoof as a barefooted girl."

15. The veteran, on whose experience they all so implicitly relied for protection, employed himself in reconnoitering objects in the distance, through the openings which the air occasionally made in the immense bodies of smoke, that by this time lay in enormous piles on every part of the plain. *James Fenimore Cooper.*

FOR PREPARATION.—I. This extract is taken from Cooper's novel, "The Prairie." Have you read "The Prairie"?—"The Spy"?—"Lionel Lincoln"? In what region is the scene laid? How do you know? (by the prairie.) The Tetons were a tribe of Indians.

II. Sŏl′-emn (-em), nīgh, o-bey′, de-cāyed′, suf-fīced′ (-fīzd′), sçȳthe, con-çēived′, sŭb′-tle (sŭt′l), hẽrb′-age (ẽrb′ej).

III. *Un-avoid-able* (a syllable placed before a word, to change its meaning, is called a *prefix—pre* meaning *before;* hence prefix = fixed before. So *un* is a prefix, meaning *not;* hence, unavoidable means *not* avoidable. A syllable, or syllables, placed after a word for the same purpose is called a *suffix.* Thus *able* is a suffix, meaning "possible to be": *avoidable* means *possible to be avoided*), unshod (prefix *un*), circumvent (*circum* = around; *circumvent* = come round, hence to gain advantage over), recede (*re* = back; *recede* = go back), diameter (*dia* = through; *meter* = measure).

IV. Aliment, area, expedient, rescued, withered, inflammable, environed, combustible, "pan of his rifle," avidity, ruminating, "wanton laziness," reconnoitering.

V. "Lined a loaded bee." (When loaded with honey, the wild bee pursues a straight line for its hive, which is generally in a hollow tree. The bee-hunter watches its course, and finds the hive.)

XLIX.—THE MOUNTAIN AND THE SQUIRREL.

1. The Mountain and the Squirrel
   Had a quarrel,
   And the former called the latter "Little Prig."

2. Bun replied:
   "You are doubtless very big;
   But all sorts of things and weather
   Must be taken in together,
   To make up a year,
   And a sphere;

3. And I think it no disgrace
   To occupy my place.
   If I'm not so large as you,
   You're not so small as I,
   And not half so spry.

4. I'll not deny you make
A very pretty squirrel-track.
Talents differ; all is well and wisely put:
If I can not carry forests on my back,
Neither can you crack a nut."

Ralph Waldo Emerson.

For Preparation.—I. What fables have you had before in this Reader? Do you remember any difference between the fable and other stories?

II. Squĭr′-rel (note the English pronunciation; see Lesson XXXIX.), mount′-ain (-in), quar′-rel, doubt′-less (dout′-), wĕath′-er, ŏc′-eu-pȳ, dĭf′-fer, nēi′-ther.

III. Explain the omissions in *I'm, you're, I'll.* Give the other forms of the pronouns *I* (my, mine, me, we, our, ours, us), *you, it, my.*

IV. Prig (conceited fellow), sphere, occupy, spry, "squirrel-track."

V. Who is called "Bun" in this fable? "All sorts of things and weather must be taken in together, to make up a year (of time), and a sphere" (of space, i. e., the world). If largeness has its advantages, so has smallness too. Does the squirrel express contempt by saying, "I'll not deny you make a very pretty squirrel-track"?

L.—THE LILLIPUTIAN WAR AT SEA.

1. The empire of Blefuscu is an island situated to the northeast of Lilliput, from which it is parted only by a channel eight hundred yards wide.

2. I had not yet seen it, and, upon this notice of an intended invasion, I avoided appearing on that side of the coast, for fear of being discovered by some of the enemy's ships, who had received no intelligence of me; all intercourse between the two empires having been

strictly forbidden during the war, upon pain of death, and an embargo laid by our emperor upon all vessels whatsoever.

3. I communicated to His Majesty a project I had formed of seizing the enemy's whole fleet; which, as our scouts assured us, lay at anchor in the harbor, ready to sail with the first fair wind. I consulted the most experienced seamen upon the depth of the channel, which they had often plumbed; who told me that in the middle, at high water, it was seventy *glumgluffs* deep, which is about six feet of European measure; and the rest of it fifty *glumgluffs* at most.

4. I walked toward the northeast coast, over against Blefuscu, where, lying down behind a hillock, I took out my small perspective glass and viewed the enemy's fleet at anchor, consisting of about fifty men-of-war and a great number of transports. I then came back to my house, and gave orders (for which I had a warrant) for a great quantity of the strongest cable and bars of iron. The cable was about as thick as pack-thread, and the bars of the length and size of a knitting-needle.

5. I trebled the cable to make it stronger, and for the same reason I twisted three of the iron bars together, bending the extremities into a hook. Having thus fixed fifty hooks to as many cables, I went back to the northeast coast, and, putting off my coat, shoes, and stockings, walked into the sea in my leathern jerkin, about half an hour before high water. I waded with what haste I could, and swam in the middle about thirty yards, till I felt ground.

6. I arrived at the fleet in less than half an hour. The enemy were so frightened when they saw me, that

they leaped out of their ships and swam to shore, where there could not be fewer than thirty thousand souls. I then took my tackling, and, fastening a hook to the hole at the prow of each, I tied all the cords together at the end.

7. While I was thus employed, the enemy discharged several thousand arrows, many of which stuck in my hands and face, and, besides the excessive smart, gave me much disturbance in my work. My greatest apprehension was for my eyes, which I should have infallibly lost if I had not suddenly thought of an expedient.

8. I kept, among other little necessaries, a pair of spectacles in a private pocket, which, as I observed before, had escaped the emperor's searchers. These I took out and fastened as strongly as I could upon my nose, and, thus armed, went on boldly with my work in spite of the enemy's arrows, many of which struck against the glasses of my spectacles, but without any other effect further than a little to discompose them.

9. I had now fastened all the hooks, and, taking the knot in my hand, began to pull; but not a ship would stir, for they were all too fast held by their anchors, so that the boldest part of my enterprise remained. I therefore let go the cord, and, leaving the hooks fixed to the ships, I resolutely cut with my knife the cables that fastened the anchors, receiving about two hundred arrows in my face and hands; then I took up the knotted end of the cables to which my hooks were tied, and with great ease drew fifty of the enemy's largest men-of-war after me.

10. The Blefuscudians, who had not the least imagination of what I intended, were at first confounded with

astonishment. They had seen me cut the cables, and thought my design was only to let the ships run adrift, or fall foul on each other; but when they perceived the whole fleet moving in order, and saw me pulling at the end, they set up such a scream of grief and despair as it is almost impossible to describe or conceive.

11. When I had got out of danger, I stopped awhile to pick out the arrows that stuck in my hands and face, and rubbed on some of the same ointment that was given me at my first arrival, as I have formerly mentioned. I then took off my spectacles, and, waiting about an hour, till the tide was a little fallen, I waded through the middle with my cargo, and arrived safe at the royal part of Lilliput.

12. The emperor and his whole court stood on the shore, expecting the issue of this great adventure. They saw the ships move forward in a large half-moon, but could not discern me, who was up to my breast in water. When I advanced to the middle of the channel, they were yet more in pain, because I was under water to my neck. The emperor concluded me to be drowned, and that the enemy's fleet was approaching in a hostile manner.

13. But he was soon eased of his fears; for, the channel growing shallower every step I made, I came in a short time within hearing, and, holding up the end of the cable by which the fleet was fastened, I cried in a loud voice, "Long live the most puissant King of Lilliput!" This great prince received me at my landing with all possible encomiums, and created me a *nardac* upon the spot, which is the highest title of honor among them.

Dean Swift.

FOR PREPARATION.—I. Have you read Swift's "Gulliver's Travels"? It is a narrative, somewhat after the manner of "Robinson Crusoe" (published eight years before), of a shipwrecked sailor who comes to a land inhabited by people not six inches high. The ludicrous incidents which would happen to men, if a giant ("man-mountain") twelve times their height and nearly two thousand times their weight should suddenly appear among them, are told with a quiet humor. This race of little men are called Lilliputians. Being at war with the neighboring nation of Blefuscu, Gulliver engages to wade across the channel and capture their whole navy.

II. Ble-fŭs′-cū, sĭt′-ū-āt-ed, for-bĭd′-den, sēiz′-ing, plŭmbed (plŭmd), knĭt′-ting-nee′-dle.

III. Correct: "They seen the ships move forward";—"They was yet more in pain because I were under water";—"The empire are an island, but I had not yet saw it";—"The fleet laid at anchor";—"They telled me."

IV. Embargo (forbidding all vessels to sail from the port), at anchor, plumbed (measured with a lead and line), perspective glass (spy-glass), pack-thread, men-of-war (vessels for fighting), transports (to carry the land army and war material), cable, trebled, jerkin, excessive, smart, apprehension, expedient, infallibly (without fail), discompose, "confounded with astonishment," adrift, cargo, "expecting the issue" (awaiting the result), growing shallower, puissant (powerful), encomiums (praises).

V. Do we more easily discover our own foibles (frailties, or weak points) from seeing other people manifest them? (By attributing to the little people the habits of his own countrymen, Swift helped the latter to see what was absurd in those habits.) The effect of reading about the habits of people widely different from ourselves is to make us tolerant and liberal (i. e., generous toward others, and willing that they should have their own views and ways of acting, even though very much unlike our own).

LI.—ALEXANDER SELKIRK.

1. I am monarch of all I survey,
 My right there is none to dispute;
From the center all round to the sea,
 I am lord of the fowl and the brute.

O Solitude! where are the charms
  That sages have seen in thy face?
Better dwell in the midst of alarms,
  Than reign in this horrible place!

2. I am out of humanity's reach,
  I must finish my journey alone;
Never hear the sweet music of speech—
  I start at the sound of my own!
The beasts that roam over the plain
  My form with indifference see;
They are so unacquainted with man,
  Their tameness is shocking to me.

3. Society, friendship, and love,
  Divinely bestowed upon man,
Oh, had I the wings of a dove,
  How soon would I taste you again!
My sorrows I then might assuage
  In the ways of religion and truth;
Might learn from the wisdom of age,
  And be cheered by the sallies of youth.

4. Religion! what treasure untold
  Resides in that heavenly word,
More precious than silver and gold,
  Or all that this earth can afford!
But the sound of the church-going bell
  These valleys and rocks never heard—
Never sighed at the sound of a knell,
  Or smiled when a Sabbath appeared!

5. Ye winds, that have made me your sport,
  Convey to this desolate shore
Some cordial, endearing report
  Of a land I shall visit no more.

My friends—do they now and then send
  A wish or a thought after me?
Oh, tell me I yet have a friend,
  Though a friend I am never to see!

6. How fleet is a glance of the mind!
  Compared with the speed of its flight,
The tempest itself lags behind,
  And the swift-wingéd arrows of light!
When I think of my own native land,
  In a moment I seem to be there;
But alas! recollection at hand
  Soon hurries me back to despair!

7. But the sea-fowl has gone to her nest,
  The beast is laid down in his lair;
Even here is a season of rest,
  And I to my cabin repair.
There's mercy in every place;
  And mercy—encouraging thought!—
Gives even affliction a grace,
  And reconciles man to his lot.

William Cowper.

FOR PREPARATION.—I. Have you read "Robinson Crusoe"? The story is said to be founded on the adventures which Selkirk met with in the island of Juan Fernandez. Find this island on the map.

II. Mŏn′-arch, sur-vẹy′, çĕn′-ter, rẹign (rān), joûr′-ney, knĕll (nĕl), văl′-leyṣ, eôr′-dĭ-al (or côrd′-ial).

III. Divide the first verse into feet, and mark the accented syllables. Which feet have three syllables?

IV. Solitude, alarms, humanity's, unacquainted, divinely, bestowed, sallies, report, glance, encouraging, assuage.

V. "Sages have seen in thy face." (Solitude is here personified. Wise men have found solitude charming, because it has aided their meditations.) What journey must he finish alone? Why is the "tameness" shocking to him? (2.) Whither would he have flown if he had had the wings of a dove? Why is the bell called "church-going"? Does a glance of the mind really travel through space, or only call up images or pictures of it?

LII.—SUSPENSE OF VOICE.

The subordinate ideas of a sentence are often neither negative nor positive, but merely circumstantial or introductory to the principal idea. They require, therefore, neither the rising nor the falling slide, but the *holding*, or continuance, of the *given pitch* on which the emphatic sound begins—that is, the *suspense* of the voice—marked thus (¯).

EXAMPLES.

"When the hours of day¯ are numbered,
  And the voices of the night¯
Wake the better soul, that slumbered,
  To a holy,¯ calm delight¯;

"Ere the evening lamps¯ are lighted¯,
  And, like phantoms grim and tall¯,
Shadows¯ from the fitful fire-light
  Dance upon the parlor-wall¯:

"Then¯ the forms of the *departed*\`
  Enter at the open door—
The *belovéd*\`, the *true-hearted*\`,
  Come to *visit*\` me once *more*\`."

From "Footsteps of Angels," by Longfellow.

"Well¯, the delightful day will come."

"Friends¯, I come not here to talk." The address, when marked by deep, tender emotion, takes the suspense.

Luke xv. 31: "And he said unto him, Son, thou art ever with me; and all that I have is thinē."

To close this verse with the suspense of voice, thus leaving the appeal unfinished, is much more *suggestive* reading than to give it the falling slide of completed sense. The sacred address takes the suspense also: "Our Father̄ which art in heaven̄."

"Rock of ages̄, cleft for me,
Let me hide myself′ in *Thee*‵."

LIII.—LILLIPUTIAN TAILORS AND COOKS.

1. It may perhaps divert the curious reader to give some account of my domestics, and my manner of living in this country during a residence of nine months and thirteen days.

2. Having a head mechanically turned, and being likewise forced by necessity, I had made for myself a table and chair convenient enough, out of the largest trees in the royal park.

3. Two hundred seamstresses were employed to make me shirts, and linen for my bed and table, all of the strongest and coarsest kind they could get; which, however, they were forced to quilt together in several folds, for the thickest was some degrees finer than lawn.

4. Their linen is usually three inches wide, and three feet make a piece. The seamstresses took my measure as I lay on the ground, one standing at my neck, and another at my knee, with a strong cord extended, that

each held by the end, while a third measured the length of the cord with a rule an inch long.

5. Then they measured my right thumb, and desired no more; for, by a mathematical computation that twice round the thumb is once round the wrist, and so on to the neck and the waist, and by the help of my old shirt which I displayed on the ground before them for a pattern, they fitted me exactly.

6. Three hundred tailors were employed in the same manner to make me clothes; but they had another contrivance for taking my measure. I kneeled down, and they raised a ladder from the ground to my neck; upon this ladder one of them mounted, and let fall a plumb-line from my collar to the floor, which just answered the length of my coat; but my waist and arms I measured myself.

7. When my clothes were finished, which was done in my house (for the largest of theirs would not have been able to hold them), they looked like the patchwork made by the ladies in England, only that mine were all of a color.

8. I had three hundred cooks to dress my victuals, in little convenient huts built about my house, where they and their families lived, and prepared me two dishes apiece. I took up twenty waiters in my hand and placed them on the table; a hundred more attended below on the ground, some with dishes of meat, and some with barrels of wine and other liquors slung on their shoulders, all which the waiters above drew up, as I wanted, in a very ingenious manner by certain cords, as we draw the bucket up a well in Europe.

9. A dish of their meat was a good mouthful, and a barrel of their liquor a reasonable draught. Their mutton

5. See the heavy clouds low-falling,
And bright Hesperus down-calling
The dead night from underground;
At whose rising, mists unsound,
Damps and vapors, fly apace,
Hovering o'er the wanton face
Of these pastures, where they come
Striking dead both bud and bloom.

6. Therefore from such danger lock
Every one his lovéd flock;
Let your dogs lie loose without,
Lest the wolf come, as a scout
From the mountain, and, ere day,
Bear a kid or lamb away;
Or the crafty, thievish fox
Break upon your simple flocks.

7. To secure yourself from these,
Be not too secure in ease;
So shall you good shepherds prove,
And deserve your master's love.
Now, good night! may sweetest slumbers
And soft silence fall in numbers
On your eyelids! So, farewell!
Thus I end my evening knell.

J. Fletcher.

FOR PREPARATION.—I. Hesperus (Venus, as evening star). In what country and at what season of the year are these scenes laid? (Note the mountains, the lark, shepherds, bitter northeast wind, dogs, wolf, heavy clouds, fox, etc.)

II. Coŭn'-try, breāk, strēak, rouşe, boughş (bouz), fruit (what sound has *u* after *r*?), căr'-olş, shĕp'-herdş, (-erdz), through (thrōō), clīmb'-ing (klīm'-), yiēld, fāith'-ful, thĭck'-en (thĭk'n), cōurse, crȳs'-tal, hŏv'-er-ing, pȧs'-tūreş, thiēv'-ish, knĕll (nĕl).

III. Make a list of five action-words in this piece that end in *ing* (denoting present time and continued action), and write out the other forms which they have (e. g., blushing, blushes, blush, blushed; gilding, gilds, gild, gilded, etc.). In solemn style, there are forms in *st* and *th* (wast, doth).

IV. Streak, "subtile fire," "morning doth unfold," erst, carols, lay, gilding, swain, chidden, decay, "air 'gins to thicken," "Hesperus downcalling the dead night" (called "dead" because it had been buried "underground" while the day lasted), "from underground" (i. e., from beyond the horizon in the east), "mists unsound" (unhealthy), "fly apace," scout, secure, "fall in numbers."

V. In the first stanza of the above, what scene is described? (the dawn.) In the second and third stanzas? (sunrise.) Note the use of the word "unfold" in the first and third stanzas. In shepherd-dialect, this means to release the sheep from the pen. In the fourth verse (scene, evening), "fold up" is used of flocks in contrast to "unfold your flocks" in the morning scene.

LV.—PERSEVERANCE OF A SPIDER.

1. I perceived, about four years ago, a large spider in one corner of my room, making its web; and, though the maid frequently leveled her fatal broom against the labors of the little animal, I had the good fortune then to prevent its destruction, and, I may say, it more than paid me by the entertainment it afforded.

2. In three days the web was, with incredible diligence, completed; nor could I avoid thinking that the insect seemed to exult in its new abode. It often traversed it round, and examined the strength of every part of it, retired into its hole, and came out very frequently. The first enemy, however, it had to encounter, was another and much larger spider, which, having no web of its own, and having probably exhausted all its stock in former labors of this kind, came to invade the property of its neighbor.

3. Soon a terrible encounter ensued, in which the invader seemed to have the victory; and the laborious spider was obliged to take refuge in its hole. Upon this I perceived the victor using every art to draw the enemy from his stronghold. He seemed to go off, but quickly returned, and, when he found all arts vain, began to demolish the new web without mercy. This brought on another battle, and, contrary to my expectations, the laborious spider became conqueror, and fairly killed his antagonist.

4. Now in peaceable possession of what was justly its own, it awaited three days with the utmost impatience, repairing the breaches of its web, and taking no sustenance that I could perceive. At last, however, a large blue fly fell into the snare, and struggled hard to get loose. The spider gave it leave to entangle itself as much as possible, but it seemed to be too strong for the cobweb.

5. I must own I was greatly surprised when I saw the spider immediately sally out, and in less than a minute weave a new net around its captive, by which the motion of its wings was stopped; and when it was fairly hampered in this manner, it was seized and dragged into the hole.

6. In this manner it lived, in a precarious state; and Nature seemed to have fitted it for such a life, for upon a single fly it subsisted for more than a week. I once put a wasp into the net; but when the spider came out in order to seize it as usual, upon perceiving what kind of an enemy it had to deal with, it instantly broke all the bands that held it fast, and contributed all that lay in its power to disengage so formidable an antagonist.

7. I had now a mind to try how many cobwebs a single spider could furnish; wherefore I destroyed this, and the insect set about another; when I destroyed the other also, its whole stock seemed entirely exhausted, and it could spin no more.

8. The arts it made use of to support itself, now deprived of its great means of subsistence, were indeed surprising. I have seen it roll up its legs like a ball, and lie motionless for hours together, but cautiously watching all the time; when a fly happened to approach sufficiently near, it would dart out all at once, and often seize its prey.

9. Of this life, however, it soon began to grow weary, and resolved to invade the possession of some other spider, since it could not make a web of its own. It formed an attack upon a neighboring fortification with great vigor, and at first was as vigorously repulsed. Not daunted, however, with one defeat, in this manner it continued to lay siege to another's web for three days, and, at length having killed the defendant, actually took possession.

10. The insect I am now describing lived three years; every year it changed its skin, and got a new set of legs. At first it dreaded my approach to its web; but at last it became so familiar as to take a fly out of my hand, and, upon my touching any part of the web, would immediately leave its hole, prepared either for a defense or an attack.

Oliver Goldsmith.

For Preparation.—I. One of the many works that Goldsmith wrote was a "History of the Earth and Animated Nature." What do you understand by "animated nature"? (all animals.) Would you suppose that the author of this piece was a poet, or only a man of science? Contrast the style of this piece with that in Lesson XV.: how simple and natural the words and expressions are in this one; how difficult and unnatural the words in that!

II. Lĕv′-eled (or levelled), in-erĕd′-i-ble, dĭl′-i-ġençe, neigh′-bor (nā′-), tĕr′-ri-ble, per-çēived′, sieġe, sēize, prey (difference from *pray*), eŏn′-quer-or (kŏnk′er-ur), pēaçe′-a-ble (why *e* retained before *able?* compare chan*ge*able), ap-prōach′, blūe.

III. What does *im* mean in *impatience?*—*dis* in *disengage?*

IV. Fatal broom, invade, demolish, antagonist, cobweb (*cob*, a word meaning *spider*), precarious, subsisted, fortification, vigor, repulsed, daunted.

V. What style is best adapted to the science of natural history? (Description or narration; not a dramatic style, for that would distract attention from the details which ought to be observed.)

LVI.—THE OLD CLOCK ON THE STAIRS.

1. Somewhat back from the village street
Stands the old-fashioned country-seat;
Across its antique portico
Tall poplar-trees their shadows throw;
And from its station in the hall
An ancient time-piece says to all:
"For ever—never!
Never—for ever!"

2. Half-way up the stairs it stands,
And points and beckons with its hands,
From its case of massive oak,
Like a monk, who, under his cloak,
Crosses himself, and sighs, alas!
With sorrowful voice to all who pass:
"For ever—never!
Never—for ever!"

3. By day its voice is low and light;
But in the silent dead of night,
Distinct as a passing footstep's fall,
It echoes along the vacant hall,

Along the ceiling, along the floor,
And seems to say, at each chamber-door:
"For ever—never!
Never—for ever!"

4. Through days of sorrow and of mirth,
Through days of death and days of birth,
Through every swift vicissitude
Of changeful time, unchanged it has stood;
And as if, like God, it all things saw,
It calmly repeats those words of awe:
"For ever—never!
Never—for ever!"

5. In that mansion used to be
Free-hearted hospitality:
His great fires up the chimney roared;
The stranger feasted at his board;
But, like the skeleton at the feast,
That warning time-piece never ceased:
"For ever—never!
Never—for ever!"

6. There, groups of merry children played;
There, youths and maidens, dreaming, strayed.
O precious hours! O golden prime,
And affluence of love and time!
Even as a miser counts his gold,
Those hours the ancient time-piece told:
"For ever—never!
Never—for ever!"

7. From that chamber, clothed in white,
The bride came forth on her wedding-night;

There, in that silent room below,
The dead lay in his shroud of snow;
And in the hush that followed the prayer
Was heard that old clock on the stair:
"For ever—never!
Never—for ever!"

8. All are scattered now, and fled;
Some are married, some are dead;
And when I ask, with throbs of pain,
"Ah! when shall they all meet again,
As in the days long since gone by?"
The ancient time-piece makes reply:
"For ever—never!
Never—for ever!"

9. Never here—for ever there,
Where all parting, pain, and care,
And death, and time, shall disappear—
For ever there, but never here!
The horologe of eternity
Sayeth this incessantly:
"For ever—never!
Never—for ever!"

H. W. Longfellow.

For Preparation.—I. See Lesson XLV. (Does this perhaps refer to Longfellow's residence?)

II. Stâirs̹, sīghs̹ (sīz), çēil′-ing, dōor, ĕv′-er-y, vĭ-çĭs′-si-tūde, chānġe′-a-ble (why *ge* before *able?*), cälm′-ly (käm′-), a̤we, çēased, gone (gŏn), skĕl′-e-ton, chĭm′-ney.

III. Why is a hyphen used in "poplar-trees"? Make a list of ten name-words in this piece that end in *s* to denote more than one (e. g., trees, shadows, etc.). What do the marks " " before and after *for ever* indicate? What kind of a letter must be used at the beginning of the word *God?* Name other words to which the same rule will apply. What does the *s* mean in sighs, beckons, stands, and *es* in crosses? Find other words to illustrate the same thing (present action). *From it's case:* correct this phrase.

IV. Find synonyms for affluence (wealth, abundance), horologe, mansion, antique, ancient, vacant.

V. "Skeleton at the feast" (in Egypt, a skeleton was placed at the table to remind all of death—death being the chief thought of the ancient Egyptian). Notice the kind of clock implied: one with a long case; long pendulum, and consequent slow ticking; room for the heavy weights to descend for a week before "running down"; "ancient time-piece." Find the accented syllables in the first stanza, and divide it into feet, marking it thus:

Some'what | back' from the | vil'lage | street'
Stands' the old- | fash'ioned | coun'try- | seat'," etc.

LVII.—GULLIVER AMONG THE GIANTS.

1. It was about twelve at noon, and a servant brought in dinner. It was only one substantial dish of meat (fit for the plain condition of a husbandman), in a dish of about four-and-twenty feet diameter. The company consisted of the farmer and his wife, three children, and an old grandmother. When they were seated, the farmer placed me at some distance from him on the table, which was thirty feet high from the floor.

2. I was in a terrible fright, and kept as far as I could from the edge, for fear of falling. The wife minced a bit of meat, then crumbled some bread on a trencher, and placed it before me. I made her a low bow, took out my knife and fork, and fell to eating, which gave them exceeding delight. The mistress sent her maid for a small dram-cup, which held about two gallons, and filled it with drink.

3. I took up the vessel with much difficulty in both hands, and in a most respectful manner drank to her

ladyship's health, expressing the words as loudly as I could in English; which made the company laugh so heartily, that I was almost deafened with the noise. This liquor tasted like a small cider, and was not unpleasant.

4. Then the master made me a sign to come to his trencher-side; but, as I walked on the table, being in great surprise all the time, as the indulgent reader will easily conceive and excuse, I happened to stumble against a crust, and fell flat on my face, but received no hurt.

5. I got up immediately, and, observing the good people to be in much concern, I took my hat (which I held under my arm, out of good manners), and, waving it over my head, gave three huzzas, to show I had received no mischief by my fall.

6. On advancing toward my master (as I shall henceforth call him), his youngest son, who sat next to him, an arch boy of about ten years old, took me up by the legs, and held me so high in the air that I trembled in every limb; but his father snatched me from him, and at the same time gave him such a box on the left ear as would have felled a European troop of horse to the earth, and ordered him to be taken from the table.

7. Being afraid the boy might owe me a spite, and well remembering how mischievous all children among us naturally are to sparrows, rabbits, young kittens, and puppy-dogs, I fell on my knees, and, pointing to the boy, made my master to understand as well as I could that I desired his son might be pardoned. The father complied, and the lad took his seat again; whereupon I went to him and kissed his hand, which my master took, and made him stroke me gently with it.

8. In the midst of dinner, my mistress's favorite cat leaped into her lap. I heard a noise behind me like that of a dozen stocking-weavers at work; and, turning my head, I found it proceeded from the purring of that animal, who seemed to be three times larger than an ox, as I computed by the view of her head and one of her paws, while her mistress was feeding and stroking her.

9. The fierceness of this creature's countenance altogether discomposed me, though I stood at the farther end of the table, above fifty feet off, and though my mistress held her fast, for fear she might give a spring and seize me in her talons. But it happened that there was no danger, for the cat took not the least notice of me when my master placed me within three yards of her.

10. As I have been always told, and found true by experience in my travels, that flying, or discovering fear before a fierce animal, is a certain way to make it pursue or attack you, so I resolved, in this dangerous juncture, to show no manner of concern.

11. I walked with intrepidity five or six times before the very head of the cat, and came within half a yard of her; whereupon she drew herself back, as if she were afraid of me. I had less apprehension concerning the dogs, whereof three or four came into the room—as it is usual in farmers' houses—one of which was a mastiff, equal in bulk to four elephants, and a greyhound somewhat taller than the mastiff, but not so large.

Dean Swift.

FOR PREPARATION.—I. From "The Voyage to Brobdingnag." Two months after Gulliver escaped from Lilliput and reached home, he goes to sea again, and, being driven by storm to the northeast of Asia, comes to an island inhabited by giants, as much larger than men as men are larger than Lilliputians. He is left on this island, and wanders into a field of barley, the stalks of which are forty feet high. He is found by one of the reapers, and is carried home by the farmer, who places him on the table at dinner, as described in the piece.

II. Tĕr′-ri-ble, frīght (frīt), knīfe (nīf), dĕaf′-ened (dĕf′nd), mĭs′-chief (-chif).

III. Correct: "The company was the farmer and his wive, three childs, and an old grandmothers";—"Me keeped away from the edge of table";—"I took two knifes";—"His son set next to him." What is the difference between "three times larger than an ox" and "three times as large as an ox"?

IV. Substantial, husbandman (farmer), trencher (wooden plate), small cider (not strong), "in great surprise" (filled with wonder), indulgent, "in much concern" (fearful that I was hurt), "an arch boy," pardoned, complied, computed (reckoned or estimated, judging of her entire size by what he could see of her), discomposed (made me uneasy), talons (do we apply the name talons to the claws of cats, or only to those of birds?), "discovering fear" (showing fear), juncture (occasion), intrepidity, apprehension.

V. Write out the last three paragraphs, using your own language. (If you read the whole story, you will see how absurd some of man's political arrangements seem, when you look at them from the point of view of a giant—e. g., man's customs in regard to war, etc.).

LVIII.—THE COMPOUND SLIDES.

The union of the simple rising and falling slides forms the "compound slide." If the voice falls first and rises last, it is called the "rising compound" slide, and is marked thus (ˇ). If the voice rises first and falls last, it is called the "falling compound" slide, and is marked thus (ˆ).

EXAMPLES.

If a friend says, "Do you like′ this work?" you answer, when you speak sincerely, with the straight slides, "Yes‵, very much‵; it is fine‵!—charming‵!"

But if you wish to make *sport* of it, or to be *sarcastic*, you say, "Ohˇ! it is finerˇ than I expectedˇ of *you*ˆ."

"Now, haven't^ you made a nice^ piece of work of it! You're a *fine*^ workman′! You deserve a prize^!"

Irony (saying one thing with the words, and another quite opposite thing with the voice) is a kind of double speaking, and therefore requires the double or compound slides. So does punning, which plays on the double meaning of words.

"To charm the fish he never spoke,
Although his voice was fine;
He found the most convenient way
Was just to *drop-a-line*^."

"Truly, sir, *all*ˇ that I live by is with the *awl*ˇ."

Sir Peter Teazle—"Very well, ma'am, very well! So a husband is to have no influence—no authority!"

Lady Teazle—"*Authority*ˇ? *No*^, to be sure! If you wanted *authority*ˇ over me, you should have *adopted*^ me, and not marriedˇ me; I am sure you were old^ enough."

In the last example Lady Teazle is *ridiculing* the idea of authority. Hence the use of the compound slides.

"SCORN" AND "SURPRISE."

"I give you a hundred dollars`." There are few persons so dull of ear or sense as not to know the difference between this positive assertion, which the simple falling slide gives, that they are to have a gift of a hundred dollars, and the scornful surprise, which the rising compound slide gives, that they are foolish enough to expect it: "*I give*ˇ *you*ˇ *a hundred*ˇ *dollars*ˇ*?*" Thus we see that the sense and spirit of what is read often depend more on the tones of the voice for their expression than on the words.

If we now generalize this lesson, we have for the use of simple and compound slides these suggestive principles:

SINCERE, HONEST, SIMPLE IDEAS SHOULD BE READ WITH THE "SIMPLE SLIDES."

JESTING, SARCASM, RIDICULE, SCORN, IRONY, ETC., SHOULD BE READ WITH THE "COMPOUND SLIDES."

LIX.—SUMMER WIND.

1. It is a sultry day; the sun has drunk
The dew that lay upon the morning grass;
There is no rustling in the lofty elm
That canopies my dwelling, and its shade
Scarce cools me.

2. All is silent save the faint
And interrupted murmur of the bee,
Settling on the thick flowers, and then again
Instantly on the wing.

3. The plants around
Feel the too potent fervors; the tall maize
Rolls up its long, green leaves; the clover droops
Its tender foliage, and declines its blooms.
But far in the fierce sunshine tower the hills,
With all the growth of woods, silent and stern,
As if the scorching heat and dazzling light
Were but an element they loved.

4. Bright clouds,
Motionless pillars of the brazen heaven—

Their bases on the mountains, their white tops
Shining in the far ether—fire the air
With a reflected radiance, and make turn
The gazer's eyes away.

5. For me, I lie
Languidly in the shade, where the thick turf,
Yet virgin from the kisses of the sun,
Retains some freshness, and I woo the wind
That still delays its coming.

6. Why so slow,
Gentle and voluble spirit of the air?
Oh, come and breathe upon the fainting earth
Coolness and life!

7. Is it that in his caves
He hears me? See, on yonder woody ridge,
The pine is bending his proud top, and now,
Among the nearer groves, chestnut and oak
Are tossing their green boughs about. He comes!
Lo! where the grassy meadow runs in waves!
The deep, distressful silence of the scene
Breaks up with mingling of unnumbered sounds
And universal motion.

8. He is come,
Shaking a shower of blossoms from the shrubs,
And bearing on their fragrance; and he brings
Music of birds, and rustling of young boughs,
And sound of swaying branches, and the voice
Of distant waterfalls.

9. All the green herbs
Are stirring in his breath; a thousand flowers,

By the road-side and the borders of the brook,
Nod gayly to each other; glossy leaves
Are twinkling in the sun, as if the dew
Were on them yet; and silver waters break
Into small waves and sparkle as he comes.

William Cullen Bryant.

For Preparation.—I. Who is the author of this piece? Did he not live in the city? Who describe country scenery best: those who live in the country constantly, or those who come from the city to visit the country? Compare this with Lesson XXXIX. in regard to season described, tone of sadness or of joy, and in regard to the images of nature called up.

II. Copy, with diacritical marks, the following words, dividing them into syllables, indicating the accent, and explaining peculiarities of spelling, as in Lesson XXXIV.: Māize (*ai* for *ā*), dăz′-zling (*zz*), hĕav′-en (hĕv′n) (*ea* for *ĕ*), fiērçe (*ie* for *ē*), eȳe (ī), brēathe, chĕst-nut (silent *t*), ōak, boughs̱ (bouz), mĕad′-ōws̱ (*ea* for *ĕ* and *ow* for *ō*), sçēne (*sc* for *s*), blŏs′-soms̱, gāy′-ly (written also *gaily*), swāy′-ing (*ay* before *i*).

III. Explain the change from canop*y* to canop*ies*;—the *'s* in gazer*'s*;—the *s* in wave*s*;—the hyphen in road-side, and not in waterfalls;—the meaning of *un* in *un*numbered;—of *ful* in distress*ful*.

IV. Define or give synonyms for potent, fervors (too potent fervors= too powerful heat), foliage, canopies, ether, radiance, languidly, voluble, blooms (blossoms), as they are used in the poem.

V. How do you distinguish poetry from prose? (By its rhythm, or regular succession of feet, each foot being composed of accented and unaccented syllables. "It *is′* a *sul′*-try *day′;* the *sun′* has *drunk′*," etc.: here there are five feet to each line, and each foot has two syllables, one accented and one unaccented.) Point out the feet of the third and fourth lines. (Besides the rhythm of a poem, there is also requisite a peculiar style of expression. Inanimate or lifeless things are conceived and described as living and acting like persons [personification]; and persons, on the other hand, are compared with things and natural forces [metaphor]; things are likewise compared with other things, as, in section 4, "bright clouds" are called "motionless pillars." Thus, the poet finds similarity or likeness of things to persons, and of things to things. He looks upon the world as filled with resemblances—one thing reflecting

Daniel Boone and his brother in their winter cottage.

("*Daniel Boone,*" p. 165.)

another, somewhat as a mirror reflects the objects before it. But rhythm, or meter, and personification and metaphor, are only the materials out of which poetry is made, just as a temple is made of hewn stone. There is a central thought in a poem, and these materials are used for its expression, just as the hewn stone is used to fill up and make solid the outlines of the temple. The central thought or subject of this poem is the summer wind—the suffering condition of animals and plants without it, and the refreshment of all upon its arrival.) "The sun has drunk" (section 1)—in what sense does the sun drink the dew? Point out the objects personified in sections 6 to 9, and name the words which indicate the personification (as "his," of pine, section 7; "voice" of waterfalls, section 8). Why "sick" flowers? (section 3.) Why "brazen" heavens? (section 4.)

Bryant's poetry is noted for the freshness and reality of its treatment of nature. Select the passage which you think to be most true to nature;—the passage which you think to be the best poetry.

LX.—DANIEL BOONE.

1. The most remarkable of all the attempts to people the Western country, during the period just preceding the Revolutionary War, was made by Colonel Daniel Boone, of North Carolina. He was a great hunter, and had rambled in the forests of the "mighty West" several years before he ventured, in defiance of wild beasts and still wilder men, to take up his residence there.

2. He first left hom[illegible] company with six other adventurers, in 17[illegible] be a fine place for [illegible]

[illegible] went in 1753);—[illegible] into what each flows);—Boonesborough (eig[illegible] of Lexington, Ky.);—also Booneville and the Femme Osage R[illegible] Missouri (whither he removed). Stuart (spelled Stewart elsewhere).

II. Indicate spelling and pronunciation (by diacritical marks, as in Lesson XXXIV.) of the following words, and explain their peculiarities: Re-cruit′ (*ui* for *u*), whōle (hōl), at-tăcked′ (not at-tackted), daugh′-ter (daw′-), prĭs′-on-er (prĭz′n-er), colonel (kûr′-nel), re-moved′. (Besides unusual combinations of vowels and consonants to represent elementary sounds, e. g., *eo* for *ē* in people, *sc* for *s*

Stuart was soon after killed by the Indians, and the other man by wolves, so that Boone and his brother alone remained. They, however, built themselves a cottage of poles and bark, and wintered there.

4. In May, 1770, the brother of Boone returned to North Carolina, in order to procure a recruit of horses and ammunition, leaving him entirely alone, and, as he himself says, "without bread, salt, or sugar, or even a horse or a dog." The preceding winter, in one of his rambles, he narrowly escaped the savages. But he was one of those men who, like Washington, seem spared for special purposes.

5. His brother returned to him late in July, and they spent the rest of the year and the following winter there. During this time they discovered and gave names to the principal rivers of the country. The whole region seemed to them a paradise, and in March, 1771, they returned home to bring their families with them.

6. In September, 1773, they set out for Kentucky. Five other families had, by their representations, been induced to join them. Forty men also joined them at Powell's Ferry, on the road. Soon after this they were attacked by the Indians, and six of the party slain, among whom was Boone's eldest son. Their cattle also were scattered

Clinch

8. This is supposed to have been the first permanent settlement in Kentucky—then a part of Virginia—though two others were made not far from the same time. The wife and daughter of Colonel Boone were, as he says, the first white women that ever stood on the banks of Kentucky River.

9. But this settlement was not made without great peril. Several times did the Indians attack Boone's party during the journey from Clinch River to Boonesborough. Five of the company were killed, and as many wounded. Others were slain after their arrival. The daughter of Boone was even carried off by the savages in 1776, but her father recovered her.

10. The whole life of this father of Kentucky is eventful and interesting. We can only add here, that he remained in his favorite State, though often much exposed and once taken prisoner, till 1798, when he removed, with a large train of relatives and friends, to Missouri, where he spent his days in hunting and trapping. He died in 1822, at the age of eighty-five. *S. G. Goodrich.*

FOR PREPARATION.—I. Explain what is alluded to by "Revolutionary War" (1);—"battle of Lexington" (7) (Bunker Hill is meant). Daniel Boone was born February 11, 1735, in Bucks County, Pennsylvania, north of Philadelphia. Locate on the map Boone's birthplace;—the Yadkin River, S. C. (whither he went in 1753);—Clinch, Powell's, and Kentucky Rivers (and tell into what each flows);—Boonesborough (eighteen miles southeast of Lexington, Ky.);—also Booneville and the Femme Osage River, Missouri (whither he removed). Stuart (spelled Stewart elsewhere).

II. Indicate spelling and pronunciation (by diacritical marks, as in Lesson XXXIV.) of the following words, and explain their peculiarities: Re-cruit′ (*ui* for *u*), whōle (hōl), at-tăcked′ (not at-tackted), daugh′-ter (daw′-), prĭṣ′-on-er (prĭz′n-er), colonel (kûr′-nel), re-mo̤ved′. (Besides unusual combinations of vowels and consonants to represent elementary sounds, e. g., *eo* for *ē* in people, *sc* for *s* in scene, or silent letters, there are short and obscure vowel-sounds in unaccented syllables, which render it difficult to tell whether the vowel should be ĭ, ĕ, or ŭ: ĭ is represented by *y*, *ui*, *u*, *ei*, *e*, *ee*, *ie*, *ia*, *o*, *ai*, *oi*; ĕ by *ea*, *ai*, *æ*, *a*, *ei*, *eo*, *ie*, *u*, *ue*; ŭ by *o*, *ou*, *oo*, *oe*.)

III. "Mighty West"—explain capital and quotation-marks; eldest—explain *est*. In section 9, change the place of the word *even*, and notice the effect on the meaning of the sentence (place it successively after daughter, Boone, off, savages).

IV. Define and substitute synonyms or phrases of your own for defiance, residence (1), ammunition (4), paradise (5), surveying (7), permanent (8), favorite, trapping (9).

V. Why is the life of Boone said to be "eventful and interesting"? (10.) Select the two most interesting events mentioned in the lesson. Contrast these with others mentioned, and give reasons for your choice.

LXI.—AFTERNOON IN FEBRUARY.

1. The day is ending,
The night is descending;
The marsh is frozen,
The river dead.

2. Through clouds like ashes,
The red sun flashes
On village windows
That glimmer red.

3. The snow recommences;
The buried fences
Mark no longer
The road o'er the plain;

4. While through the meadows,
Like fearful shadows,
Slowly passes
A funeral train.

5. The bell is pealing,
And every feeling
Within me responds
To the dismal knell.

6. Shadows are trailing,
My heart is bewailing
And tolling within
Like a funeral bell.

H. W. Longfellow.

For Preparation.—I. What pieces of this author have you read before? (Lessons XXVI., XXXIII., XLV., LVI.)

II. De-sçĕnd'-ing, vĭl'-lage, glĭm'-mer, mĕad'-ōws, dĭs'-mal, knĕll (nĕl).

III. What force has *er* in long*er*?—*es* in ash*es*?—*es* in pass*es*?—*en* in froz*en*?

IV. Trailing, responds, bewailing.

V. "The river dead"—why does it seem dead? (frozen.) Note the description of outward nature (all wintry, gloomy, and forlorn), and the correspondence of the world without to the internal feelings of the heart, as stated in the last stanza. Compare the composition of the above piece, in this respect, with that of Lesson XXXIII.

LXII.—THE SOLDIER'S REPRIEVE.

EXAMPLE OF NOBLE PATHOS AND TENDERNESS.

PART I.

"I thought, Mr. Allan, when I gave my *Bennie*\ to his *country*, that not a father in all this broad land\ made so *precious*\ a gift—no, not *one*\. The *dear boy* only slept a minute', just one little *minute'*, at his post'. I *know*\ that was all, for Bennie never *dozed'* over a *duty'*. How *prompt*\ and *reliable*\ he was! I know\ he only slept one *little second'* ;—he was so *young*\`, and *not strong*\`, that *boy*¯ of mine! Why, he was as *tall'* as *I*\`, and only eighteen'! And now they SHOOT\` him—because he was found *asleep*\` when doing *sentinel*\`-duty. 'Twenty-four hours\`,' the telegram said. Only *twenty-four hours*\` ! *W-h-e-r-e i-s*\` Bennie *n-o-w*\` ?"

"We will hope, with his HEAVENLY\` *Father*," said Mr. Allan, soothingly.

"*Yes, yes*\` ; let us *hope*\`. *God*^ is very *merciful*\` ! 'I should be *ashamed*\`, father,' Bennie said, 'when I am a *man*¯, to think I never used this great right arm' (and he held it out so proudly before me¯) 'for my *country*\`, when it needed\` it. P-A-L-SY\` it, rather than keep it at the *plow'*.' '*Go*\`, then—GO\`, my boy,' I said, 'and *God keep*\` you!' God *has*\` kept him, I think¯, Mr. Allan."

"Like the *apple* of his *eye*\`, Mr. Owen; *doubt* it *not*\`."

Little *Blossom*\` sat near them, listening, with blanched cheek. She had not shed a tear. Her anxiety had been so concealed that no one had noticed\` it. Now she answered a gentle tap at the kitchen door, opening it to receive a *letter*\` from a neighbor's hand. "It is from *him*\`," was all she said.

It was like a message from the *dead*\` ! Mr. Owen *took* the letter, but could not *break*¯ the *envelope* on account of his *trembling* fingers, and held it toward Mr. *Allan*\`, with the *helplessness* of a *child*\`.

The minister opened it, and read as follows:—

"DEAR FATHER\`: When *this* reaches *you*¯—*I—shall —be in—eternity*\`. At first¯ it seemed *a-w-ful*\` to me; but I have thought about it so *much now'*, that it has *no terror*\`. They say they will not *bind'* me nor *blind'* me, but that I may meet my death like a MAN\`. I *thought*, father, it might have been on the *battle-field* for my *country*, and that, when I fell, it would be *f-i-g-h-t-ing g-l-o-r-i-ously*; but to be shot down like a *dog* for nearly *betraying* it—to die for *neglect*-of-duty!—*oh, father*, I wonder the very *thought* does not *kill* me! But I shall not disgrace *you*. I am going to write you all about it; and, when *I-am-gone*, *you* may *tell* my *comrades*. *I* can not *now*. You know I promised Jimmie Carr's mother I would *look after* her boy; and, when he fell *sick*, I *did all* I *could* for him. He was not strong when ordered back into the ranks, and the day before *that night I carried all* HIS luggage, besides my *own*, on our march. Toward night we went in on *double-quick*, and though the luggage began to feel very *heavy*, everybody *else* was tired *too*. And as for *Jimmie*, if I had not lent him an *arm* now and then, he would have dropped by the way. I was ALL-TIRED-OUT when we went into camp, and then it was *Jimmie's* turn to be *sentry*, and I-*would*-take-*his-place*; but I was *too tired*, father. I could not have kept *awake* if a *gun* had been pointed at my head; but I did not *know* it *until*—well—*until-it-was* TOO LATE."

"GOD *be* THANKED!" said MR. OWEN. "I *knew* Bennie was not the boy to *sleep carelessly* at his post."

"They tell me, to-day, that I have a short *reprieve*—'time to *write* to *you*,' our good colonel says. Forgive him, father; he only does his *duty*; he would gladly *save* me if he could. And do not lay my death up against *Jimmie*. The *poor* boy is *broken-hearted*, and does nothing but *beg-and-entreat* them to let H-I-M *die* in *m-y* stead.

"I can't *bear* to think of *mother* and *Blossom*. COMFORT them, father! Tell them I die as a *brave boy* should, and that, when the *war* is *over*, they will not be *ashamed*` of me, as they *must* be now`. *God* help` me; it *is*` *very hard*` to bear! Good-by`, father! *God*` seems *near*` and *dear*` to me, as if he felt *sorry*` for his *poor*, *broken-hearted* childˉ, and would take me to be with *him*` —in a *better*`, BETTER` life.

"To-night I shall see the cows′ all coming home from pasture′, and precious little *Blossom*′ standing on the back stoop, waiting′ for me; but—Iˉ—SHALL NEVERˉ—NEVERˉ—COME`! *God*ˉ BLESS` you *all! Forgive*` your *poor* BENNIE`."

PART II.

Late that night a *little figure* glided down the foot-path toward the Mill Depot`. The conductor, as he reached down to lift her into the carˉ, *wondered*` at the *tear*-stained face that was upturned toward the dim lantern` he held in his hand.

A few questions and ready answers told him *all*`; and no *father*` could have cared more *tenderly* for his *only child*`, than *he* for our little *Blossom*`. She was on her way to Washington`, to ask President Lincoln` for her *brother's life*`. She had brought Bennie's letter` with her; no *good, kind* heart, like the *President's*ˉ, could *refuse* to be *melted*` by it.

The next morning they reached New Yorkˉ, and the conductor hurried her on to Washington`. Every minute`, now, might be the means of *saving*` her *brother's life*`.

The President had but just seated himself to his evening's taskˉ, when the door softly openedˉ, and *Blossom*`, with downcast eyes and folded hands, stood before him.

"Well′, my child′," he said, in his pleasant, cheerful tones, "what do *you′ want?*"

"*Bennie's* LIFE\`, *p-l-e-a-s-e*\`, sir," faltered Blossom.

"*Bennie′!* Who *is*\` Bennie?"

"My *brother*\`, sir. They are going to *shoot*\` him for *sleeping*\` at his *post*\`."

"Oh, yes\`; I remember. It was a FATAL\` sleep. You see, child, it was a time of *special danger*\`. THOUSANDS\` of *lives might* have been *lost* by HIS *negligence*\`."

"*So* my *father*\` said," replied Blossom, gravely. "But *poor-Bennie* was *s-o*-T-I-R-E-D\`, sir, and *Jimmie so weak*\`. HE did the work of *two*\`, sir, and it was *Jimmie's*\` night, *not his;* but *Jimmie* was too *tired*\`, and *Bennie* never thought about *himself′*, that HE′ was *tired too′*."

"*What is this you say′*, child? Come here\`; I do not understand\`." And the kind man, as ever, caught eagerly at what seemed to be a *justification*\` of an offense.

Blossom went to him. He put his hand tenderly on her shoulder, and turned up the pale, anxious face toward his\`. How *tall*\` he seemed! And he was *President* of the *United States*\`, too! A dim thought of this kind passed for a moment through Blossom's mind¯; but she *told* her *simple, straightforward story*\`, and handed Bennie's *letter*\` to Mr. Lincoln to read.

He read it *carefully*\`; then, taking up his pen, wrote a few hasty lines and rang his bell. Blossom heard *this order*\` given: "*Send* THIS *dispatch at* ONCE\`."

The President then turned to the girl, and said¯: "Go *home*\`, my child, and tell that *father*\` of yours, who could *approve* his *country's* sentence, even when it took the *life* of a *child* like THAT¯, that Abraham Lincoln thinks the life far too PRECIOUS\` to be *lost.* Go back\`, or—wait until to-morrow\`; *Bennie*\` will need a *change* after he has so *bravely faced death*\`; *he*\` shall go *with*\` you."

"*God* BLESS\` *you,* sir!" said Blossom.

Two days after this interview, the young *soldier*\` came to the White House with his little *sister*\`. He was called into the President's private room, and a *strap*\` fastened upon his shoulder. Mr. Lincoln then said: "The soldier that could carry a sick *comrade's baggage*ˉ, and *die*\` for the act so *uncomplainingly,* DESERVES WELL\` of his *country*\`."

Then Bennie and Blossom took their way to their Green-Mountain-*home*\`. A *crowd*\` gathered at the Mill Depot to *welcome*\` them back; and, as Farmer *Owen's* hand grasped that of his *boy,* TEARS\` flowed down his cheeks, and he was heard to say fervently, "THE LORD\` BE PRAISED\`!"

Mrs. R. D. C. Robbins.

LXIII.—THE TALENTS.

1. The kingdom of heaven is as a man traveling into a far country, who called his own servants, and delivered unto them his goods. And unto one he gave five talents, to another two, and to another one: to every man according to his several ability; and straightway took his journey.

2. Then he that had received the five talents went and traded with the same, and made them other five talents. And likewise he that had received two, he also gained other two. But he that had received one went and digged in the earth, and hid his lord's money.

3. After a long time the lord of those servants cometh, and reckoneth with them. And so he that had re-

ceived five talents came and brought other five talents, saying, Lord, thou deliveredst unto me five talents: behold, I have gained beside them five talents more. His lord said unto him, Well done, thou good and faithful servant; thou hast been faithful over a few things, I will make thee ruler over many things: enter thou into the joy of thy Lord.

4. He also that had received two talents came and said, Lord, thou deliveredst unto me two talents: behold, I have gained two other talents beside them. His lord said unto him, Well done, good and faithful servant; thou hast been faithful over a few things, I will make thee ruler over many things: enter thou into the joy of thy lord.

5. Then he which had received the one talent came and said, Lord, I knew thee that thou art an hard man, reaping where thou hast not sown, and gathering where thou hast not strewed: and I was afraid, and went and hid thy talent in the earth. Lo, there thou hast that is thine.

6. His lord answered and said unto him, Thou wicked and slothful servant, thou knewest that I reap where I sowed not, and gather where I have not strewed: thou oughtest therefore to have put my money to the exchangers, and then at my coming I should have received mine own with usury. Take therefore the talent from him, and give it unto him which hath ten talents.

7. For unto every one that hath shall be given, and he shall have abundance: but from him that hath not shall be taken away even that which he hath. And cast ye the unprofitable servant into outer darkness: there shall be weeping and gnashing of teeth.

Matthew, Chapter XXV.

FOR PREPARATION.—I. How much, in our money, is the value of the talent as used in Judea in the time of Christ? ($1,645 to $1,916.) Our word "talent," as meaning mental endowment, is derived from the figurative application made in this parable. All words relating to the mind, or to what is spiritual, are derived by the same process from words used first for material things.

II. Gnăsh′-ing (năsh′-), strāight′-way (strāt′-), joûr′-ney, brôught (brawt), a-frāid′, ăn′-swered (-serd).

III. Likewise (*wise* meaning manner, or *guise*, in this word, as also in other*wise* and length*wise*). "Sown" and "strewed"—what two ways of indicating past time or completed action, illustrated in these words? Note the use of "which" (5 and 6), referring to "him" and "he." What word do we use to refer to persons? (who.) Note also the use of "that" ("thou hast that is thine"). (The style of the Bible is that of good English of the time of the settlement of this country by the English—1600 to 1630.) Make a list of expressions that are no longer used—e. g., "unto one," "straightway took," "he that" for "he who," "other two," "cometh" (*eth* = *s*, denoting present time and continued action), "thou deliveredst" (*st* to agree with *thou*), "behold," "thee," "mine own," "an hard," etc.

IV. Slothful, unprofitable.

V. What figure of speech is used in the parable? (The allegory is a continued *metaphor*, wherein imaginary events are told as though they were realities, but with the unexpressed intention that a figurative application shall be made of them. The parable is a continued *simile*, the figurative application being expressly stated: "The kingdom of heaven is *as* [like] a man traveling," etc.) Do faculties of the mind—memory, attention, power of thought—all increase by frequent use? Does one's character improve by repetition of good acts? Can we all increase the "talents" we have, by making good use of them?

LXIV.—SOLDIER, REST!

1. Soldier, rest! Thy warfare o'er,
   Sleep the sleep that knows not breaking;
Dream of battled fields no more,
   Days of danger, nights of waking.

2. In our isle's enchanted hall,
   Hands unseen thy couch are strewing;
Fairy strains of music fall,
   Every sense in slumber dewing.

3. Soldier, rest! Thy warfare o'er,
Dream of fighting fields no more;
Sleep the sleep that knows not breaking,
Morn of toil, nor night of waking.

4. No rude sound shall reach thine ear,
   Armor's clang, or war-steed champing;
Trump nor pibroch summon here
   Mustering clan, or squadron tramping.

5. Yet the lark's shrill fife may come,
   At the daybreak, from the fallow,
And the bittern sound his drum,
   Booming from the sedgy shallow.

6. Ruder sounds shall none be near;
Guards nor warders challenge here;
Here's no war-steed's neigh and champing,
Shouting clans, or squadrons stamping.

Sir Walter Scott.

FOR PREPARATION.—I. This song is found in Scott's "Lady of the Lake," and is sung by the Lady of the Lake herself. What is a bittern?—a lark? In what country are they found? What is a pibroch, and where used? (The scene of this piece is a beautiful island in Loch Katrine, a lake of Scotland surrounded by woody hills; on the south are Ben Venue and Aberfoyle, on the east Loch Achray, on the north the Trossachs, Ben Voirlich, Uam-Var, etc. See Lessons XX. and XXII.: the lady sings for the huntsman there described, who is lost, and has wandered to this island.

II. Wąr'-fâre, breāk'-ing, bĭt'-tern, squạd'-ron, neigh (nā), chăl-lenge.

III. When would you use *thy*, and when *thou?* (Note the use of "thy" and "thou," and words of this style, in modern poetry as well as in old English prose.) What is omitted in *o'er?* Why not say "sleep *who* knows not," etc., instead of "*that* knows not"? Explain *'s* in isle's, armor's, lark's, here's.

IV. "Battled fields," clang, fallow (uncultivated land), clan, sedgy, champing.

V. Contrast the first and second stanzas: the allusion to battle-scenes in the former, and the quiet, peaceful surroundings of the latter. Make the same contrast between the third and fourth stanzas, and the fifth (the lark's fife instead of the soldier's fife, and the bittern's drum instead of the soldier's drum). Note the difference between squadrons (of the regular Scotch army) and the "shouting clans" (of wild mountaineers, who strove to be independent).

LXV.—BENJAMIN FRANKLIN.

1. One of the Americans who rendered the greatest services to the liberty of their country was Dr. Benjamin Franklin. He was born in Boston in 1706, and was the son of a poor tallow-chandler. When a boy, he learned the printer's trade; at seventeen he left home, and established himself in Philadelphia.

2. He and a young partner began business with no capital, and felt very grateful to a friend whom they met in the street and who gave them a five-shilling job. Afterward they set up a newspaper, and published an almanac called "Poor Richard's Almanac," which had a great circulation. They also dealt in all sorts of small wares—rags, ink, soap, feathers, and coffee.

3. Franklin was a great reader, and a great student of science, and especially of electricity. He formed the

theory that lightning and the electrical fluid are the same thing. This he said in a pamphlet, and some readers thought it a very absurd view. Then he resolved to prove it. He and his young son made a great kite of a silk handkerchief, fastened a piece of sharpened wire to the stick, and went out to fly the kite in a thunder-storm.

4. As the low thunder-cloud passed, the electric fluid came down the string of the kite. When Franklin touched a key that he had fastened to the string, his knuckles drew sparks from it, and proved that there was electricity there. This led him to invent the lightning-rod, which is now in almost universal use. This discovery at once made him very famous in Europe, as well as in America.

5. He was afterward sent to England on a public mission, and remained there till the outbreak of the Revolution. Returning to America, he was one of the framers and signers of the Declaration of Independence. He was sent to France as ambassador, and aided in making the treaty with France which secured the independence of the American colonies.

6. He was a man of the greatest activity, public spirit, and wit. He exercised great influence in all public affairs, and founded more good institutions and benevolent enterprises than any other American of his time. His last public act was to sign a memorial to Congress in behalf of the Philadelphia Antislavery Society, of which he was president, asking the abolition of slavery.

7. He lived to the age of eighty-four, dying in 1790. The whole nation mourned when he died. Mirabeau,

then the leader of the French Assembly, called him "the sage whom two worlds claim as their own," and proposed that the Assembly should wear mourning on the arm for him during three days, which was done. It was said of him after his death, by a celebrated Frenchman (Turgot), that "he snatched the lightning from the sky, and the scepter from tyrants!" *T. W. Higginson.*

FOR PREPARATION.—I. From Higginson's "Young Folks' History of the United States." To whom is the word "Americans" applied? Why not to Mexicans and Canadians? The literature relative to the Revolutionary War fixed the word in a national meaning, partly from the difficulty of forming a descriptive word from the name of our nation (United Statesians!).

II. Sçī′-ençe, knŭck′-leş (nŭk′lz), al′-ma năe, out′-breāk, Mī-ra-beau′ (-bō′), Tūr-gōt′ (-gō′).

III. Make a list of ten abbreviations that you remember, and write opposite each the full word, thus: Dr.—Doctor; N. A.—North America; U. S.—United States; Mo.—Missouri; N. Y.—New York, etc.

IV. Rendered, universal, famous, sage, memorial, "electric fluid" (is it really a "fluid"?), partner, capital (money, and other means, to carry on business), lightning-rod, "Declaration of Independence."

V. "With no capital" (2). Some capital was furnished by his partner. He withdrew in 1729, and Franklin afterward started the store and the almanac alone. The famous experiment of Franklin "drew electricity from the clouds." Doubtless it can be drawn from the upper air on a cloudless day. Had the lightning really descended his kite-string, it would have killed Franklin, as it did the Russian who undertook to repeat the experiment.

LXVI.—THE THREE BLACK CROWS.

1. Two honest tradesmen meeting in the Strand,
One took the other briskly by the hand.
"Hark ye," said he, "'tis an odd story, this,
About the crows!" "I don't know what it is,"

Replied his friend. "No? I'm surprised at that.
Where I come from, it is the common chat.

2. "But you shall hear—an odd affair, indeed!
And that it happened, they are all agreed.
Not to detain you from a thing so strange:
A gentleman, who lives not far from 'Change,
This week, in short, as all the Alley knows,
Taking a vomit, threw up three black crows!"

3. "Impossible!" "Nay, but 'tis really true;
I had it from good hands, and so may you."
"From whose, I pray?" So, having named the man,
Straight to inquire his curious comrade ran:
"Sir, did you tell—" (relating the affair).
"Yes, sir, I did; and, if 'tis worth your care,
'Twas Mr. Such-a-one who told it me.
But, by-the-by, 'twas two black crows—not three."

4. Resolved to trace so wondrous an event,
Quick to the third the virtuoso went:
"Sir—" (and so forth). "Why, yes—the thing is fact,
Though, in regard to number, not exact:
It was not two black crows—'twas only one.
The truth of that you may depend upon:
The gentleman himself told me the case."
"Where may I find him?" "Why, in such a place."

5. Away he went; and, having found him out:
"Sir, be so good as to resolve a doubt."
Then to his last informant he referred,
And begged to know if true what he had heard:

"Did you, sir, throw up a black crow?" "Not I!"
"Bless me, how people propagate a lie!
Black crows have been thrown up, three, two, and one;
And here, I find, all comes at last to none!

6. "Did you say anything of a crow at all?"
"Crow?—crow? Perhaps I might, now I recall
The matter over." "And pray, sir, what was't?"
"Why, I was horrid sick, and, at last,
I did throw up—and told my neighbor so—
Something that was as black, sir, as a crow!"

John Byrom.

For Preparation.—I. What locality is indicated by "the Strand"?—"'Change" (Exchange)?—"Alley"? (Is it London?)

II. Two (too͞), straight (strāt), cŏm′-rade (kŏm′răd *or* kŭm′răd), bĕgged, prŏp′-a-gāte, nōne (nŭn).

III. Supply omission in *'tis*;—meaning of *im* in impossible;—of *se* in whose (like *'s*, it denotes possession). Of what is *Mr.* an abbreviation? What punctuation-mark must always be placed after an abbreviation? Meaning of *n* in thrown? (like *ed*, it denotes past or completed action.) "Horrid sick"—is this proper language to use? (Such expressions are called vulgarisms, or slang.)

IV. "Curious comrade" (curious for *anxious*, or *inquiring*), "by-the-by," virtuoso, "and so forth" (stands for what remarks in the line where it occurs?), "such a place" (stands for the name of the locality given by the speaker), "resolve a doubt."

V. Make a list of the different steps in reducing this street-rumor to its foundation. Which party says, "Bless me, how people propagate a lie!" "All the Alley"—what is meant?

LXVII.—THE BIRTHDAY OF WASHINGTON.

MARKED FOR LOGICAL ANALYSIS AND EMPHASIS.

The *birthday* of the "FATHER OF HIS COUNTRY!" May it ever be *freshly remembered* by AMERICAN HEARTS! May it ever reawaken in them a *filial* VENERATION for his memory; ever rekindle the fires of *patriotic regard* for the COUNTRY he loved so well; to which he gave his *youthful vigor* and his *youthful energy* during the perilous period of the early *Indian warfare;* to which he *devoted his life* in the *maturity* of his powers in the *field;* to which again he offered the counsels of his *wisdom* and his *experience* as *president* of the *convention* that framed our *Constitution;* which he guided and directed while in the chair of *State;* and for which the *last prayer* of his earthly supplication was offered up, when it came the moment for him so *well*, and so *grandly*, and so *calmly* TO DIE.

He was the FIRST *man* of the *time* in which he grew. His *memory* is *first* and *most* SACRED in our LOVE; and *ever* hereafter, till the *last drop of blood* shall *freeze* in the *last* AMERICAN HEART, *his name* shall be a *spell* of *power* and of *might.*

Yes, gentlemen, there is *one personal,* one VAST FELICITY, which *no* man can *share* with him. It was the *daily beauty* and *towering* and *matchless glory* of his *life* which enabled him to CREATE HIS COUNTRY, and at the same time secure an *undying love* and *regard* from the WHOLE *American people.* "The *first* in the HEARTS of his *countrymen!*" Undoubtedly there were *brave* and *wise* and *good* men, before his day, in every colony. But the *American nation,* as a NATION, I do not reckon to have begun before 1774. And the FIRST LOVE of that YOUNG AMERICA was WASHINGTON. *Rufus Choate.*

LXVIII.—THE BROOK.

1. I come from haunts of coot and hern;
   I make a sudden sally,
And sparkle out among the fern,
   To bicker down a valley.

2. By thirty hills I hurry down,
   Or slip between the ridges,
By twenty thorps, a little town,
   And half a hundred bridges.

3. I chatter over stony ways,
   In little sharps and trebles;
I bubble into eddying bays,
   I babble on the pebbles.

4. I chatter, chatter, as I flow
   To join the brimming river;
For men may come and men may go,
   But I go on for ever.

5. I wind about, and in and out,
   With here a blossom sailing,
And here and there a lusty trout,
   And here and there a grayling,

6. And here and there a foamy flake
   Upon me, as I travel,
With many a silvery water-break,
   Above the golden gravel.

7. I steal by lawns and grassy plots,
   I slide by hazel covers;

"I chatter over stony ways,
In little sharps and trebles."

(*"The Brook,"* p. 184.)

I move the sweet forget-me-nots
  That grow for happy lovers.

8. I murmur under moon and stars
  In brambly wildernesses;
I linger by my shingly bars;
  I loiter round my cresses.

9. And out again I curve and flow
  To join the brimming river;
For men may come and men may go,
  But I go on for ever.

Alfred Tennyson.

For Preparation.—I. "The Brook: An Idyl," is the name that Tennyson gives to the poem from which this is taken. The song of the brook winds along through the poem like a silver thread, suggesting melancholy memories to the poet, which he relates in longer and less musical lines that interrupt the song of the brook at irregular intervals. (The "Scene by the Brook," in Beethoven's "Pastoral Symphony," is suggested.) Let the pupil select the names of animals, and other things, that indicate the country in which the scene is laid.

II. Häunts, loi′-ter, brĭdġ′-es̱, pĕb′-ble.

III. Copy the first stanza, and mark the feet and accented syllables. Change the order of the words in the second stanza, adding words where needed to make good prose.

IV. Coot (a water-fowl), hern (heron), bicker (to quiver), thorps (small villages), eddying, cresses.

V. What is "a sudden sally"? "Little sharps and trebles" (it describes the tones of the chattering—in high, shrill tones). River (4)—why "brimming"? Is the brook represented as being gay and chattering because it goes on for ever, while men come and go, meet and part, and are sad in consequence? What kind of a fish is a "grayling"? "Hazel covers" (in England, the expression used by hunters to describe underbrush that *covers* or conceals game). "Shingly bars" (shallow places, with gravel—shingle—bottoms).

LXIX.—THE SERMON ON THE MOUNT.

1. And there followed him great multitudes of people from Galilee, and from Decapolis, and from Jerusalem, and from Judea, and from beyond Jordan. And seeing the multitudes, he went up into a mountain: and when he was set, his disciples came unto him: And he opened his mouth, and taught them, saying: Blessed are the poor in spirit: for theirs is the kingdom of heaven. Blessed are they that mourn: for they shall be comforted. Blessed are the meek: for they shall inherit the earth. Blessed are they which do hunger and thirst after righteousness: for they shall be filled.

2. Blessed are the merciful: for they shall obtain mercy. Blessed are the pure in heart: for they shall see God. Blessed are the peacemakers: for they shall be called the children of God. Blessed are they which are persecuted for righteousness' sake: for theirs is the kingdom of heaven. Blessed are ye, when men shall revile you, and persecute you, and shall say all manner of evil against you falsely, for my sake. Rejoice, and be exceeding glad: for great is your reward in heaven: for so persecuted they the prophets which were before you.

3. Ye are the salt of the earth: but if the salt have lost his savor, wherewith shall it be salted? it is thenceforth good for nothing, but to be cast out, and to be trodden under foot of men. Ye are the light of the world. A city that is set on an hill can not be hid. Neither do men light a candle, and put it under a bushel, but on a candlestick; and it giveth light unto all that are in the house. Let your light so shine before men, that they may see your good works, and glorify your Father which is in heaven.

4. Think not that I am come to destroy the law, or the prophets: I am not come to destroy, but to fulfill. For verily I say unto you, Till heaven and earth pass, one jot or one tittle shall in no wise pass from the law, till all be fulfilled. Whosoever therefore shall break one of these least commandments, and shall teach men so, he shall be called the least in the kingdom of heaven: but whosoever shall do and teach them, the same shall be called great in the kingdom of heaven. For I say unto you, That except your righteousness shall exceed the righteousness of the scribes and Pharisees, ye shall in no case enter into the kingdom of heaven.

5. Ye have heard that it was said by them of old time, Thou shalt not kill; and whosoever shall kill shall be in danger of the judgment: but I say unto you, That whosoever is angry with his brother without a cause shall be in danger of the judgment. . . . Therefore if thou bring thy gift to the altar, and there rememberest that thy brother hath aught against thee; leave there thy gift before the altar, and go thy way; first be reconciled to thy brother, and then come and offer thy gift. . . .

6. And if thy right eye offend thee, pluck it out, and cast it from thee: for it is profitable for thee that one of thy members should perish, and not that thy whole body should be cast into hell. And if thy right hand offend thee, cut it off, and cast it from thee: for it is profitable for thee that one of thy members should perish, and not that thy whole body should be cast into hell. . . .

7. Again, ye have heard that it hath been said by them of old time, Thou shalt not forswear thyself, but shalt perform unto the Lord thine oaths: but I say unto you, Swear not at all; neither by heaven; for it is God's

throne: nor by the earth; for it is his footstool: neither by Jerusalem; for it is the city of the great King. Neither shalt thou swear by thy head, because thou canst not make one hair white or black. But let your communication be, Yea, yea; Nay, nay: for whatsoever is more than these cometh of evil.

8. Ye have heard that it hath been said, An eye for an eye, and a tooth for a tooth: but I say unto you, That ye resist not evil: but whosoever shall smite thee on thy right cheek, turn to him the other also. And if any man will sue thee at the law, and take away thy coat, let him have thy cloak also. And whosoever shall compel thee to go a mile, go with him twain. Give to him that asketh thee, and from him that would borrow of thee turn not thou away.

9. Ye have heard that it hath been said, Thou shalt love thy neighbor, and hate thine ememy. But I say unto you, Love your enemies, bless them that curse you, do good to them that hate you, and pray for them which despitefully use you, and persecute you; that ye may be the children of your Father which is in heaven: for he maketh his sun to rise on the evil and on the good, and sendeth rain on the just and on the unjust. For if ye love them which love you, what reward have ye? do not even the publicans the same? And if ye salute your brethren only, what do ye more than others? do not even the publicans so? Be ye therefore perfect, even as your Father which is in heaven is perfect.

Matthew, Chapter V.

FOR PREPARATION.—I. Point out, on the map, Decapolis, Jerusalem, Judea, Jordan River. What mountain (near Capernaum) did Christ ascend? Point out the passages known as "The Beatitudes" (1 and 2).

II. Com-pĕl′, pēo′-ple (pē′pl), mount′-ain (-in), dis-çī′-pleṣ, ō′-pened (-pnd), mōurn, rīght′-eoŭs-ness (rī′chŭs-nes), taught (tawt), a-gainst′ (-gĕnst′), fạlse′-ly, prŏph′-ets, nŏth′-ing, fụl-fĭlled′.

III. Do you find the word *its* used anywhere in the Bible? What word was used instead in the time when the Bible was translated? (3: "if the salt have lost his savor.") What is our use of "his"? Note the use of "which" for "who" and "that" (Lesson LXIII.); "an" ("on an hill").

IV. Bushel, reconciled, multitudes, comforted, meek, inherit, merciful, obtain, persecuted, revile, reward, savor, trodden, glorify, destroy, jot, tittle, except, exceed, scribes, Pharisees, danger, judgment, altar, offend, pluck, profitable, perish, forswear, perform, oaths, communication, yea, nay, resist, smite, twain, borrow, despitefully, salute, perfect.

V. Note, in the fifth paragraph, the distinction between legal and religious views. The law (enforced by the state, or the courts of the land) takes notice of a deed actually done, not of one merely wished to be done (hence it is called an "overt act," i. e., an open, public act); but religion takes cognizance of the frame of mind—the wish, or desire, or intention of the inmost heart—rather than of the overt act. The same distinction exists between *sin* and *crime* (crime—a breach of the law of the land; sin—a breach of the law of God. Of course, some acts may be both sins and crimes, and some may be one or the other only). Note, further, the expiation of the two kinds of transgressions: crime being expiated by a definite limited punishment; but sin being infinite in its nature, and not expiated by external acts, but only escaped by internal repentance, which is met by mercy and pardon on the part of the lawgiver. So, in the ninth paragraph, the distinction between kindness, or love, which is good toward all men, and (*a*) *politeness*, which merely treats all with the external show of good feeling, or (*b*) *justice*, which returns upon each his own deed—love for love, or hate for hate.

LXX.—THE SERMON ON THE MOUNT (Continued).

1. Take heed that ye do not your alms before men, to be seen of them: otherwise ye have no reward of your Father which is in heaven. Therefore when thou doest thine alms, do not sound a trumpet before thee, as the hypocrites do in the synagogues and in the streets, that they may have glory of men. Verily I say unto you,

They have their reward. But when thou doest alms, let not thy left hand know what thy right hand doeth: that thine alms may be in secret: and thy Father which seeth in secret himself shall reward thee openly.

2. And when thou prayest, thou shalt not be as the hypocrites are: for they love to pray standing in the synagogues and in the corners of the streets, that they may be seen of men. Verily I say unto you, They have their reward. But thou, when thou prayest, enter into thy closet, and when thou hast shut thy door, pray to thy Father which is in secret: and thy Father which seeth in secret shall reward thee openly. But when ye pray, use not vain repetitions, as the heathen do: for they think that they shall be heard for their much speaking. Be not ye therefore like unto them: for your Father knoweth what things ye have need of, before ye ask him.

3. After this manner therefore pray ye: Our Father which art in heaven, Hallowed be thy name. Thy kingdom come. Thy will be done in earth, as it is in heaven. Give us this day our daily bread. And forgive us our debts, as we forgive our debtors. And lead us not into temptation, but deliver us from evil: For thine is the kingdom, and the power, and the glory, for ever. Amen. For if ye forgive men their trespasses, your heavenly Father will also forgive you: but if ye forgive not men their trespasses, neither will your Father forgive your trespasses.

4. Moreover, when ye fast, be not, as the hypocrites, of a sad countenance: for they disfigure their faces, that they may appear unto men to fast. Verily I say unto you, They have their reward. But thou, when thou fastest, anoint thy head, and wash thy face; that thou appear not unto men to fast, but unto thy Father which is in

secret: and thy Father, which seeth in secret, shall reward thee openly.

5. Lay not up for yourselves treasures upon earth, where moth and rust doth corrupt, and where thieves break through and steal: but lay up for yourselves treasures in heaven, where neither moth nor rust doth corrupt, and where thieves do not break through nor steal: for where your treasure is, there will your heart be also. The light of the body is the eye: if therefore thine eye be single, thy whole body shall be full of light. But if thine eye be evil, thy whole body shall be full of darkness. If therefore the light that is in thee be darkness, how great is that darkness!

No man can serve two masters: for either he will hate the one, and love the other; or else he will hold to the one, and despise the other. Ye can not serve God and mammon.

6. Therefore I say unto you, Take no thought for your life, what ye shall eat, or what ye shall drink; nor yet for your body, what ye shall put on. Is not the life more than meat, and the body than raiment? Behold the fowls of the air: for they sow not, neither do they reap, nor gather into barns; yet your heavenly Father feedeth them. Are ye not much better than they? Which of you by taking thought can add one cubit unto his stature? And why take ye thought for raiment? Consider the lilies of the field, how they grow; they toil not, neither do they spin: and yet I say unto you, That even Solomon in all his glory was not arrayed like one of these.

7. Wherefore, if God so clothe the grass of the field, which to-day is, and to-morrow is cast into the oven, shall he not much more clothe you, O ye of little faith?

Therefore take no thought, saying, What shall we eat? or, What shall we drink? or, Wherewithal shall we be clothed? . . . For your heavenly Father knoweth that ye have need of all these things. But seek ye first the kingdom of God, and his righteousness; and all these things shall be added unto you. Take therefore no thought for the morrow: for the morrow shall take thought for the things of itself. Sufficient unto the day is the evil thereof. *Matthew, Chapter VI.*

For Preparation.—I. Who was Solomon? People of what religion meet in synagogues? "Mammon"—what is meant?

II. Hy̆p′-o-crītes, sy̆n′-a-gŏgues (-gŏgz), ālms (āmz), prāy′-est, ēi′-ther, rāi′-ment, sōw, rēap, ȯv′-en (ŭv′n), hĕav′-en (hĕv′n), dĕbts (dĕts), trĕas′-ūres (trĕzh′ụrz).

III. What meaning is given by *e* in men?—capital *F* in Father?—*est* in doest?—*ine* in thine?—*ee* in thee?—*y* in thy?—*th* in seeth?—*ne* in done?—*ily* in daily?—*r* in your?—*ies* in lilies?

IV. Repetitions, hallowed, forgive, trespasses, reward, verily, secret, "eye be single," else, despise, arrayed, temptation, deliver, fast, disfigure, anoint, moth, rust, corrupt, morrow, sufficient.

V. What do moths attack? What things rust? What is the original meaning of the word *cubit*, and what does it signify when used as a measure of length?

LXXI.—THE FIGHT OF PASO DEL MAR.

1. Gusty and raw was the morning;
 A fog hung over the seas,
And its gray skirts, rolling inland,
 Were torn by the mountain-trees.
No sound was heard but the dashing
 Of waves on the sandy bar,
When Pablo of San Diego
 Rode down to the Paso del Mar.

2. The pescador, out in his shallop,
Gathering his harvest so wide,
Sees the dim bulk of the headland
Loom over the waste of the tide;
He sees, like a white thread, the pathway
Wind round on the terrible wall,
Where the faint, moving speck of the rider
Seems hovering close to its fall!

3. Stout Pablo of San Diego
Rode down from the hills behind;
With the bells on his gray mule tinkling,
He sang through the fog and wind.
Under his thick, misted eyebrows
Twinkled his eye like a star,
And fiercer he sang as the sea-winds
Drove cold on the Paso del Mar.

4. Now Bernal, the herdsman of Corral,
Had traveled the shore since dawn,
Leaving the ranches behind him:
Good reason had he to be gone!
The blood was still red on his dagger,
The fury was hot in his brain,
And the chill, driving scud of the breakers
Beat thick on his forehead in vain.

5. With his blanket wrapped gloomily round him,
He mounted the dizzying road,
And the chasms and steeps of the headland
Were slippery and wet as he trode.
Wild swept the wind of the ocean,
Rolling the fog from afar,
When near him a mule-bell came tinkling,
Midway on the Paso del Mar.

6. "Back!" shouted Bernal full fiercely,
   And "Back!" shouted Pablo in wrath,
As his mule halted, startled and shrinking,
   On the perilous line of the path.
The roar of devouring surges
   Came up from the breakers' hoarse war;
And "Back, or you perish!" cried Bernal;
   "I turn not on Paso del Mar!"

7. The gray mule stood firm as the headland;
   He clutched at the jingling rein,
When Pablo rose up in his saddle
   And smote till he dropped it again.
A wild oath of passion swore Bernal,
   And brandished his dagger still red;
While fiercely stout Pablo leaned forward,
   And fought o'er his trusty mule's head.

8. They fought till the black wall below them
   Shone red through the misty blast.
Stout Pablo then struck, leaning farther,
   The broad breast of Bernal at last;
And, frenzied with pain, the swart herdsman
   Closed round him with terrible clasp,
And jerked him, despite of his struggles,
   Down from the mule in his grasp.

9. They grappled with desperate madness
   On the slippery edge of the wall;
They swayed on the brink, and together
   Reeled out to the rush of the fall!
A cry of the wildest death-anguish
   Rang faint through the mist afar,
And the riderless mule went homeward
   From the fight of the Paso del Mar!

Bayard Taylor.

FOR PREPARATION.—I. Find San Diego (de-ā'go) (in California). "Pä'so del Mar" (Spanish, Pass of the Sea); "pĕs-ca-dōr'" (fisherman); "ranches" (rude huts of herdsmen, called "*ranchos*" by the Mexicans).

II. Pä'-blo, mount'-ain (-in), shăl'-lop, tĕr'-ri-ble, hŏv'-er-ing, twĭnk'-led (-ld), fŏre'-head (fŏr'ed), dĭz'-zy-ing, de-vour'-ing, grăp'-pled (-pld), slĭp'-per-y.

III. What is denoted by *er* in fiercer?—*ther* in farther? (*Ther*, *ter*, *der*, and similar forms, occur often in English and Latin, to denote that the word expresses something that stands in contrast to something else, or depends on it, as *father* is related to *child*, or *under* to *over*; e. g., father, mother, brother, sister, under, sunder, further, hither, yonder; Latin: *mater*, *pater*, *frater*, *contra*, *intra*, etc. The syllable *er* is not so ancient a termination to denote comparison as *ter* and its kindred forms.)

IV. Gusty, shallop, loom, "misted eyebrows," "scud of the breakers," swayed, death-anguish, swart.

V. The figure of speech by which the fog has its gray skirts torn by the trees, is called what? (Personification.) Why are the fisherman's gainings called *so wide a harvest?*

LXXII.—ROBERT BRUCE AND THE SPIDER.

1. It was about the time when King Robert Bruce was in his greatest difficulties, that an incident took place which, although it rests only on tradition in families of the name of Bruce, is rendered probable by the manners of the time. After receiving the last unpleasing intelligence from Scotland, Bruce was one morning lying on his wretched bed, and deliberating with himself whether he had not better resign all thoughts of again attempting to make good his right to the Scottish crown, and, dismissing his followers, transport himself and his brothers to the Holy Land, and spend the rest of his life in fighting against the Saracens.

2. But then, on the other hand, he thought it would be both criminal and cowardly to give up his attempts to

restore freedom to Scotland, while there yet remained the least chance of his being successful in an undertaking which, rightly considered, was much more his duty than to drive the infidels out of Palestine, though the superstition of his age might think otherwise. While he was divided between these reflections, and doubtful of what he should do, Bruce was looking upward to the roof of the cabin in which he lay, and his attention was attracted by a spider, which, hanging at the end of a long thread of its own spinning, was endeavoring, as is the fashion of that creature, to swing itself from one beam in the roof to another, for the purpose of fixing the line on which it meant to stretch its web.

3. The insect made the attempt again and again, without success; and at length Bruce counted that it had tried to carry its point six times, and been as often unable to do so. It came into his head that he had himself fought just six battles against the English and their allies, and that the poor, persevering spider was exactly in the same situation with himself, having made as many trials and been as often disappointed in what it aimed at.

4. "Now," thought Bruce, "as I have no means of knowing what is best to be done, I will be guided by the luck which shall attend this spider. If the insect shall make another effort to fix its thread, and shall be successful, I will venture a seventh time to try my fortune in Scotland; but if the spider shall fail, I will go to the wars in Palestine, and never return to my native country more."

5. While Bruce was forming this resolution, the spider made another exertion with all the force it could muster, and fairly succeeded in fastening its thread to the beam which it had so often in vain attempted to reach. Bruce,

seeing the success of the spider, resolved to try his own fortune; and as he had never before gained a victory, so he never afterward sustained any considerable or decisive check or defeat. I have often met with people of the name of Bruce so completely persuaded of the truth of this story that they would not on any account kill a spider, because it was that insect which had shown the example of perseverance, and given a signal of good luck, to their great namesake.

6. Having determined to renew his efforts to obtain possession of Scotland, notwithstanding the smallness of the means which he had for accomplishing so great a purpose, the Bruce removed himself and his followers from Rachlin to the island of Arran, which lies in the Firth of Clyde. The king landed, and inquired of the first woman he met what armed men were on the island. She returned for answer that there had arrived there very lately a body of armed strangers, who had defeated an English officer—the governor of the castle of Brodick—had killed him and most of his men, and were now amusing themselves with hunting about the island.

7. The king, having caused himself to be guided to the woods which these strangers most frequented, there blew his horn repeatedly. Now, the chief of the strangers who had taken the castle was James Douglas, one of the best of Bruce's friends, and he was accompanied by some of the bravest of that patriotic band.

8. When he heard Robert Bruce's horn, he knew the sound well, and cried out that yonder was the king—he knew by his manner of blowing. So he and his companions hastened to meet King Robert, and there was great joy on both sides; while, at the same time, they could not help weeping when they considered their own

forlorn condition, and the great loss that had taken place among their friends since they had last parted. But they were stout-hearted men, and looked forward to freeing their country, in spite of all that had yet happened.

Sir Walter Scott.

FOR PREPARATION.—I. From "Tales of a Grandfather," First Series. "Holy Land" (this was a short time after the eighth Crusade). Who were the Saracens? Palestine—where? Location of Rachlin (Rathlin) (on the northeastern coast of Ireland) and Arran?

II. Dĭf′-fi-cul-tieṣ, re-çēiv′-ing, wrĕtch′-ed (rĕtch′-), re-ṣign′ (-zīn′), ŏf′-ten (ŏf′n), fre-quĕnt′-ed.

III. Why is *which* (2) used, instead of *who*, to relate to the spider? "Best to be done" (4)—what word for *best*, when no comparison is intended?—when comparison between two objects? Of what use is the word "more" after return? (end of 4.)

IV. Incident, tradition, intelligence, deliberating, transport, infidels, cabin, exertion, considerable, decisive, defeat, patriotic, yonder. "While he was divided" (body or mind?).

V. "Superstition of his age" (2). Was not the act of Bruce, in casting his fate upon luck, also a superstitious act? Is not a superstitious habit also mentioned of people of his name? (5.)

LXXIII.—THE SWIFTEST RUNNERS.

EXAMPLE OF "RIDICULE" FOR THE COMPOUND SLIDES.

There was a prizeˋ offered—or rather twoˋ prizes, a large′ and a smallˋ one—for the *greatest speed*ˋ, not in a single′ race, but to such as had raced the *whole year*ˋ.

"*I*ˇ took the firstˆ prize," said the Hareˋ. "One had a right to expect justiceˇ when one's own familyˆ and best friendsˆ were in the council; but that the *Snail*ˆ should have got the *second*ˆ prizeˇ, I consider as almost an *insult*ˇ to *me*ˆ."

"No," observed the Fence-rail`, who had been a witness to the distribution of the prizes; "you must take *diligence*^ and *good-will*^ into consideration. The Snailˇ, to be sure, took *half a year*^ to cross the threshold^; but he broke his thigh-boneˇ in the *haste*ˇ he made. He devoted himself *entirely*^ to this race^; and, moreover, he ran with his *house*^ on his back. And so *he*ˇ took the *second*^ prize."

"I think *my*^ claims might also have been taken into account," said the *Swallow*`. "More speedy than Iˇ, in flight and motion, I believe no one has shown′ himself. And where have I *not* been? *Far, far* away`!"

"And that is just your misfortune^," said the Fence-rail. "You *gad about*^ too much. You are *always*^ on the *wing*."

"I can declare upon my *honor*` that each prize—at least, as far as *my*ˇ voice in the matter went—was accorded with strict *justice*`," said the old Sign-post` in the wood. "My plan was to give the *first*^ *prize*ˇ to one of the *first*ˇ *letters*^ in the alphabet, and the *second*ˇ prize to one of the *last*^ letters. If you will be so good as to grant me your attention, I will explain` it to you. The eighthˇ letter in the alphabet from Aˇ is *H*^; that stands for *Hare*^, and therefore I awarded the *greatest*ˇ prize to the *Hare*^; and the eighth letter from the *end*ˇ is *S*^, therefore the *Snail*^ obtained the *second*^ prize. Everything should go by *rule*`. Rule^ must precede merit`."

"*I*ˇ should certainly have voted for *myself*^, had I not been among the *judges*ˇ," said the *Mule*`. "There is *one*^ thing which ought never to be disregarded`: it is called The Beautiful`. I saw *that*^ in the *Hare's*^ charming, well-grown *ears*^; it is quite a pleasure to see how *long*` they are. I fancied that I beheld *myself*^ when I was *little*`, and so I voted for *him*^. I must say, I expect great things from the *future*ˇ—we have made so good a *beginning*^."

Hans Christian Andersen.

LXXIV.—OFT IN THE STILLY NIGHT.

1. Oft in the stilly night,
   Ere Slumber's chain has bound me,
Fond Memory brings the light
   Of other days around me:
      The smiles, the tears
      Of boyhood's years,
The words of love then spoken;
      The eyes that shone,
      Now dimmed and gone,
The cheerful hearts now broken!
Thus, in the stilly night,
   Ere Slumber's chain has bound me,
Sad Memory brings the light
   Of other days around me.

2. When I remember all
   The friends, so linked together,
I've seen around me fall,
   Like leaves in wintry weather,
      I feel like one
      Who treads alone
Some banquet-hall deserted,
      Whose lights are fled,
      Whose garlands dead,
And all but he departed!

Thus, in the stilly night,
  Ere Slumber's chain has bound me,
Sad Memory brings the light
  Of other days around me.

Thomas Moore.

FOR PREPARATION.—I. Compare the sad feeling of this poem with that of Hood's "I Remember," or of Longfellow's "Rainy Day." (In this one, and in Hood's, memory of the past brings sadness, because of its contrast with the present, which has lost the charming personal relations that were enjoyed in the past. The present condition is empty—only a shell—the delightful social meetings of other days being only suggested, but no longer contained in it.) (This poem, like Lesson XLVII., is intended to be sung rather than read. It is inserted here to afford practice in reading this difficult species of poetry.)

II. Mĕm'-o-ry, lĭn̲ked, băn̲'-quet-ha̤ll, de-pärt'-ed, de-ṡẽrt'-ed, shone (shŏn), gone (gŏn).

III. Mark the feet, underscoring the accented syllables in the first four lines. Why are "Slumber" and "Memory" printed with capitals?

IV. Dimmed, banquet-hall, garlands.

V. Point out the similes in this piece (i. e., comparisons, or *figures of speech*, expressed by *like* or *as*); also the personifications (inanimate things made to act as persons—Slumber, Memory).

LXXV.—HARVEY BIRCH.

1. "What animal is moving through the field on our right?"

"'Tis a man," said Mason, looking intently at the suspicious object.

"By his hump, 'tis a dromedary!" added the captain, eying it keenly. Wheeling his horse suddenly from the highway, he exclaimed, "Harvey Birch! Take him, dead or alive!"

Mason, and a few of the leading dragoons only, understood the sudden cry, but it was heard throughout the line. A dozen of the men, with the lieutenant at their head, followed the impetuous Lawton, and their speed threatened the pursued with a sudden termination of the race.

2. Birch prudently kept his position on the rock, where he had been seen by Henry Wharton, until evening had begun to shroud the surrounding objects in darkness. From this height he had observed all the events of the day as they occurred. He had watched with a beating heart the departure of the troops under Dunwoodie, and with difficulty had curbed his impatience until the obscurity of night should render his moving free from danger.

3. He had not, however, completed a fourth of his way to his own residence, when his quick ear distinguished the tread of the approaching horse. Trusting to the increasing darkness, he determined to persevere. By crouching, and moving quickly along the surface of the ground, he hoped yet to escape unseen.

4. Captain Lawton was too much engrossed with the foregoing conversation to suffer his eyes to indulge in their usual wanderings; and the peddler, perceiving by the voices that the enemy he most feared had passed, yielded to his impatience, and stood erect, in order to make greater progress. The moment his body rose above the shadow of the ground it was seen, and the chase commenced.

5. For a single instant Birch was helpless, his blood curdling in his veins at the imminence of the danger, and his legs refusing their natural and necessary office. But it was only for a moment. Casting down his pack where he stood, and instinctively tightening the belt he wore,

the peddler betook himself to flight. He knew that, while bringing himself on a line with his pursuers and the wood, his form would be lost to sight.

6. This he soon effected, and was straining every nerve to gain the wood itself, when several horsemen rode by him a short distance on his left, and cut him off from this place of refuge. The peddler threw himself on the ground as they came near him, and was passed unseen.

7. But delay now became too dangerous for him to remain in that position. He accordingly arose, and, still keeping in the shadow of the wood, along the skirts of which he heard voices crying to each other to be watchful, he ran with incredible speed in a parallel line, but in an opposite direction, to the march of the dragoons.

8. The confusion of the chase had been heard by the whole of the men, though none distinctly understood the order of Lawton but those who followed. The remainder were lost in doubt as to the duty that was required of them; and the cornet was making eager inquiries of the trooper near him on the subject, when a man, at a short distance in his rear, crossed the road at a single bound.

9. At the same instant the stentorian voice of Lawton rang through the valley, shouting: "Harvey Birch! Take him, dead or alive!" Fifty pistols lighted the scene, and the bullets whistled in every direction round the head of the devoted peddler. A feeling of despair seized his heart, and in the bitterness of that moment he exclaimed: "Hunted like a beast of the forest!"

10. He felt life and its accompaniments to be a burden, and was about to yield himself to his enemies. Na-

ture, however, prevailed. If taken, there was great reason to apprehend that he would not be honored with the forms of a trial, but that, most probably, the morning's sun would witness his ignominious execution; for he had already been condemned to death, and had only escaped that fate by stratagem.

11. These considerations, with the approaching footsteps of his pursuers, aroused him to new exertions. He again fled before them. A fragment of a wall, that had withstood the ravages made by war in the adjoining fences of the wood, fortunately crossed his path. He hardly had time to throw his exhausted limbs over this barrier, before twenty of his enemies reached its opposite side.

12. Their horses refused to take the leap in the dark, and, amid the confusion of the rearing chargers and the execrations of their riders, Birch was enabled to gain a sight of the base of a hill, on whose summit was a place of perfect security. The heart of the peddler now beat high with hope, when the voice of Captain Lawton again rang in his ears, shouting to his men to make room.

13. The order was obeyed, and the fearless trooper rode at the wall at the top of his horse's speed, plunged the rowels into his charger, and flew over the obstacle in safety. The triumphant hurrahs of the men, and the thundering tread of the horse, too plainly assured the peddler of the imminence of his danger. He was nearly exhausted, and his fate no longer seemed doubtful.

14. "Stop, or die!" was uttered above his head, and in fearful proximity to his ears.

Harvey stole a glance over his shoulder, and saw, within a bound of him, the man he most dreaded. By the light of the stars he beheld the uplifted arm and the threatening saber. Fear, exhaustion, and despair seized his heart, and the intended victim fell at the feet of the dragoon. The horse of Lawton struck the prostrate peddler, and both steed and rider came violently to the earth.

15. As quick as thought, Birch was on his feet again, with the sword of the discomfited dragoon in his hand. Vengeance seems but too natural to human passions. There are few who have not felt the seductive pleasure of making our injuries recoil on their authors; and yet there are some who know how much sweeter it is to return good for evil.

16. All the wrongs of the peddler shone on his brain with a dazzling brightness. For a moment the demon within him prevailed, and Birch brandished the powerful weapon in the air; in the next, it fell harmless on the reviving but helpless trooper. The peddler vanished up the side of the friendly rock. *James Fenimore Cooper.*

FOR PREPARATION.—I. In "The Spy," Cooper makes Harvey Birch to be a secret spy, through whom Washington gets intelligence of the plans and movements of the British. He is obliged to play a part that makes him suspected by the American troops, and they constantly endeavor to capture him. Captain Lawton, of Dunwoodie's Virginia cavalry, has succeeded in this twice, but Harvey has escaped both times, although condemned to death on the second occasion. He was allowed by the American commander to enter into the service of the British general, and this circumstance heightened the difficulty and danger of his delicate position in the greatest degree. In the extract given here, we have a vivid account of one of his narrow escapes from Lawton's troops.

II. Sŭs-pĭ′-cioŭs (-pish′us), yiēld′-ed, vẹinṣ, văl′-ley, străt′-a-ġem, pĕd′-dler, e̱x-hạust′-ed, cȳ′-ing, lieū-tĕn′-ant, heīght (hīt), nĕrve, păr′-al-lel, ēa′-ġer, in-quīr′-ieṣ, sēized, rēa′-ṣon (-zn), rēar′-ing, pre-vāiled′.

III. Change the following so as to indicate more than one: Man, woman, child, ox, thou, he, it, son-in-law.

IV. Intently, dromedary, dragoons, impetuous, termination, prudently, obscurity, persevere, crouching, engrossed, indulge, erect, curdling, imminence (and eminence), instinctively, incredible, stentorian, apprehend, ignominious, execution, condemned, stratagem, ravages, exhausted, barrier, rowels, charger, triumphant, proximity, saber, prostrate, discomfited, brandished, recoil.

V. "Curbed his impatience" (as an impatient horse is curbed by the rein and bit).

LXXVI.—BURIAL OF SIR JOHN MOORE.

1. Not a drum was heard, nor a funeral note,
   As his corse to the rampart we hurried;
Not a soldier discharged his farewell shot
   O'er the grave where our hero we buried.

2. We buried him darkly, at dead of night,
   The sods with our bayonets turning,
By the struggling moonbeams' misty light,
   And the lantern dimly burning.

3. No useless coffin inclosed his breast,
   Nor in sheet nor in shroud we wound him;
But he lay, like a warrior taking his rest,
   With his martial cloak around him.

4. Few and short were the prayers we said,
   And we spoke not a word of sorrow;
But we steadfastly gazed on the face of the dead,
   And we bitterly thought of the morrow.

5. We thought, as we hollowed his narrow bed,
   And smoothed down his lonely pillow,
That the foe and the stranger would tread o'er his head,
   And we far away on the billow!

6. Lightly they'll talk of the spirit that's gone,
   And o'er his cold ashes upbraid him;
But little he'll reck, if they let him sleep on,
   In the grave where a Briton has laid him!

7. But half of our heavy task was done
   When the clock tolled the hour for retiring,
And we heard the distant and random gun
   That the foe was sullenly firing.

8. Slowly and sadly we laid him down,
   From the field of his fame fresh and gory!
We carved not a line, we raised not a stone,
   But we left him alone in his glory.

Charles Wolfe.

For Preparation.—I. Lord Byron pronounced this poem the most perfect in the language. Sir John Moore was killed by a cannon-ball at Corunna, Spain, in 1809. His army repulsed Marshal Soult, one of Napoleon's generals, but embarked for England immediately afterward.

II. Bāy'-o-nets, wạr'-rior (wŏr'yur), strŭg'-gling, bur'-ied (bĕr'-id).

III. Explain the use of the apostrophe in *o'er*, *they'll*, *he'll*, *that's*.

IV. Corse, rampart, random, sullenly, upbraid, reck.

V. Make a list of rhymes used in this poem, and mark the imperfect ones (note, shot; hurried, buried; down, stone). Divide the lines of the first stanza into feet, marking the accented syllables ("Not a *drum* | was *heard*, | nor a *fu-* | neral *note*"). Do you pronounce *gone* so as to rhyme with *on*, or with *lawn?* (See Lesson LXXIV.)

LXXVII.—THE CASTLE BY THE SEA.

EXAMPLE OF JOYOUS AND SAD EXPRESSION FOR THE SIMPLE RISING AND FALLING SLIDES.

[The *happy* spirit of the questions requires *faster* time, and louder and smoother force, and longer slides, and clearer, happier tones, to express the cumulating, eager *joy;* while the *sad* spirit of the answers requires *slow* and *slower* time, with softer force, and shorter slides, and a slightly abrupt stress, to give the cumulating *sorrow* so vividly suggested.]

"Hast thou *seen'* that *lordly' castle'*,
That castle by the *sea'?*
Golden and *red`* above it
The *clouds`* float *gorgeously`*.

"And fain it would stoop *downward`*
To the mirrored *wave`* below;
And fain it would soar *upward`*
In the evening's crimson glow."

"*Well`* have I *seen* that *castle`*,
That castle by the *sea`*,
And the *moon`* above it standing,
And the *mist`* rise *solemnly`*."

"The *winds* and the *waves'* of ocean,
Had they a *merry'* chime?
Didst thou hear, from those lofty chambers,
The *harp'* and the *minstrel's'* rhyme?"

"The *winds* and the *waves* of ocean¯,
They *rested`* *quietly`*;
But I heard on the gale¯ a sound of WAIL`,
And *tears`* came to mine eye."

"And sawest thou on the turrets
The *king'* and his *royal bride'?*—
And the wave of their *crimson mantles'?*—
And the *golden crown* of *pride'?*

"Led they not forth, in *rapture*,
A beauteous MAIDEN′ there,
Resplendent as the *morning sun′*,
Beaming with *golden hair′ ?*"

"*Well*\` saw I the *ancient parents*ˉ,
WITHOUT\` the *crown* of *pride*\` ;
They were moving *slow*ˉ, in *weeds* of *woe*\` ;
No *maiden*\` was by their side!"

Uhland (translated by H. W. Longfellow).

LXXVIII.—HOHENLINDEN.

1. On Linden, when the sun was low,
All bloodless lay th' untrodden snow,
And dark as winter was the flow
Of Iser, rolling rapidly.

2. But Linden saw another sight,
When the drum beat at dead of night,
Commanding fires of death to light
The darkness of her scenery.

3. By torch and trumpet fast arrayed,
Each horseman drew his battle-blade,
And furious every charger neighed,
To join the dreadful revelry.

4. Then shook the hills, with thunder riven;
Then rushed the steed, to battle driven;
And, louder than the bolts of heaven,
Far flashed the red artillery.

5. But redder yet that light shall glow
On Linden's hills of stainéd snow,

And bloodier yet the torrent flow
Of Iser, rolling rapidly.

6. 'Tis morn, but scarce yon lurid sun
Can pierce the war-clouds, rolling dun,
Where furious Frank and fiery Hun
Shout in their sulph'rous canopy.

7. The combat deepens. On, ye brave,
Who rush to glory or the grave!
Wave, Munich! all thy banners wave,
And charge with all thy chivalry!

8. Few, few shall part where many meet!
The snow shall be their winding-sheet,
And every turf beneath their feet
Shall be a soldier's sepulcher.

Thomas Campbell.

FOR PREPARATION.—I. Campbell, at the age of twenty-three, on a visit to Germany to study its literature, witnessed, from a safe position, this battle between the French ("furious Frank"), under Moreau, and the Austrians ("fiery Hun," named from the Huns, who settled in Austria, or Hungary, after overrunning Europe in the fifth century), under Archduke John. (Hohenlinden means *linden* [kind of tree] *heights.*) Find, on the map, the Ĭ'ṣer, and trace its waters to the sea. Mū'nich is the capital of Bavaria; find it on the map.

II. Sçēn'-er-y, neighed (nād), piērçe, sōl'-dier (-jer), sĕp'-ul-cher (-kŭr), rōll'-ing, sīght (sīt), tŏr'-rent.

III. "Sulph'rous"—why *u* omitted? Explain the meaning of the prefix *un* and the suffix *en* in untrodden. Note the alliteration in this poem (recurrence of *l* (1), *d* (2), *b*, battle-blade (3), *f*, far flashed (4), etc.).

IV. "Dead of night," arrayed, charger, revelry, riven, "bolts of heaven," artillery, dun, canopy, combat, banners, chivalry, winding-sheet, "fires of death."

V. Note the succession of scenes and their contrasts: (1) Snow untrodden; bloodless; near sunset; dark and rapid river. (2) The night follows; drums beat the alarm; torches light up the troops arrayed for battle. (3) The charging of squadrons, and the flashing and thundering of artillery. (4) Morning; but the sun is lurid as seen through the smoke rising from the field. (5) Munich (the Bavarians were allies of the French in this battle) troops are distinguished in the fierce charges. (6) On the hills of blood-stained snow lie seven thousand Austrian and five thousand French soldiers, dead or wounded.

LXXIX.—OVER THE RIVER.

1. Over the river they beckon to me,
   Loved ones who've crossed to the farther side;
The gleam of their snowy robes I see,
   But their voices are lost in the dashing tide.
There's one, with ringlets of sunny gold,
   And eyes the reflection of heaven's own blue;
He crossed in the twilight gray and cold,
   And the pale mist hid him from mortal view.
We saw not the angels who met him there;
   The gates of the city we could not see:
Over the river, over the river,
   My brother stands waiting to welcome me.

2. Over the river the boatman pale
   Carried another, the household pet;
Her brown curls waved in the gentle gale—
   Darling Minnie! I see her yet.
She crossed on her bosom her dimpled hands,
   And fearlessly entered the phantom-bark;
We felt it glide from the silver sands,
   And all our sunshine grew strangely dark.
We know she is safe on the farther side,
   Where all the ransomed and angels be:
Over the river, the mystic river,
   My childhood's idol is waiting for me.

3. For none return from those quiet shores,
   Who cross with the boatman cold and pale;
We hear the dip of the golden oars,
   And catch a gleam of the snowy sail,
And lo! they have passed from our yearning heart;
   They cross the stream and are gone for aye.
We may not sunder the veil apart
   That hides from our vision the gates of day;
We only know that their barks no more
   May sail with us o'er life's stormy sea;
Yet somewhere, I know, on the unseen shore,
   They watch, and beckon, and wait for me.

4. And I sit and think, when the sunset's gold
   Is flushing river, and hill, and shore,
I shall one day stand by the water cold,
   And list for the sound of the boatman's oar;
I shall watch for a gleam of the flapping sail,
   I shall hear the boat as it gains the strand;
I shall pass from sight with the boatman pale,
   To the better shore of the spirit-land;
I shall know the loved who have gone before,
   And joyfully sweet will the meeting be,
When over the river, the peaceful river,
   The angel of death shall carry me.

Nancy Priest Wakefield.

FOR PREPARATION.—I. The authoress lived on the banks of the Connecticut River. Do you think there may be something in this fact that suggested the imagery of the piece (see fourth stanza), or was it, rather, the allegory in the "Pilgrim's Progress"?

II. Bĕck'-on (bĕk'n), re-flĕc'-tion (-shun), view (vū), rĭng'-lets, wĕl'-come, bōat'-man, veil.

III. Why is *ha* omitted in who've?—*i* in there's? Difference in meaning caused by adding *let* to *ring*?

IV. Gleam, phantom, ransomed, mystic, dimpled, "childhood's idol."

V. Is the metaphor, "their barks no more may sail with us o'er life's stormy sea" (3), in keeping with the fundamental metaphor of the poem, in which we stand on the bank of a river? (If they had had barks of their own, and were used to the terrors of the "stormy sea," a mere river would scarcely be the gulf of separation that it is. This is called "mixed metaphor.")

LXXX.—A LETTER OF DR. FRANKLIN.

EASTON, PA., *Saturday Morning, November* 13, 1756.

MY DEAR CHILD:

I wrote to you a few days since by a special messenger, and inclosed letters for all our wives and sweethearts: expecting to hear from you by his return, and to have the Northern newspapers and English letters, per the packet; but he is just now returned, without a scrap for poor us. So I had a good mind not to write you by this opportunity; but I can never be ill-natured enough, even when there is the most occasion. The messenger says he left the letters at your house, and saw you afterward at Mr. Dentic's, and told you when he would go, and that he lodged at Honey's, next door to you, and yet you did not write; so let Goody Smith give one more just judgment, and say what should be done to you. I think I won't tell you that we are well, nor that we expect to return about the middle of the week, nor will send you a word of news; that's poz. My duty to mother, love to the children and to Miss Betsey and Gracey, etc., etc.

I am your loving husband,

BENJAMIN FRANKLIN.

P. S.—I have *scratched out the loving words*, being written in haste by mistake, when I *forgot I was angry.*

FOR PREPARATION.—I. A letter of Dr. Franklin to his wife (he married Deborah Read).

II. Spĕ′-cial (spĕsh′al), jŭdġ′-ment, dône, scrătched.

III. In the above letter, point out what is called the *date*. What items does it include? (Name of post-office, town, or city, and State [and, if the place is small, the county], day of month, and year.) Point out the *address;* —the *subscription*. Where should the *superscription* be? (On the envelope of the letter, thus:

MRS DEBORAH FRANKLIN,
Philadelphia, Pa.)

What does "P. S." mean?

IV. Inclosed, return, packet, scrap, opportunity, occasion, lodged.

V. Notice the humor of the style. (He pretends to be angry, and to forget that he is angry; then to remember it, and scratch out the loving words; calls himself "we," and "poor us"; calls his wife "all our wives and sweethearts"; playfully says that he won't tell her that he is well, etc., and tells it all.) "That's poz" (positively so). Write a letter to some friend, and give an account of your visit to the country, or of some other event that you may select, taking care to have the *date*, *address*, *subscription*, and *superscription* right.

LXXXI.—LITTLE HAL.

EXAMPLE FOR VARIED AND IMPASSIONED EXPRESSION.

"Old Ironsides\ at anchor\ lay,
In the harbor of Mahon\;
A dead c-a-l-m\ rested on the bay—
The w-a-v-e-s to s-l-e-e-p\ had gone—
When little *Hal*\, the captain's\ son,
A lad both *b-r-a-v-e* and *g-o-o-d*¯,
In *sport* up *shroud* and *rigging* ran,
And on the m-a-i-n\-truck stood!

"A *shudder*\ shot through every *vein*\;
All eyes were turned on *high*\;
There stood the boy, with *dizzy*\ brain,
Between the *s-e-a*′ and *s-k-y*\.

No *h-o-l-d*\` had he *above*', *below*\`;
A-l-o-n-e\` he stood in *air*\`:
To that *f-a-r*\` height none *d-a-r-e-d*\` to go—
No *a-i-d*\` could *r-e-a-c-h*\` him there."

[The word "shudder" is *very* abrupt in emphasis; it expresses *sudden pain* and *fear.* The first syllable is *short*, and time can not be given to it. Sound sharply the "*sh*," with a little prolongation, to *aspirate* it, and bring out thus the *shock* and *terror.*]

"We g-a-z-e-d, but not a *man* could *speak*\` !
With *horror*\` *a-l-l* aghast,
In groups, with *pallid* brow and cheek,
We *watched*\` the quivering *mast*\`.
The atmosphere grew *thick*\` and *hot*\`,
And of a *l-u-rid*\` hue,
As, *riveted* unto the spot,
Stood officers and crew\`."

[Half whisper the word "horror," to suit the quality of voice to the spirit—on the general principle that all painful, disagreeable ideas demand the disagreeable *aspiration;* all pure and pleasing ideas require a clear, *pure* tone, to suit the *sound* to the *sense.*]

"The *f-a-ther*\` came on deck. He gasped¯,
'O *God*\` ! *t-h-y*\` will be done!'
Then suddenly a *rifle*\` grasped,
And aimed it at his *son*\`:
'*Jump*\`—*f-a-r* - out, boy, into the *wave*\`!
Jump\`, or I *f-i-r-e*\`!' he said;
'That o-n-l-y chance your *l-i-f-e*\` can s-a-v-e\`!
Jump\` ! JUMP\`, boy!' He obeyed\`.

"He *sank*\`—he *r-o-s-e*\`—he *lived*\`—he *m-o-v-e-d*\`,
And for the *ship*\` struck out:

On *board* we *h-a-l-e-d*\` the lad beloved,
  With many a *manly shout*\`.
His *f-a-ther* drew, in *s-i-lent*\` *j-o-y*,
  Those wet a-r-m-s round his *neck*\`,
And folded to his *h-e-a-r-t*\` his boy—
  Then *f-a-i-n-t-e-d*\` on the deck."

Colton.

["*Jump*" should be *shouted* louder and *louder* as it is repeated. "He sank—he rose—he lived—he moved," should be read with very *long pauses* between the ideas, and with very long quantity on "rose" and "moved," so as to give *time enough* for all this to take place. You must *see* it all, *imagine* it, and speak it very *earnestly.* In the third and fourth lines, *smooth, loud,* and *pure* tones should shout with joy that little Hal is *safe.* But the *father* is too deeply moved to shout, or even to *speak;* his *silent* joy we should read with *subdued* tenderness.]

LXXXII.—GOODY BLAKE AND HARRY GILL.

1. Oh! what's the matter?—what's the matter?
  What is't that ails young Harry Gill,
That evermore his teeth they chatter—
  Chatter, chatter, chatter still?
Of waistcoats Harry has no lack,
  Good duffel gray and flannel fine;
He has a blanket on his back,
  And coats enough to smother nine.

2. In March, December, and in July,
  'Tis all the same with Harry Gill;
The neighbors tell, and tell you truly,
  His teeth they chatter, chatter still.

At night, at morning, and at noon,
'Tis all the same with Harry Gill;
Beneath the sun, beneath the moon,
His teeth they chatter, chatter still!

3. Young Harry was a lusty drover—
And who so stout of limb as he?
His cheeks were red as ruddy clover;
His voice was like the voice of three.
Old Goody Blake was old and poor;
Ill-fed she was, and thinly clad;
And any man who passed her door
Might see how poor a hut she had.

4. All day she spun in her poor dwelling,
And then her three hours' work at night—
Alas! 'twas hardly worth the telling—
It would not pay for candle-light.
Remote from sheltering village green,
On a hill's northern side she dwelt,
Where from sea-blasts the hawthorns lean,
And hoary dews are slow to melt.

5. By the same fire to boil their pottage,
Two poor old dames, as I have known,
Will often live in one small cottage;
But she—poor woman!—housed alone.
'Twas well enough when summer came,
The long, warm, lightsome summer-day;
Then at her door the canty dame
Would sit, as any linnet gay.

6. But when the ice our streams did fetter,
Oh, then how her old bones would shake!
You would have said, if you had met her,
'Twas a hard time for Goody Blake.

Her evenings then were dull and dead;
Sad case it was, as you may think,
For very cold to go to bed,
And then for cold not sleep a wink!

7. Oh, joy for her! whene'er in winter
The winds at night had made a rout,
And scattered many a lusty splinter
And many a rotten bough about.
Yet never had she, well or sick,
As every man who knew her says,
A pile beforehand, turf or stick,
Enough to warm her for three days.

8. Now, when the frost was past enduring,
And made her poor old bones to ache,
Could anything be more alluring
Than an old hedge to Goody Blake?
And now and then, it must be said,
When her old bones were cold and chill,
She left her fire, or left her bed,
To seek the hedge of Harry Gill.

9. Now, Harry he had long suspected
This trespass of old Goody Blake,
And vowed that she should be detected,
And he on her would vengeance take.
And oft from his warm fire he'd go,
And to the fields his road would take;
And there at night, in frost and snow,
He watched to seize old Goody Blake.

10. And once, behind a rick of barley,
Thus looking out did Harry stand;
The moon was full and shining clearly,
And crisp with frost the stubble-land.

He hears a noise!—he's all awake!—
  Again!—on tiptoe down the hill
He softly creeps. 'Tis Goody Blake!
  She's at the hedge of Harry Gill!

11. Right glad was he when he beheld her!
  Stick after stick did Goody pull;
He stood behind a bush of elder,
  Till she had filled her apron full.
When with her load she turned about,
  The byway back again to take,
He started forward with a shout,
  And sprang upon poor Goody Blake;

12. And fiercely by the arm he took her,
  And by the arm he held her fast;
And fiercely by the arm he shook her,
  And cried, "I've caught you, then, at last!"
Then Goody, who had nothing said,
  Her bundle from her lap let fall;
And, kneeling on the sticks, she prayed
  To God, who is the Judge of all.

13. She prayed, her withered hand uprearing,
  While Harry held her by the arm—
"God, who art never out of hearing,
  Oh, may he never more be warm!"
The cold, cold moon above her head,
  Thus on her knees did Goody pray.
Young Harry heard what she had said,
  And, icy cold, he turned away.

14. He went complaining all the morrow
  That he was cold and very chill:
His face was gloom, his heart was sorrow—
  Alas! that day for Harry Gill!

That day he wore a riding-coat,
  But not a whit the warmer he;
Another was on Thursday brought,
  And ere the Sabbath he had three.

15. 'Twas all in vain—a useless matter—
  And blankets were about him pinned;
Yet still his jaws and teeth they clatter,
  Like a loose casement in the wind.
And Harry's flesh it fell away;
  And all who see him say, "'Tis plain
That, live as long as live he may,
  He never will be warm again."

16. No word to any man he utters,
  Abed or up, to young or old;
But ever to himself he mutters,
  "Poor Harry Gill is very cold!"
Abed or up, by night or day,
  His teeth they chatter, chatter still.
Now, think, ye farmers all, I pray,
  Of Goody Blake and Harry Gill!

William Wordsworth.

FOR PREPARATION.—I. What pieces of Wordsworth have you read before? (Lessons II., XIII., XXXV.) Mention some of the qualities of his poems (kindness to animals and to poor children, simplicity, etc.). He calls this piece "A True Story."

II. Wāist'-eōats, flăn'-nel, neigh'-bors (nā'-), nôrth'-ern, hōar'-y, light'-sôme (līt'sum), lĭn'-net, al-lūr'-ing, trĕs'-pass, vĕn'-ġeançe, fiēlds, sēize, fiērçe'-ly, up-rēar'-ing.

III. Correct.: "Three hour's work";—"t'was";—"on a hills' side." What is omitted in "he'd"?

IV. "Hoary dews," canty, "fetter streams," rout, "lusty splinter," alluring, casement.

V. "Good duffel gray"—do you remember what Alice Fell's warm cloak was to be made of? (Lesson XIII.) ("Duffel"—a coarse woolen, with a thick nap left on it, so that it is very warm.) "March, December, and July"—why select these three months? (whether in moderate, cold, or hot weather.) "From sea-blasts the hawthorns lean" (i. e., owing to the incessant wind, they have grown in a leaning position). "For very cold to go to bed" (i. e., to be obliged to go to bed for reason of the cold; very = actual). "Right glad was he when he beheld her" (11)—what kind of a spirit did this show? What kind of a spirit did Goody Blake show when she prayed that Harry Gill might never be warm again?

LXXXIII.—TWO VIEWS OF CHRISTMAS.

[The following is a good example for the very smooth and the very abrupt stress, from the "Christmas Carol," by Dickens. The part of the nephew is good and pleasing in spirit, and calls for the smooth, happy stress. The part of old Scrooge is hateful in spirit, and should have the most abrupt stress, to suit the sound to the sense.]

Nephew—A merry Christmas, uncle! God save you!

Scrooge—Bah! humbug!

Neph.—Christmas a humbug, uncle! You don't mean that, I am sure.

Scrooge—I do. Out upon "Merry Christmas"! If I had my will, every idiot who goes about with "Merry Christmas" on his lips should be boiled with his own pudding, and buried with a stake of holly through his heart. He should!

Neph.—Uncle!

Scrooge—Nephew, keep Christmas-time in your own way, and let me keep it in mine.

Neph.—Keep it? But you don't keep it!

Scrooge—Let me leave it alone, then! Much good may it do you! Much good it has ever done you!

Neph.—I am sure I have always thought of Christmas as a good time—a kind, forgiving, charitable, pleasant time; and therefore, uncle, though it has never put a scrap of gold or silver in my pocket, I believe it has done me good, and will do me good; and I say, God bless it!

LXXXIV.—THE THREE FISHERS.

1. Three fishers went sailing out into the west—
   Out into the west, as the sun went down;
Each thought on the woman who loved him the best,
   And the children stood watching them out of the town:
For men must work, and women must weep,
And there's little to earn, and many to keep,
   Though the harbor-bar be moaning.

2. Three wives sat up in the lighthouse tower,
   And they trimmed the lamps as the sun went down;
They looked at the squall, and they looked at the shower,
   And the night-rack came rolling up ragged and brown:
But men must work, and women must weep,
Though storms be sudden, and waters deep,
   And the harbor-bar be moaning.

3. Three corpses lie out on the shining sands,
   In the morning gleam, as the tide goes down,
And the women are weeping, and wringing their hands,
   For those who will never come home to the town:

For men must work, and women must weep,
And the sooner it's over, the sooner to sleep,
And good-by to the bar and its moaning.

Charles Kingsley.

FOR PREPARATION.—I. Harbor-bar. (At the entrance of a harbor where the shores approach, the water is often very shallow, and the shoal thus formed is called a "bar." When the high waves break over it, a "moaning" sound is caused.)

II. Mōan′-ing, thôught, wom′-en (wĭm′-), răg′-ḡed, wrĭng′-ing.

III. What change, in pronunciation and spelling, in the word "woman," to make it mean more than one?

IV. Gleam, tide, night-rack, corpses.

V. What state of the waves is indicated by the "moaning" on the bar? By the fact of the three wives sitting up in the tower and trimming the lamps, do you infer that the men were lighthouse-keepers? Write out, or tell, the story implied in the last stanza.

LXXXV.—JULIUS CÆSAR.

EXAMPLE OF ANGRY EARNESTNESS AND JESTING.

[The *anger* of Flavius and Marullus requires the *very abrupt force*, and their direct questions and earnestness demand the *simple slides*. The second citizen is *jesting* and *fooling*, and his part, therefore, should be read with the *compound slides*. The last answer alone is spoken directly, with straightforward honesty, and this only should have the *straight* or *simple slides*.]

Act I., Scene 1.

Flavius—Hence\! home\, you idle\ creatures—get you home\!
Is this a holiday′? What! know you not,
Being mechanical, you ought not walk,

Upon a laboring day, without the sign′
Of your profession′? Speak`—what trade` art thou?

1 *Citizen*—Why, sir, a carpenter`.

Marullus—Where is thy leather apron`, and thy rule`?
What dost thou with thy *best`* apparel on?—
You`*, sir—what trade are *you`?

2 *Cit.*—Truly, sir, in respect of a *fineˇ* workman, I am but, as you would say, a *cobˇbler.*

Mar.—But what trade` art thou? Answer me directly`.

2 *Cit.*—A trade, sir, that, I hope, I may use with a safeˇ conˇscience; which is, indeed, sir, a mendˇer of badˇ soles^.

Mar.—What trade`, thou knave?—thou naughty knave, what trade`?

2 *Cit.*—Nay, I beseech you, sir, be not outˇ with me: yet, if you be outˇ, sir, I can mendˇ you.

Mar.—What meanest thou by that`? Mend′ me?—thou saucy fellow!

2 *Cit.*—Why, sir, cob^ble you.

Flavius—Thou art a cobbler`, art′ thou?

2 *Cit.*—Truly, sir, *allˇ* that I live by is with the *awlˇ*. I meddle with no tradesman'sˇ matters, nor women'sˇ matters, but with awlˇ. I am, indeed, sir, a *surˇgeon* to *old shoes^;* when they are in great danger, I recov^er them. As proper men as ever trod upon neat'sˇ leather have gone upon myˇ handiwork.

Flavius—But wherefore art not in thy shop` to-day? Why dost thou lead these men about the streets`?

2 *Cit.*—Truly, sir, to wear outˇ their shoes^, to get myself into moreˇ work^. But, indeed, sir, we make holiday to see *Cæsar`*, and to rejoice` in *his triumph`*.

Shakespeare.

LXXXVI.—ROBIN HOOD.

1. A target was placed at the upper end of the southern avenue which led to the lists. The contending archers took their station in turn, at the bottom of the southern access; the distance between that station and the mark allowing full distance for what was called a "shot at rovers." The archers, having previously determined by lot their order of precedence, were to shoot each three shafts in succession. The sports were regulated by an officer of inferior rank, termed the provost of the games; for the high rank of the marshals of the lists would have been held degraded had they condescended to superintend the sports of the yeomanry.

2. One by one the archers, stepping forward, delivered their shafts yeomanlike and bravely. Of twenty-four arrows shot in succession, ten were fixed in the target, and the others ranged so near it that, considering the distance of the mark, it was accounted good archery. Of the ten shafts which hit the target, two within the inner ring were shot by Hubert, a forester in the service of Malvoisin, who was accordingly pronounced victorious.

3. "Now, Locksley," said Prince John to the bold yeoman, with a bitter smile, "wilt thou try conclusions with Hubert, or wilt thou yield up bow, baldric, and quiver to the provost of the sports?"

"Sith it be no better," said Locksley, "I am content to try my fortune; on condition that, when I have shot two shafts at yonder mark of Hubert's, he shall be bound to shoot one at that which I shall propose."

"That is but fair," answered Prince John, "and it shall not be refused thee. If thou dost beat this braggart, Hubert, I will fill the bugle with silver pennies for thee."

"A man can but do his best," answered Hubert; "but my grandsire drew a good long-bow at Hastings, and I trust not to dishonor his memory."

4. The former target was now removed, and a fresh one of the same size placed in its room. Hubert, who, as victor in the first trial of skill, had the right to shoot first, took his aim with great deliberation, long measuring the distance with his eye, while he held in his hand his bended bow, with the arrow placed on the string. At length he made a step forward, and, raising the bow at the full stretch of his left arm, till the center or grasping-place was nigh level with his face, he drew the bowstring to his ear. The arrow whistled through the air, and lighted within the inner ring of the target, but not exactly in the center.

"You have not allowed for the wind, Hubert," said his antagonist, bending his bow, "or that had been a better shot."

5. So saying, and without showing the least anxiety to pause upon his aim, Locksley stepped to the appointed station, and shot his arrow as carelessly in appearance as if he had not even looked at the mark. He was speaking almost at the instant that the shaft left the bowstring, yet it alighted in the target two inches nearer to the white spot which marked the center than that of Hubert.

"By the light of heaven!" said Prince John to Hubert, "an thou suffer that runagate knave to overcome thee, thou art worthy of the gallows!"

6. Hubert had but one set speech for all occasions. "An your highness were to hang me," he said, "a man can but do his best. Nevertheless, my grandsire drew a good bow—"

"The foul fiend on thy grandsire and all his generation!" interrupted John. "Shoot, knave, and shoot thy best, or it shall be the worse for thee!"

Thus exhorted, Hubert resumed his place, and, not neglecting the caution which he had received from his adversary, he made the necessary allowance for a very light breath of wind which had just arisen, and shot so successfully that his arrow alighted in the very center of the target.

"A Hubert! a Hubert!" shouted the populace, more interested in a known person than in a stranger. "In the clout!—in the clout! A Hubert for ever!"

7. "Thou canst not mend that shot, Locksley," said the prince, with an insulting smile.

"I will notch his shaft for him, however," replied Locksley. And, letting fly his arrow with a little more precaution than before, it lighted right upon that of his competitor, which it split to shivers. The people who stood around were so astonished at his wonderful dexterity, that they could not even give vent to their surprise in their usual clamor.

"This must be the devil, and no man of flesh and blood," whispered the yeomen to each other; "such archery was never seen since a bow was first bent in Britain!"

8. "And now," said Locksley, "I will crave your grace's permission to plant such a mark as is used in the north country, and welcome every brave yeoman to try a shot at it."

He then turned to leave the lists. "Let your guards attend me," he said, "if you please. I go but to cut a rod from the next willow-bush."

Prince John made a signal that some attendants

should follow him, in case of his escape; but the cry of "Shame! shame!" which burst from the multitude, induced him to alter his ungenerous purpose.

9. Locksley returned almost instantly, with a willow wand about six feet in length, perfectly straight, and rather thicker than a man's thumb. He began to peel this with great composure, observing, at the same time, that to ask a good woodsman to shoot at a target so broad as had hitherto been used was to put shame upon his skill. "For my own part," said he, "in the land where I was bred, men would as soon take for their mark King Arthur's round table, which held sixty knights around it. A child of seven years old might hit yonder target with a headless shaft; but," he added, walking deliberately to the other end of the lists and sticking the willow wand upright in the ground, "he that hits that rod at five-score yards, I call him an archer fit to bear both bow and quiver before a king, an it were the stout King Richard himself!"

10. "My grandsire," said Hubert, "drew a good bow at the battle of Hastings, and never shot at such a mark in his life; and neither will I. If this yeoman can cleave that rod, I give him the bucklers—or, rather, I yield to the devil that is in his jerkin, and not to any human skill. A man can but do his best, and I will not shoot where I am sure to miss. I might as well shoot at the edge of our parson's whittle, or at a wheat-straw, or at a sunbeam, as at a twinkling white streak which I can hardly see."

"Cowardly dog!" exclaimed Prince John.—"Sirrah Locksley, do thou shoot; but if thou hittest such a mark, I will say thou art the first man ever did so. Howe'er it be, thou shalt not crow over us with a mere show of superior skill."

"'A man can but do his best!' as Hubert says," answered Locksley.

11. So saying, he again bent his bow, but, on the present occasion, looked with attention to his weapon, and changed the string, which he thought was no longer truly round, having been a little frayed by the two former shots. He then took his aim with some deliberation, and the multitude awaited the event in breathless silence. The archer vindicated their opinion of his skill: his arrow split the willow rod against which it was aimed. A jubilee of acclamations followed; and even Prince John, in admiration of Locksley's skill, lost for an instant his dislike to his person.

12. "These twenty nobles," he said, "which with the bugle thou hast fairly won, are thine own: we will make them fifty if thou wilt take livery and service with us as a yeoman of our body-guard, and be near to our person; for never did so strong a hand bend a bow, or so true an eye direct a shaft."

"Pardon me, noble prince," said Locksley; "but I have vowed that, if ever I take service, it should be with your royal brother King Richard. These twenty nobles I leave to Hubert, who has this day drawn as brave a bow as his grandsire did at Hastings. Had his modesty not refused the trial, he would have hit the wand as well as I."

Hubert shook his head as he received with reluctance the bounty of the stranger; and Locksley, anxious to escape further observation, mixed with the crowd and was seen no more. *Sir Walter Scott.*

For Preparation.—I. This piece is taken from Scott's greatest novel, "Ivanhoe." The scene is laid in England, in the time of John, who had usurped the place of Richard I., the Lion-hearted, while the latter was away on a crusade. Richard has returned *incognito*, and is looking on at the various tournaments held by his brother John, and now and then exhibiting his prodigious strength and skill in behalf of those oppressed by the tyranny of John or his minions. Robin Hood, the ideal of perfection in English archery, makes his appearance at the trial of archers here described, under the name of Locksley. He has been chief of the highwaymen in Sherwood Forest, and desires to attach himself to Richard's service. Malvoisin (măl-vwä-zăng′) is one of the favorites of Prince John, who finally succeeded Richard as king.

II. Sou̇th′-ern (sŭth′-), al-low′-ing, pre-çēd′-ence, prŏv′-ȯst (prŏv′ust). yeō′-man-līke, fŏr′-est-er, ăn′-swered (-serd), whĭs′-tled (hwĭs′ld), ĭn-ter-rŭpt′-ed, e̤x-hôrt′-ed, guärds (gärdz), strāight (strāt).

III. "Sith" (old form for *since*); "it be no better" ("be" was the correct form in old English; we should now say, "Since it *is* no better").

IV. Target, lists, "contending archers," access, previously, "order of precedence," shafts, inferior, provost, "held degraded," ranged, "try conclusions," baldric, jerkin, braggart, deliberation, runagate, "set speech," resumed, competitor, antagonist, adversary, dexterity, composure, "headless shaft," bucklers, whittle, vindicated, "jubilee of acclamations," livery, reluctance.

V. "Sports of the yeomanry." (Archery belonged to the common people; to fight, or "joust," with spears, and on horseback, belonged to the nobles.) "In the clout" (piece of white cloth on the center of the target). "An it were the stout King Richard himself" ("an" was formerly much used where we now use *if*). Is there any sarcasm in Locksley's allusion to Hubert's grandsire at Hastings, as he gives him the twenty nobles?

LXXXVII.—ELEGY WRITTEN IN A COUNTRY CHURCHYARD.

1. The curfew tolls the knell of parting day;
The lowing herd winds slowly o'er the lea;
The plowman homeward plods his weary way,
And leaves the world to darkness and to me.

2. Now fades the glimmering landscape on the sight,
   And all the air a solemn stillness holds,
Save where the beetle wheels his droning flight,
   And drowsy tinklings lull the distant folds;

3. Save that, from yonder ivy-mantled tower,
   The moping owl does to the moon complain
Of such as, wand'ring near her secret bower,
   Molest her ancient, solitary reign.

4. Beneath those rugged elms, that yew-tree's shade,
   Where heaves the turf in many a moldering heap,
Each in his narrow cell for ever laid,
   The rude forefathers of the hamlet sleep.

5. The breezy call of incense-breathing morn,
   The swallow twitt'ring from the straw-built shed,
The cock's shrill clarion, or the echoing horn,
   No more shall rouse them from their lowly bed.

6. For them no more the blazing hearth shall burn,
   Or busy housewife ply her evening care;
No children run to lisp their sire's return,
   Or climb his knees the envied kiss to share.

7. Oft did the harvest to their sickle yield,
   Their furrow oft the stubborn glebe has broke;
How jocund did they drive their team a-field!
   How bowed the woods beneath their sturdy stroke!

8. Let not Ambition mock their useful toil,
   Their homely joys, and destiny obscure;
Nor Grandeur hear with a disdainful smile
   The short and simple annals of the poor.

9. The boast of heraldry, the pomp of power,
   And all that beauty, all that wealth e'er gave,
Await alike the inevitable hour:
   The paths of glory lead but to the grave.

10. Nor you, ye proud, impute to these the fault,
   If Memory o'er their tomb no trophies raise,
Where, through the long-drawn aisle and fretted vault,
   The pealing anthem swells the note of praise.

11. Can storied urn, or animated bust,
   Back to its mansion call the fleeting breath?
Can Honor's voice provoke the silent dust,
   Or Flattery soothe the dull, cold ear of Death?

12. Perhaps in this neglected spot is laid
   Some heart once pregnant with celestial fire—
Hands that the rod of empire might have swayed,
   Or waked to ecstasy the living lyre:

13. But Knowledge to their eyes her ample page,
   Rich with the spoils of time, did ne'er unroll;
Chill Penury repressed their noble rage,
   And froze the genial current of the soul.

14. Full many a gem of purest ray serene
   The dark, unfathomed caves of ocean bear;
Full many a flower is born to blush unseen,
   And waste its sweetness on the desert air.

15. Some village Hampden, that, with dauntless breast,
   The little tyrant of his fields withstood;

Some mute, inglorious Milton here may rest—
Some Cromwell, guiltless of his country's blood.

16. The applause of listening senates to command,
The threats of pain and ruin to despise,
To scatter plenty o'er a smiling land,
And read their history in a nation's eyes,

17. Their lot forbade; nor circumscribed alone
Their growing virtues, but their crimes confined;
Forbade to wade through slaughter to a throne,
And shut the gates of mercy on mankind;

18. The struggling pangs of conscious truth to hide,
To quench the blushes of ingenuous shame,
Or heap the shrine of Luxury and Pride
With incense kindled at the Muse's flame.

19. Far from the madding crowd's ignoble strife,
Their sober wishes never learned to stray;
Along the cool, sequestered vale of life
They kept the noiseless tenor of their way.

20. Yet e'en these bones from insult to protect,
Some frail memorial still erected nigh,
With uncouth rhymes and shapeless sculpture decked,
Implores the passing tribute of a sigh.

21. Their name, their years, spelt by the unlettered Muse,
The place of fame and elegy supply;
And many a holy text around she strews,
That teach the rustic moralist to die.

22. For who, to dumb forgetfulness a prey,
 This pleasing, anxious being e'er resigned,
Left the warm precincts of the cheerful day,
 Nor cast one longing, lingering look behind?

23. On some fond breast the parting soul relies,
 Some pious drops the closing eye requires;
E'en from the tomb the voice of Nature cries,
 E'en in our ashes live their wonted fires.

24. For thee, who, mindful of the unhonored dead,
 Dost in these lines their artless tale relate,
If chance, by lonely contemplation led,
 Some kindred spirit shall inquire thy fate—

25. Haply some hoary-headed swain may say:
 "Oft have we seen him, at the peep of dawn,
Brushing with hasty steps the dews away,
 To meet the sun upon the upland lawn.

26. "There, at the foot of yonder nodding beech,
 That wreathes its old, fantastic roots so high,
His listless length at noontide would he stretch,
 And pore upon the brook that babbles by.

27. "Hard by yon wood, now smiling as in scorn,
 Muttering his wayward fancies, he would rove;
Now drooping, woful-wan, like one forlorn,
 Or crazed with care, or crossed in hopeless love.

28. "One morn I missed him on the customed hill,
 Along the heath, and near his fav'rite tree;
Another came, nor yet beside the rill,
 Nor up the lawn, nor at the wood was he;

29. "The next, with dirges due, in sad array,
Slow through the church-way path we saw him borne:
Approach and read (for thou canst read) the lay
Graved on the stone beneath yon aged thorn."

THE EPITAPH.

30. Here rests his head, upon the lap of earth,
A youth to Fortune and to Fame unknown;
Fair Science frowned not on his humble birth,
And Melancholy marked him for her own.

31. Large was his bounty, and his soul sincere;
Heaven did a recompense as largely send:
He gave to misery—all he had—a tear;
He gained from Heaven—'twas all he wished—a friend.

32. No further seek his merits to disclose,
Or draw his frailties from their dread abode—
There they alike in trembling hope repose—
The bosom of his Father and his God.

Thomas Gray.

FOR PREPARATION.—I. Of this elegy General Wolfe said, as he repeated it on the evening before Quebec: "I would rather have written that poem than beat the French to-morrow." Hampden, Milton, Cromwell—three great names connected with the English Revolution that overthrew Charles I.

II. Knĕll (nĕl), ĕch'-o-ing, house'-wīfe, grănd'-eūr (-yụr), trō'phieṣ, ĕc'-sta-sy, dăunt'-less, sçī'-ençe, mĕl'-an-chŏl-y, jŏc'-und.

III. Transpose stanzas 16 and 17 into prose.

IV. Solitary, folds, moping, rugged, hamlet, incense-breathing, envied, glebe, jocund, sturdy, ambition, destiny, obscure, annals, disdainful, heraldry, pomp, inevitable, impute, long-drawn aisle, fretted vault, anthem, storied urn, animated bust, celestial fire, ample page, penury, genial, serene, unfathomed, "little tyrant of his fields," mute applause, senate, circumscribed, ingenuous, shrine, ignoble, sequestered, tenor, memorial, erected, uncouth, sculpture, "passing tribute," "unlettered Muse," elegy, "rustic moralist," pleasing, anxious, resigned, precincts, pious, wonted, artless, contemplation, kindred, haply, swain, fantastic, heath, dirges, bounty, recompense, merits, disclose.

V. "Curfew" (*cover fire.* On the ringing of the curfew at 8 P. M., the English people were required to extinguish their fires and candles. The law was enacted by William the Conqueror in 1068, and abolished by Henry I. in 1100; but the ringing of bells at sunset, practiced for centuries afterward, was still called the curfew). What "ivy-mantled tower" is referred to here? (of the church in this "country churchyard.") What is meant by "heaves the turf"?—"narrow cell"?—"shrill clarion"?—"echoing horn"? Why are these mentioned as sounds that will rouse the sleeper? (the first sounds heard in the morning.) "Lowly bed" (lowly means *low in the grave*, or *poor and humble*—such beds as they slept on in their cottages). "Evening care" means what? (Is *care* used for the sake of rhyme with *share?* If so, why not let the rhymes be *task—ask?*) "Their furrow oft," etc. (the effect is used for the cause: the *furrow* for the *plow.* This figure of speech is called *metonomy*, which means *name-changing*). "Nor Grandeur" ("Grandeur" used for "grand people"). "If Memory o'er their tomb," etc. (referring to the memorials erected by the rich and powerful within the churches). "Repressed their noble rage" (i. e., the celestial fire of poetry). "Guiltless of his country's blood" (i. e., was not at the head of armies, as Cromwell was). "For thee," etc. (24)—(i. e., the poet describes himself in the speech of the hoary-headed swain and in the epitaph. The description tells us how much like an idiot a poet seems to an uneducated "swain"; while absorbed in his reveries and constructing his rhymes (i. e., "Muttering his wayward fancies"), his behavior could not be accounted for on the hoary-headed swain's theory of life). "Another came" (i. e., another morn). "The next" (morn). "Large was his bounty"—what is meant? (he was very generous, for he gave to people in misery all he had.) Heaven, as "recompense" for his "bounty," became his "friend."

APPENDIX.

WORDS DIFFICULT TO SPELL.

THE difficulty of spelling English words arises from uncertainty in regard to the combinations used to represent elementary sounds. For instance, the sound ĕ is represented in eleven different ways in the words ebb, dead, again, æsthetics, many, nonpareil, jeopardy, friend, bury, guest, says. Again, the words bead, head, great, heart, wear, ocean, earth, present *ea* with seven sounds.

The pupil will readily learn to spell all words in which the sounds are represented by the usual combinations of letters, by seeing them in print whenever he reads a book or newspaper.

A list of words to spell should not be cumbered by the introduction of easy words, such as contain only the usual combinations, but should have only those that are difficult because of the exceptional combinations of letters used.

The spelling-book, then, may be a very small book, containing about fifteen hundred words. This small list of words should be so thoroughly learned that the pupil can spell orally or write *every word* in it without hesitation. This can be accomplished by the pupil of twelve years of age in six months' time, having one lesson of twenty words a day to write from dictation, and using every fifth day for an oral review of all words from the beginning.

This thorough drill on a few words will train the child's faculty of observing unusual combinations of letters, and his memory thus trained will make him a good speller without spending any further time over the spelling-book. His memory will absorb and retain hard words wherever he sees them, just as a sponge absorbs and retains water.

The words are arranged in the following list so as not to bring together a number of words of the same combination, and thereby paralyze the memory, as is too frequently the case in the lists given in spelling-books, which, for example, collect in one lesson the words ending in *tion*, or *tain*, or *ture*, or *cious*, etc., thus giving to the pupil by the first word that is spelled a key to all that follow.

Correct pronunciation is as important as correct spelling, and the rare combinations of letters are the ones most likely to be mispronounced. The following list contains the words liable to be mispronounced as well as misspelled, and even some words easy to spell that are often mispronounced. The following mode of analysis is recommended as an excellent auxiliary to the oral and written spelling-lesson. It should always be practiced in connection with the reading-lesson, and with the book open before the pupil, in preference to the usual plan.

Spelling Analysis.—The pupils and teacher have reading-books or spelling-books open at the lesson. The pupils, in the order of recitation, analyze the list of difficult words one after the other, as follows:

First Pupil—Groat, g-r-o-a-t (pronounces and reads its spelling from the book). It is a difficult word, because the sound *aw* is represented by the rare combination *oa;* it is usually represented by *aw* or *au* (*awl*, *fraud*), and by *o* before *r* (*born*). This sound may be represented in nine ways.

Second Pupil—Police, p-o-l-i-c-e. It is a difficult word, because the sound ē is represented by *i*, and not by one of the more frequent modes, *e*, *ea*, *ee*, *ie*, and *ei*. There are twelve ways of representing this sound. The word is also more difficult to spell, because it represents the sound of *s* by *ce*.

Third Pupil—Sacrifice, s-a-c-r-i-f-i-c-e. It is difficult, because the sound ĭ (before *f*) is obscure, and may be represented by any one of twelve ways. The letter *c* in *fice* has here the sound of *z*, a very rare use of that letter. The word is liable to be mispronounced sā′-krĭ-fĭs or săk′-rĭ-fĭs for săk′-rĭ-fīz.

A.—Table of Equivalents representing Elementary Sounds.

I.—The sound ā is represented in eleven ways: 1. In many words by ā (āle), āi (āid), and āy (bāy); 2. In a few words by e̱y (the̱y), e̱i (ve̱il), eā (breāk), āu (gāuge), āo (gāol, for *jail*), e̱ and e̱e (mêlée), āye (meaning *ever*).

II.—The sound ă is represented in three ways: 1. In many words by ă (ăt); 2. In a few words by ăi (plăid), uă (guărantee).

III.—The sound ä is represented in six ways: 1. In many words by ä (fäther); 2. In a few words by äu (täunt), eä (heärt), uä (guärd), e (sergeant), äa (bazäar).

IV.—The sound â is represented in seven ways: 1. In many words by â (câre); 2. In a few words by âi (fâir), eâ (peâr), ây (prâyer), ê (thêre), êi (thêir), aâ (Aâron). â is the sound ȧ (ȧsk) followed by the guttural vowel-sound which clings to the smooth r (see below, No. XV.).

V.—The sound ȧ is represented only by ȧ (ȧsk) in a few words.

VI.—The sound a̤ is represented in nine ways: 1. In many words by a̤ (a̤ll), a̤w (a̤wl), a̤u (fra̤ud), ô (bôrn); 2. In a few words by ôu (bôught), ôa (brôad), eô (Geôrge), aô (extraôrdinary), a̤we.

VII.—The sound ē is represented in twelve ways: 1. In many words by ē (ēve), ēa (bēat), ēe (bēef), iē (chiēf); 2. In a few words by ēi (decēive), ï (marïne), ēy (kēy), ēo (pēople), uay (quay), uē (Portuguēse), æ (Cæsar), œ̄ (Phœbus).

VIII.—The sound ĕ is represented in twelve ways: 1. In many words by ĕ (mĕt), ĕa (brĕad); 2. In a few words by ai (said), æ (diæresis), a (any), ĕi (hĕifer), ĕo (lĕopard), iĕ (friĕnd), u (bury), uĕ (guĕst), ay (says), œ (Œdipus).

IX.—The sound ī (a diphthong composed of the sounds ä-ē, pronounced so briefly as to reduce them nearly to ẽ-ĭ [hẽr, ĭt]) is represented in ten ways: 1. In many words by ī (īce), ȳ (bȳ), īe (dīe); 2. In a few words by uī (guīde), eī (heīght), uȳ (buȳ), aī (aīsle), ȳe (rȳe), eȳe, aȳ (or aȳe, meaning *yes*).

X.—The sound ĭ is represented in twelve ways: 1. In many words by ĭ (ĭt), ў (lўnx), ĭe (dutĭes); 2. In a few words by uĭ (buĭld), aĭ (certaĭn), u (busy), e (pretty), ee (been), o (women), eĭ (foreĭgn), ĭa (carrĭage), oĭ (tortoĭse).

XI.—The sound ō is represented in ten ways: 1. In many words by ō (nōte), ōa (bōat), ōw (blōw); 2. In a few words by ōu (fōur), ōe (fōe), ōo (dōor), au (hautboy), ew (sew), eau (beau), eō (yeōman).

XII.—The sound ŏ is represented in four ways: 1. In many words by ŏ (nŏt), a̤ (wa̤s); 2. In a few words by ŏu (lŏugh), ŏw (knŏwledge).

XIII.—The sound ū (a diphthong composed of ĭ-o͝o; the accent placed on the ĭ gives the prevalent American pronunciation, placed on the o͝o converts the ĭ into a y-sound, and gives the current English sound) is represented in nine ways: 1. In many words by ū (tūbe), ew (few); 2. In a few words by ūe (hūe), ūi (jūice), eū (neūter), ieū (lieū), iew (view), eaū (beaūty), ūa (mantūa-maker).

XIV.—The sound ŭ is represented in eight ways: 1. In many words by ŭ (bŭt), ȯ (sȯn, and terminations in ion), oŭ (toŭch, and terminations in ous); 2. In a few words by ȯo (blȯod), ȯe (dȯes), ȯi (porpȯise), iȯ (cushiȯn), eȯ (dungeȯn).

XV.—The sound û is represented in nine ways: 1. In many words by û (bûrn), ẽ (hẽr), ĩ (fĩrst); 2. In a few words by ẽa (hẽard), õ (wõrk), oû (scoûrge), ỹ (mỹrtle), a (liar), uẽ (guẽrdon). This sound, like â in âir (ȧ in ȧsk, and the guttural ŭh), is diphthongal, occasioned by the transmutation of the rough or trilled r to the smooth or palatal r, the effort expended in trilling the tongue having weakened into a guttural vowel-sound ŭh, heard as a glide from the previous vowel-sound to the r. Very careful speakers preserve enough of the original sounds of e, i, and y to distinguish them from o or u, although the common usage, here and in England, is to pronounce them all alike, except before a trilled r. Smart says: "Even in the refined classes of society in England *sur*, *durt*, *burd*, etc., are the current pronunciation of *sir*, *dirt*, *bird;* and, indeed, in all very common words it would be somewhat affected to insist on the delicate shade of difference." The careful teacher will, however, practice his pupils in this delicate distinction enough to make them well acquainted with it. The same guttural vowel-sound ŭh occurs as a vanish after ē (mere), ī (fire), ō (more), ū (pure), etc.

XVI.—The sound u̥ is represented in nine ways: 1. In many words by o͞o (blo͞om); 2. In a few words by ou̥ (grou̥p), o̥ (do̥), u̥ (ru̥le), ew (grew), ewe (yu̥), u̥e (tru̥e), u̥i (fru̥it), o̥e (sho̥e), œu̥ (manœu̥vre). This is the general sound of ū after an r or sh sound, because the first part of the diphthong (ĭ-o͝o) is lost (after r) or absorbed (in sh).

XVII.—The sound u̇ is represented in four ways: 1. In many words by o͝o (bro͝ok); 2. In a few by u̇ (bu̇sh), ou̇ (wou̇ld), o̩ (wo̩lf).

XVIII.—The diphthong oi (= a̤-ĭ or aw-e), as in coil, is represented also by oy (boy).

XIX.—The diphthong ou (= ä-o͝o), as in bound, is represented also by ow (crowd).

XX.—The sounds of ġ in ġem, of ḡ in ḡet, of s in so, of ṣ in waṣ, of ç in çell, of c in cat, of ch in child, of ch in chorus, of çh in maçhine, of x in ox, of x̣ in ex̣act (ḡz), of n in no, of ṉ in coṉcord (kongkord), of th in thing, of th in the, are marked, when marked, as here indicated.

XXI.—The sound of f is represented by ph (philosopher) in many words, and by gh (cough) in a few words. The sound of v is represented by f in of and ph (Stephen) in a few words. The sound of sh is represented by c (oceanic), s (nauseate), t (negotiation), ce (ocean), ci (social), se (nauseous), si (tension), ti (captious), ch (chaise), sc (conscientious), sch (schorl), sci (conscience). xi = ksh in noxious, xu = kshu in luxury, su = shu in sure; zh is represented by si (fusion), zi (grazier), s (symposium), ti (transition), ssi (abscission), g (rouge); zu = zhu in azure.

B.—Table of Sounds represented by Letters and Combinations.

1. a—eight sounds: āle, ăt, ärms, ȧsk, câre, ạll, wạs, any (ĕ).
2. e—five sounds: ēve, mĕt, thêre, hẽr, pretty (ĭ).
3. i—four sounds: īce, ĭt, fatïgue, fĩr.
4. o—eight sounds: nōte, nôr, nŏt, mo̤ve, wo̩lf, wõrk, sȯn, women (ĭ).
5. u—eight sounds: ūse (yu̇), cūbe, bŭt, rṳde, pu̩ll, fûr, busy (ĭ), bury (ĕ).
6. y—three sounds: bȳ, lўric, myrrh.
7. aa = ä, ă; æ = ē, ĕ; ai = ā, â, ă, ĕ, ī, ĭ; ao = ā, ạ; au = ä, ā, ạ, ō; aw = ạ; awe = ạ; ay = ā, â, ĕ, ī; aye = ā.
8. ea = ā, â, ä, ē, ĕ, ŭ, û; ee = ē, ĭ, ā; ei = ā, â, ē, ĕ, ī, ĭ; ey = ā, ē, ī; eo = ē, ĕ, ō, ô, ŭ; eu = ū, yu̇, yŭ; ew = ū, ō, ṳ, yṳ; eau = ō, ū; ewe = yṳ; eye = ī; eou = yŭ.
9. ia = ĭ, yă; ie = ē, ĕ, ī, ĭ, yĕ, yŭ; io = yō, yŭ, ŭ; iu = yṳ; ieu = ū; iew = ū; iou = yŭ.
10. oa = ō, ạ; oe = ē, ĕ, ō, ṳ, ŭ; oi = oy, ĭ, ŭ, wī, wạ; œu = ṳ; oo = ō, ṳ, u̩ ŭ; ou = ow, ạ, ō, o̤, o̩, ŭ; ow = ou, ō, ŏ; oy = oi.
11. ua = ă, ā, ū, wā, wă, wä, wạ, wạ; ue = ē, ĕ, wē, wĕ, ū, û, ṳ, yṳ; ui = ī, ĭ, ū, ṳ, wī, wĭ, wī, wē; uo = wō, wŏ; uy = ē, ī; uay = ē; uea = wē; uee = wē; uoy = woi; uay = wā, ē.

D.—Less Common Words.

I.	II.	III.
fŏs'sil	dī-ær'e-sĭs	de-çĕp'tion
găm'ut	ŏs'si-fȳ	fa-çē'tious (-shus)
scăb'bard	ma-nœū'vre (-nū-)	vĭ'ti-āte (-shĭ-)
stŭe'ȼo	myrrh (mẽr)	in-ĭ'tial (-ĭsh'-)
vĭe'ar	nā'dir	in-sĭ'tion (-sĭsh'un)
vĭs'çid	phā'lanx	se-dĭ'tious
tĕr'raçe	phœ'nix (fē'-)	tu-ĭ'tion
sôr'tiē	sī'phon	ȼŏn'sciençe (-shens)
tŏn-tīne'	nā'şal	au-dā'cioŭs
pæ'an	sĕn'ti-ent (-shĭ-)	pre-ȼō'cioŭs

IV.	V.	VI.
pug-nā'cioŭs (-shus)	sūt'ūre (-yur)	ex-chĕq'uer (-chĕk'er)
ăv-a-lănçhe'	stăt'ūe	mos-quī'to (mŭs-ke'-)
nau'se-āte (-she-)	stăt'ūte	ăn-tīque' (-teek')
tran-sĭ'tion (-sizh'-un)	ġĕn'ū-ĭne	gro-tĕsque' (-tĕsk')
āl'ien	strĕn'ū-oŭs	mŏsque
pŏn'iard	ăq'ue-duet (-we-)	o-pāque'
çĭ-vĭl'ian	ĕq'uĭ-paġe (-pej)	ȼhȳme (kīm)
ȼŏll'ier-y (-yer-)	ĕq'uĭ-ty	bur-lĕsque'
pa-vĭl'ion (-yun)	rĕq'uĭ-şĭte	ȼrĭ'tīque'
stăt'ūre (-yur)	ȼo-quĕtte' (-kĕt')	ȼhī-mē'rā

VII.	VIII.	IX.
ȼhro-nŏl'o-ġy	dŏç'ĭle	ĕl'i-ġi-ble
strȳȼh'nīne	mĭs'sĭle	in-dĕl'i-ble
är'ȼhe-tȳpe	ȼrȳs'tal-līne	re-ġĭst'i-ble
lăȼh'ry-mal	tûr'pen-tīne	çȳ'ȼle
mĕȼh'a-nĭşm	ȼŏr'al-līne	pĭn'na-ȼle
Pĕn'ta-teūȼh (-tūk)	săt'el-līte	re-çĕp'ta-ȼle
ga̱n'grene	grăn'ĭte	ḡrĭz'zle
triph-thŏn'gal	suȼ-çĕs'sĭve	măs'sa-ȼre (-ker)
dis-bûrse'	ăr'a-ble	drĭv'el (v'l)
ĭn'çense	rĭş'i-ble	wee'vil (v'l)

X.	XI.	XII.
bēa′con (-kn)	ăc-quĭ-ĕsçe′	ăp-ro-pos′ (-pō′)
ob-lĭque′ (-leek′)	gnärl (närl)	trĕs′tle (s′l)
dĕe′a-lŏgue	phlĕgm (flĕm)	schĭşm (sĭzm)
sy̆n′a-gŏgue	dī′a-phrăgm (-frăm)	môrt′gaġe (môr′ġej)
băi′liff	ăsth′ma (ăst′-)	mĭş′tle-tōe (mĭz′l-)
hăr′ass	năph′thȧ (năp′-)	in-făl′li-ble
sŭbt′le (sŭt′l)	hal̤s′er (haws′-)	fĭl′a-ment
czär (zär)	pneū-mō′ni-ȧ (nū-)	măn′aġe-a-ble
ăb′sçess	psal̤′ter-y (sawl′-)	lĭn′i-ment
Ġĭ-bral̤′tar	pĕr′emp-to-ry	nū′tri-ment

XIII.	XIV.	XV.
sĕd′i-ment	re-çĭp′ro-eal	de-lūde′
ea-tărrh′ (-tär′)	lăs′si-tūde	de-lĭn′e-āte
făs′çi-nāte	a-trŏç′i-ty	dĭ-mĕn′sion
sŭp′pli-eāte	ea-păç′i-ty	e-lū′çi-dāte
ē-qui-lĭb′ri-ŭm	ē-las-tĭç′i-ty	im-mĕn′si-ty
eo-mē′di-an	ăl-le-gŏr′ie-al	in-ŏe′ū-lāte
gram-mā′ri-an	ăn-te-çēd′ent	fĕr-men-tā′tion
ea-lŭm′ni-oŭs	ăn′tĭ-dōte	fĭr′ma-ment
de-lĭr′i-um	nĭç′e-ty	sŭs′te-nançe
ăe-a-dĕm′ie-al	ăn-tĭ-ehrĭs′tian	eon-eŭr′rençe

XVI.	XVII.	XVIII
de-çēase′	sū-per-in-tĕnd′ent	pro-bŏs′çis
ae-çĕpt′ançe	çy̆l′in-der	eon-tā′ġioŭs
chȧn′çel-lor	ăt′mos-phēre	măr′çhion-ess (-shun-)
sur-vey̤′or (-vā′-)	fĭn-an-çiēr′ (-seer′)	vo-rā′cioŭs
ae-eou′ter (-kōō′-)	eo-ērçe′	dis-pērse′
ăm-phi-thē′a-ter	as-pērse′	fie-tĭ′tioŭs
eon-çĕn′ter	rē-im-bûrse′	sū-per-stĭ′tioŭs
ĭn-ter-çēde′	ăv′a-rĭçe	ġe-ŏm-e-trĭ′cian (-trĭsh′an)
sū-per-sēde	ŏr′i-fĭce	eŏn-de-sçĕn′sion
găz-et-teer′	trēa′tĭse	ĭn-ter-mĭs′sion (-mĭsh′un)

XIX.

ac-çĕl-er-ā'tion
ex̱-hĭl-a-rā'tion (gz)
sçĭn-til-lā'tion
ĕm'bas-sy
court'e-sy (kûrt'-)
făl'la-çy
mil-lĕn'ni-um
blīthe'sôme
mälm'ṣey (mäm'-)
ăm'e-thy̆st

XX.

bĭg'ot
căl'um-ny
căt'e-chīṣe
cŏm'ic
flăg'on
frĭg'ate
ŏb'e-lĭsk
pĕl'i-can
tĕn'or
vĭg'or

XXI.

păn'ic
com-mŏd'i-ty
de-vĕl'op
e-lăb'o-rāte
en-ăm'el
ĕp-i-dĕm'ic
e-văp'o-rāte
ex-pĕr'i-ment
pī-răt'i-cal
re-tăl'i-āte

XXII.

ăg'gre-gāte
ăc-a-dĕm'ic
ba-rŏm'e-ter
băr-ri-cāde'
băt'ter-y
brăg'gart
crăb'bed
dĭs'si-pāte
dĭt'ty
căv-a-liēr'

XXIII.

flĭp'pant
fŏp'pish
mŏt'to
mŭm'my
păl'lid
pĕn'nant
pŏl'len
sĕn'na
stĕl'lar
trăf'fic

XXIV.

wĭt'ti-çĭṣm
ac-cŏm'mo-dāte
am-băs'sa-dor
ban-dĭt'tĭ
bri-tăn'ni-ȧ
co-lŏs'sus
com-mĭt'tee
em-băr'rass
ex̱-ăġ'ġer-āte
sŭf'fo-cāte

XXV.

in-flăm'ma-to-ry
ty̆-răn'nic-al
a-chiēve'ment
pī-ăz'zȧ
ac-knŏwl'edġ-ment
ăd'mi-ra-ble
ăd-van-tā'ġeoŭs
am-phĭb'i-oŭs
a-năl'y-sĭs
ăn-ni-vēr'sa-ry

XXVI.

a-nŏn'y-moŭs
a-pŏc'ry-phȧ
as-çĕnd'en-çy
ăt'tri-būte
aux̱-ĭl'ia-ry
be-nĕf'i-çençe
a-pŏth'e-ca-ry
blăs'phe-my
bo-hēa'
bŏm-ba-zïne'

XXVII.

bûrg'la-ry
car-touch' (-tōōtch')
chĭr'rup
chŏr'is-ter
çĭt'a-del
brĭll'ian-çy
çĕl'er-y
çĕm'e-tĕr-y
çĕr'e-mo-ny
con-fĕc'tion-er-y

XXVIII.	XXIX.	XXX.
erĕv'ïçe	ĕr-y-sĭp'e-las	hȳ-dro-phō'bi-ȧ
dĭm-i-nū'tion	ĕt-y-mŏl'o-ġy	ĭl-lĭt'er-ate
dis-pĕn'sa-ry	păr'a-çhute	ĭn-dĭe'a-tĭve
drăm'a-tĭst	ex-erĕs'çençe	ĭn-stan-tā'ne-oŭs
e-eŏn'o-my	dȳs'en-tĕr-y	ĭn-tĕl'li-ġi-ble
ĕf-fer-vĕs'çençe	en-dĕav'or	ĩrk'sŏme
ē-lec-trĭç'i-ty	er-rō'ne-oŭs	jăg-u-är'
e-lĭx'ir	em-bĕd'ded	jăve'lin (jăv'-)
en-çȳ-elo-pæ'di-ȧ	fu-nē're-al	joûr'ney-man
e-thē're-al	ġym-năs'ties	kẽr'ṣey-mēre

XXXI.	XXXII.	XXXIII.
lăt'tĭçe	pĕn-i-tĕn'tia-ry (-sha-)	săp'phire (săf'ĭr)
lĭt'er-a-tūre	ve-neer'	prŏd'i-ġy
lĭq'ue-fȳ (-we-)	phā'e-tŏn	pȳr'a-mĭd
lū'era-tĭve	phȳṣ-i-ŏl'o-ġy	dĭs-a-gree'ing
ma-lā'ri-ȧ	păr'al-lel	skĩr'mish
păl'pa-ble	prŏm'i-nent	so-lĭç'i-tūde
păm'phlet	rĕe'om-pĕnse	sŏl'i-ta-ry
pa-răl'y-sĭs	re-pŏṣ'i-to-ry	stûr'di-ly
pär'lĭa-ment	rĕṣ-ur-rĕe'tion	sûr'ġer-y
fĭs'sūre (fĭsh'ụr)	rĭ-dĭe'u-loŭs	sȳm'me-try

XXXIV.	XXXV.	XXXVI.
sȳn-ŏn'y-moŭs	văn̤'quish	An-năp'o-lis
sȳr'inġe	Ra̤'leĭgh	Hāy'ti
tăn'ta-līze	Sa-văn'nah	Clēve'land
tăm'a-rĭnd	Băt'ŏn Ro̤uge (roozh)	Mil-wa̤u'kee
tĕl'e-seōpe	Du-būque'	Des Moines' (de moin')
tĕn'e-ment	Pōugh-keep'sie (-kĭp'-)	Ĭn-dĭ-an-ăp'o-lis
tȳr'an-nīze	Prāi'rĭe du̥ Chiēn (sheen)	Pĭtts'burg
ve-lŏç'i-pēde	Worces'ter (wo͝os'-)	Ja-māi'ea
vĭct'ual-er (vĭt'l-)	Tĕr're Haute (hōt)	Căr-ib-bē'an
vo-lū'mi-noŭs	Ra-çīne'	Schuyl'kill (sko͞ol'-)

LV.*	LVI.*	LVII.*
(2) plain	(2) wring	(2) tier
(2) plait	(3) road	(2) through
(2) plumb	(2) roar	(2) thrown
(2) prey	(2) rood	(2) thyme
(3) praise	(2) sail	(2) toe
(3) rein	(2) scene	(2) tun
(2) wrap	(2) seam	(2) vein
(2) red	(2) seize	(2) veil
(2) reed	(2) sleigh	(3) viol
(2) rice	(3) so	(2) waist

LVIII.*	LIX.†	LX.†
(2) week	(2) abuse	(2) slough
(2) wood	(2) bow	(2) wind
(2) throe	(2) cleanly	(2) mall
(2) rime	(2) hinder	(2) gallant
(2) moat	(2) lead	(2) grease
(2) meed	(2) live	(2) gill
(2) grieves	(2) lower	(2) close
(2) cygnet	(2) minute	(2) rise
(2) corol	(2) mow	(2) irony
(2) bruit	(2) row	(2) wound

* When the teacher pronounces a word from these lessons (XLIX.-LVIII.), the pupil should spell and define the two or more words having the same pronunciation.

† When the teacher pronounces a word from these lessons (LIX., LX.), the pupil should give its two pronunciations and the definition in each case: e. g., bow (bou), to incline the head; bow (bō), a weapon for propelling arrows, or the doubling of a string in a knot, etc.

DESCHANEL'S Natural Philosophy. Complete........................ $5 70
Natural Philosophy. 1. Mechanics, Hydrostatics, etc. 1 50
Natural Philosophy. 2. Heat........................ 1 50
Natural Philosophy. 3. Electricity.................... 1 50
Natural Philosophy. 4. Sound and Light............ 1 50
DEW'S Digest of Ancient and Modern History.......................... 2 20
GILLESPIE'S Land Surveying.. 2 60
Higher Surveying.. 2 20
GRAHAM'S English Synonymes.. 1 30
GREENE'S History of the Middle Ages.................................. 1 30
Primary Botany 1 10
Class-Book of Botany.. 1 70
GUIZOT'S History of Civilization 1 30
HADLEY. Twelve Lectures on Roman Law.............................. 1 30
HAND-BOOK of Anglo-Saxon Root-Words.............................. 85
of Anglo-Saxon Derivations.............................. 1 10
of the Engrafted Words of the English Language....... 1 30
HASWELL'S Book-keeping.. 3 00
Blanks for the same.. 1 70
HENSLOW'S Botanical Charts..................................Per set, 15 75
Key to do.. 25
HISTORY PRIMERS. Edited by J. R. Green:
Greece. By C. A. Fyffe.. 45
Rome. By M. Creighton.. 45
Europe. By E. A. Freeman.. 45
Old Greek Life. By J. P. Mahaffy.................................. 45
Geography. By George Grove.. 45
Roman Antiquities. By A. S. Wilkins.............................. 45
England. By J. R. Green..*(In press.)*
France. By Charlotte M. Yonge..................................*(In press.)*
HOME PICTURES of English Poets.................................. 85
HOOKER'S Penmanship..Per dozen, 1 20
HOWS'S Historical Shakespearian Reader.............................. 1 30
Shakespearian Reader.. 1 30
HUXLEY and YOUMANS'S Elements of Physiology and Hygiene. 1 50
JACOBS'S Learning to Spell, to Read, to Write, and to Compose....... 65
The same, in two volumes.. 1 10
JAEGER'S Class-Book in Zoölogy.. 45
KEIGHTLEY'S Mythology of Greece and Rome.......................... 65
KÖPPEN'S Historical Geography.. 3 00
KRÜSI'S System of Free-Hand and Industrial Drawing:
Synthetic Series. Four Books..............................Each, 18
Analytical Series. Six Books..............................Each, 22
Perspective Series. Four Books..............................Each, 27
Advanced Perspective and Shading Series. Four Books.
Nos. 1 and 2..Each, 27
Nos. 3 and 4..Each, 35
Manuals. (One to each Series.)..Cloth, each, 65c.; paper, each, 50

KRÜSI'S Industrial Series. — Textile Designs. Six Books .. Per set,	$2 00
Mechanical. Six Books.........Per set,	2 00
Architectural. Nine Books......Per set,	4 00
Machinery..............................	*(In press.)*
Outline and Relief Designs..........	*(In press.)*
LATHAM'S Hand-Book of the English Language......................	1 50
LITERATURE PRIMERS. Edited by J. R. Green:	
English Grammar. By R. Morris................................	45
English Literature. By Stopford Brooke........................	45
Philology. By J. Peile..	45
Classical Geography. By H. F. Tozer...........................	45
Shakespeare. By Edward Dowden..........	45
Greek Literature. By R. C. Jebb...............................	45
English Grammar Exercises. By R. Morris......................	45
Studies in Bryant. By J. Alden................................	45
Homer. By W. E. Gladstone....................................	45
LOCKYER'S Elementary Lessons in Astronomy......................	1 50
MACAULAY'S Biographical Sketches..............	85
MANDEVILLE'S Elements of Reading and Oratory.	1 10
Course of Reading...............	1 10
MANGNALL'S Historical Questions........	1 30
MARCET. Mary's Grammar..	1 10
MARKHAM'S School History of England............................	1 30
MARSH'S Course of Practice in Single Entry Book-keeping............	1 70
A Set of Blank Books for ditto................................	1 30
Science of Double Entry Book-keeping.........................	2 20
A Set of Blank Books for ditto.......	1 30
Bank Book-keeping and Joint Stock Accounts..............	6 00
MARSHALL'S Book of Oratory.......................................	30
First Book of Oratory.................................	1 10
MODEL COPY-BOOKS. In Six Numbers................Per dozen,	1 55
MORSE'S First Book in Zoölogy....................................	1 10
MULLIGAN'S Exposition of English Grammatical Structure..........	1 70
MUNSELL'S Psychology..	1 70
NICHOLSON'S Text-Book of Zoölogy...	1 50
Text-Book of Geology................................	1 30
Introduction to the Study of Biology..................	65
NORTHEND'S Memory Gems.........................	20
Choice Thoughts..	30
OTIS'S Drawing-Books of Landscape. Six Parts........................	2 60
" " Parts I., II., and III.......Each,	40
" " Parts IV., V., and VI......Each,	50
" " The same in 1 volume.....Cloth,	3 00
Drawing-Books of Animals. Five Parts.........................	2 60
" " Parts I. and II..............Each,	45
" " Part III...........................	50
" " Parts IV. and V.............Each,	65
" " The same, in 1 volume.......Cloth,	3 00

PERKINS'S	Elementary Arithmetic	$0 65
	Practical Arithmetic	1 10
	Key to ditto	1 30
	Elementary Geometry	1 10
	Plane and Solid Geometry	1 70
	Elements of Algebra	1 30
	Treatise on ditto	1 70
	Plane Trigonometry and Surveying	1 70
PRENDERGAST'S	Hand-Book to the Mastery Series	45
PUTZ and ARNOLD'S	Manual of Ancient Geography and History	1 30
	Mediæval Geography and History	1 30
	Modern Geography and History	1 30
QUACKENBOS'S	Primary Arithmetic	22
	Mental Arithmetic	35
	Elementary Arithmetic	40
	Practical Arithmetic	80
	Part I	45
	Practical Arithmetic. Part II	45
	Key to ditto	18
	Higher Arithmetic	1 10
	Key to ditto	65
	First Lessons in English Composition	80
	Advanced Course of Composition and Rhetoric	1 30
	Primary History of the United States. (Old edition.)	80
	Elementary History of the United States. (New ed.)	65
	American History for Schools	1 25
	History of the United States for Schools	1 30
	Primary Grammar	45
	English Grammar	80
	Natural Philosophy	1 50
	Illustrated School History of the World	1 50
	Illustrated Lessons in our Language	55
REID'S	Dictionary of the English Language	1 10
RICHARDS'S	Elements of Plane Trigonometry	75
RICORD'S	Youth's Grammar	35
ROBBINS'S	Class-Book of Poetry	1 10
	Guide to Knowledge	85
ROEMER'S	Polyglot Reader and Guide for Translation	1 30
SCHMIDT'S	Course of Ancient Geography	1 10
SCIENCE PRIMERS:		
	Chemistry. By H. E. Roscoe	45
	Physics. By Balfour Stewart	45
	Physical Geography. By Archibald Geikie	45
	Geology. By Archibald Geikie	45
	Physiology. By M. Foster	45
	Astronomy. By J. Norman Lockyer	45
	Botany. By J. D. Hooker	45
	Logic. By W. S. Jevons	45

SCIENCE PRIMERS:

	Inventional Geometry. By W. G. Spencer	$0 45
	Pianoforte Playing. By F. Taylor	45
	Political Economy. By W. S. Jevons	45
SEWELL'S	First History of Greece	65
	First History of Rome	65
SPALDING'S	History of English Literature	1 30
TAPPAN'S	Elements of Logic	1 30
TAYLOR'S (BAYARD)	School History of Germany	1 50
TENNEY'S	Grammatical Analyzer	1 30
WEBSTER'S	Elementary Spelling-Book	15
	Elementary Reader	15
WILLARD'S	Synopsis of General History	2 00
WILLIAMS and PACKARD'S	Gems of Penmanship	5 00
WILLIAMSON'S	Elementary Treatise on Differential Calculus	3 75
	Elementary Treatise on Integral Calculus	3 75
WILSON'S	Elementary Treatise on Logic	1 30
WINSLOW'S	Elements of Moral Philosophy	1 30
WORTHEN'S	First Lessons in Mechanics	65
	Rudimentary Drawing	65
WRIGHT'S	Primary Lessons	25
YOUMANS'S	(Professor) Class-Book of Chemistry	1 50
	(Eliza A.) First Book of Botany	85
	Second Book of Botany	1 30
	Botanical Charts	15 75
	Key to same	25

Elementary Works on Mechanical and Physical Science, forming a Series of

TEXT-BOOKS OF SCIENCE,

ADAPTED FOR THE USE OF

ARTISANS AND STUDENTS IN PUBLIC AND SCIENCE SCHOOLS.

EDITED BY

Prof. T. M. GOODEVE, M. A., and C. W. MERRIFIELD, F. R. S.

Fully illustrated, and handsomely printed in 16mo. Price, cloth, $1.50 per volume, with the exception of a single volume of nearly 400 pages, the price of which is $2.50. Sixteen volumes of the series have been published, and others are in preparation.

D. APPLETON & CO., PUBLISHERS,

1, 3, & 5 BOND STREET, NEW YORK.